MW00748891

LIVERPOOL OF THE SOUTH SEAS

Dear Marilynn
With love and
gratitude for all
your generousity
to my family and I.
Debbie
P.S. Chapter 2 is my work
- my friends Sandi & Hud.

OTHER BOOKS IN THE CONTEMPORARY ISSUES SERIES

The Salinity Crisis: Landscapes, Communities and Politics
Quentin Beresford, Hugo Bekle, Harry Phillips and Jane Mulcock

Left Directions: Is There a Third Way?
edited by Paul Nursey-Bray and Carol Bacchi

More than Refuge: Changing Responses to Domestic Violence
Suellen Murray

Power and Freedom in Modern Politics
edited by Bruce Stone and Jeremy Moon

Legacies of White Australia: Race, Culture and Nation
edited by Laksiri Jayasuriya, David Walker and Jan Gothard

Reform and Resistance in Aboriginal Education
edited by Quentin Beresford and Gary Partington

The People Next Door: Understanding Indonesia
Duncan Graham

A Jury of Whose Peers?
edited by Kate Auty and Sandy Toussaint. Preface by Chris Cunneen

LIVERPOOL OF THE SOUTH SEAS

PERTH AND ITS POPULAR MUSIC

Edited by
TARA BRABAZON

University of Western Australia Press

First published in 2005 by
University of Western Australia Press
Crawley, Western Australia 6009
www.uwapress.uwa.edu.au

This book is copyright. Apart from any fair dealing for the purpose of private study, research, criticism or review, as permitted under the Copyright Act 1968, no part may be reproduced by any process without written permission. Enquiries should be made to the publisher.

Copyright © Introduction Tara Brabazon 2005; all other copyright is retained by the individual contributors.

Every reasonable effort has been made to obtain permission to reproduce copyright material in this publication. Copyright holders who have not received a request for permission to reproduce material should contact the publisher.

National Library of Australia Cataloguing-in-Publication entry:

Liverpool of the south seas: Perth and its popular music.

Bibliography.
Includes index.

ISBN 1 920694 30 7 (pbk.).

1. Popular music—Western Australia—Perth.
2. Music trade—Western Australia—Perth. I. Brabazon, Tara.

781.64099411

Cover photograph by Tara Brabazon
Designed by Pages in Action, Melbourne
Typeset in 10.5pt Adobe Garamond
Printed by BPA Print Group, Melbourne

Contents

Acknowledgments

Tara Brabazon wishes to thank all the talented and passionate contributors to this volume. They are accustomed to following their supervisor through all manner of schemes and dreams, but their efforts in this book have excelled far beyond even her lofty expectations. It is a tribute to our universities that punchy, courageous and committed work is still being produced during difficult times. Thanks to the Popular Culture Collective. You remind the editor—every day—why cultural studies is the coolest theory on the block.

On behalf of the contributors, it is important to recognise and thank those who shared their views and voices. Paul Higgins, Eve Arnold and many local DJs discussed the Higgins Hyde Park Hotel with Angela Jones. For the work on hip hop and b-boying, respect to Maze and the Systematic Crew, including Beni Benz and Taka in particular. Simon Collins and Julian Tompkin discussed with Carrie Kilpin the nature of writing and music. Sandi and Geoff Hudson took time from their business to talk to Debbie Hindley about 78 Records. Giovana Neves and the members of Seychelles Rhythms assisted in the writing of a chapter. RTR-FM has been a fount of expertise for this project. Major thanks are due to Pete Carroll and Stephen Mallinder. They are great people, and it has been a pleasure and privilege to work with them and tell their histories.

This work has been produced without vested interests imposing a direction, opinion or restriction on the research conducted or the arguments presented. Appropriately for a book on Western Australian popular music, the chapters that follow are staunchly independent and defiantly creative. The aim has been to produce prose that captures the quality of the music flowing from Perth and Western Australia. This goal was impossible to reach but in the flashes that follow, the best of writing matches sound with style and rhythm with respect.

Contributors

REBECCA BENNETT is a PhD student with a specialist expertise in travel, migration, marginalisation and popular culture. The relationship between cultural studies and tourist studies is a major focus for her work. She is fascinated with how notions of home and abroad are challenged through backpacker tourism. Rebecca also has an interest in multiliteracies.

TARA BRABAZON is an Associate Professor in Cultural Studies at Murdoch University. She has written five books, including *Tracking the Jack*, *Ladies Who Lunge* and *Digital Hemlock*. She has published widely in academic and journalistic publications, maintaining research commitments in popular cultural studies, popular music, sport, Internet studies, cultural difference, educational policy, city imaging and the night-time economy.

FELICITY CULL is a PhD student with interests in the politics of popular music. Billy Bragg's words and music are a particular focus of her research. Felicity's research in drum 'n' bass is matched by expertise and interest in 1980s pop music. Popular memory remains a theory and paradigm of great relevance in her work.

AMANDA EVANS completed her PhD in 2000 on style journalism. Her research expertise encompasses writing, literacy and popular culture, publishing in the areas of journalism and popular memory. Also of long-term focus has been the link between popular culture and space. She is currently a staff member at Curtin International College, specialising in ESL and media studies.

DEBBIE HINDLEY is a PhD student exploring the role of women in Australian Rules Football. Her expertise in sports studies is extended through a questioning of how cultural differences challenge the idea of a national, inclusive culture. Such work is seen in her research project on John Curtin. Debbie also has experience in cultural policy, governance structures and the regulation of popular culture.

ANGELA JONES is a PhD student researching the formulation of professional women. Fashion, as a creative industry and facilitator for power and social structures, is a hub of her research. She is also a musician, while maintaining expertise in technology, gender and cultural geography.

CARRIE KILPIN has completed a PhD specialising in women's use of the World Wide Web. She also maintains an independent writing career, working between journalistic and academic modes, with an interest in the politics of publishing. Carrie is also a web designer, and the web designer for the Popular Culture Collective.

CHRISTINA LEE is a PhD student working on Generation X film. She has expertise in screen theory and popular memory studies, matched by a strong grasp of youth studies and cultural studies. Her writing interests extend from film criticism to style journalism, while also maintaining an interest in popular memory studies.

KATHRYN LOCKE is a PhD student researching city imaging and the regulation of night-time economies. The application of the cultural studies framework to creative industries is a primary concern. She is focused on how cultural studies ideas, theories and concepts can be used to make the political economy more socially just, open and accessible.

LEANNE MCRAE was an Honorary Research Fellow at Murdoch University in 2003, having graduated from her PhD. She has also worked as a lecturer and tutor in Western Australian universities. Leanne has published in the areas of 'cult' television, film and fiction.

She is also an expert in hip hop cultures, media convergence and post-colonial theory, with a major concentration on the development of creative industries pedagogy.

RACHEL SHAVE is a PhD student with interests in feminism, multiculturalism, media and diversity. She has chapters featured in a soon-to-be-released book on slash fiction. Bodies, their meanings and limits, remain a long-term research trajectory. Rachel also works with—and researches—independent fan fiction. Writing and creativity are her passion.

CARLEY SMITH is an honours student at Murdoch University with expertise in fandom and fan cultures. The relationship between popular culture and its audiences is a particular emphasis in her scholarship. While fascinated by televisual science fiction, particularly 'Star Trek Voyager', she is committed to presenting fan voices and theories within an academic context.

ADAM TRAINER is a PhD student and a musician. His research interests encompass both film and music, particularly stressing the relationships between the two media. Not surprisingly, he has published material focusing on the sound and vision of David Bowie. This innovative convergence of film and music provides the basis for many of his current research projects.

You've Got About a Year: An Introduction

Tara Brabazon

> The city sucks us in, though. The city is moving towards us. The city is so alive we can hear it breathe. We can hear its stomach rumble.[1]
>
> *Paul Morley*

Throughout my professional life, there has been a subtle—but sometimes overt—pressure to leave Perth, vacate the West Coast and get into 'the main game'. The cloak of power enfolding Sydney, Melbourne and Canberra supposedly hems in the creative people and important networks. Sydney, the population capital, Melbourne, the cultural capital, and Canberra, the political capital, seem to sap the talent and passion from the rest of the nation. Travelling east on the Nullarbor, the sweaty road that connects the two sides of the continent, supposedly lifts the IQ of the traveller by some thirty points.

Perth has—either wistfully or derisively—been labelled the most isolated capital city in the world. Ensconced in the western corner of the country, its closest cities are Adelaide and Darwin located over two thousand kilometres away and separated by desert. This distance shapes identity and consciousness, requiring strategies to manage marginality. The isolation has consequences for literature, sport, politics and the performing arts but also popular music. The great centres of innovation in popular music during the last fifty years have been on the periphery of global cites. Seattle, the 'origin' of grunge, was culturally partitioned from Los Angeles and New York. Liverpool, the fuse of a musical—rather than territorial—British invasion, was removed from the blistering influence of London. Manchester, as the hotbed of acid house, gathered cultural influences from beyond the south of England. Dunedin, the long-time base for Flying Nun Records in New Zealand, was neither the nation's capital nor most populated city. Isolation from the economic or political centre shapes not only the relationship between music and community, but also widens the database of cultural influences. This network of ideas and identities is even more complex in Perth, which forges an intricate relationship with the rest of Western Australia. A huge state that is larger than many European countries, it is punctuated by a diversity of industries including mining, farming, gas production and tourism. The urban and rural relationship is important for popular music, with bands such as Spencer Tracy sourced from Collie and two of the three Waifs from Albany.[2] The relationship between Perth and the vast state of Western Australia has created a city-region of potency and complexity, forging a web of self-standing economic and social relationships and possibilities.[3]

Outsiders to social and economic power have built the most significant musical movements in the last fifty years. The Beatles' Liverpool, the Happy Mondays' Manchester and Nirvana's Seattle are three examples of musical cities that plucked above their weight. It is the pressure-cooker intensity of being excluded from the complacency of cultural main games that creates energetic and creative work. There are two elements that frame distinctiveness for Perth music. Extreme isolation generates insularity, protectiveness and self-satisfaction. Interweaving with this inwardness is a huge immigrant population that creates an associative web between cities, thereby encouraging extreme outwardness and interconnectedness. This combination forges Perth's cultural environment. The specificity of this popular cultural framework is rarely acknowledged, and often flattened or condensed to a division between the east and west coasts of Australia.

Globalisation, as a word and idea, infers a series of equivalent relationships, but there are profound inequalities that prevent a fair and equitable trade in ideas, immigrants or capital. Local, national and global relationships are interdependent, not adversarial. Local identities remain important, not because they are authentic or real, but because they demonstrate what happens to global formations of popular culture in specific spaces.

ABOUT A YEAR IN DULLSVILLE

> You've got about a year.
>
> *A & R Officer, Festival Mushroom*

Through all the hype, hope and promise of Perth music, there are doubters and dreamers who reside within old and frequently destructive models for managing music. As part of the Western Australian Music Industry (WAMI) Festival for 2003, a Technical and Further Education (TAFE) campus in Perth hosted a panel of 'experts' on the music industry. All were from Sydney and Melbourne. Once more, the great and good gurus from the south-eastern states of Australia explained to Perth-based musicians why gatekeepers such as themselves were important and necessary to the popular music industry. Such self-fulfilling prophecies are often delivered with great commitment and confidence. The room was burgeoning with young and talented musicians, desperately wanting information and a mirror to their excitement for this city at a special time. The version of music marketing the experts sold was pre-Kazaa,[4] capturing and performing the problems confronting national music industries and international recording conglomerates.

The panel assumed and interlinked three mistaken assumptions of popular music: nationalism, rock and capitalism. During this seminar, a worldview was summoned that was as outmoded as it was dangerous. Firstly, they assumed that Sydney and Melbourne record companies, producers and managers had a reach that encompassed the entire continent, with entrees into the wider world of music. These A & R executives admitted that they 'make it' to Perth twice a year, but remain 'excited' by 'the scene' (man). In other words, through two annual trips, they assume that they can hoover up the talent and move the bands to Sydney. They have no understanding that popular music is—and has been for some time—a relationship between cities and not nations. Perth's industry has as many relationships with Manchester, Sheffield, Seattle, Bristol and Austin as Sydney. With the distribution mechanism of record companies being fire-bombed by the Internet, it is no longer clear—precisely—what a record label can do for a band. By working in a national mode, these executives were able to demean a significant city, reducing Perth's music industry to a trend or fashion. Nationalism has always been a mask for industry executives in Sydney and Melbourne to maintain a power base and confirm that they are really not redundant—that inter-city relationships for producing, mixing, downloading and touring have not over-written the tired nation state.

The next error perpetuated by this distinguished panel was to apply a rock discourse to the diverse and exciting plurality that is popular music. The only model of instrumentation in which they held either expertise or interest was three men (invariably) with guitars, backed by a drummer. This mode of music is fifty years old. There is little fresh or exciting about rock. Certainly great rock songs are being written, but the genre itself is as tired and craggy as Keith Richards' face, and probably less interesting. For this panel, it was as if dance music never happened. The innovative, edgy rhythms in the last twenty years that have shaken up the sonic palette have emerged from dance music. Those of us who have lived though the dance revolution laugh long and hard at those who argue that pub and stadium rock, with four-minute songs in predictable time signatures and—at best—eight chords in a major key, is innovative. The rock ideology is not redundant, but it is boring. It is the relationship *between* guitars and keyboards, drums and drum programming that provides the basis for innovative music. Listening to these executives, it was like nothing had changed since The Beatles played in Hamburg.

The final problem expressed by the panel was probably the most interesting. Those of us who live in Perth expect Sydney, Melbourne and Canberra residents to think they run the country economically, socially or politically. What was most surprising is the blatant and obvious acceptance by both the panel and the punters at the seminar that music and market capitalism is the way forward. The panel—although split between major and independent labels—assumed that the performers in the room would continue to create music for love, while record companies would make profit *for them.* Continually, the executives affirmed that musicians must not enter the industry for the money, but the love of music. Such a maxim seems very convenient for shareholders, if not performers. Clearly, none of the panel had heard of creative industry initiatives or how city policy makers throughout the world are instigating strategies and policies to grow music, fashion, design, architecture, film, sport and tourism. They not only believed in the nation and rock: they were espousing an old mode of capitalism where Post-Fordism, niche marketing, customisation and casualised workforces never emerged.

Trapped in the musical nirvana of the late 1950s, these A & R men and women—who rarely hold on to their jobs for more than two years—are perpetuating a myth of the music industry that has been challenged for two decades and is effectively being replaced. The notion that they could come to Perth with little knowledge of the city's intricate musical economy, which has social tentacles throughout the world, and perpetuate a myth that bands must move east before they can go north, is arrogant, outdated and wrong. Unfortunately, the young music students did not yet see the nakedness of the entrepreneurial emperors before them. When asked by one of the students about the long-term fortunes of the Perth scene, an A & R executive from Festival Mushroom replied that 'You've got about a year.' After that time, supposedly another musical trend will take the attention of Sydney and Melbourne companies, to make another fast buck on the back—and hopes—of another few talented but desperate musicians. Perth's music is not a trend, fashion or quirky intervention in national programming. It is an industry like any other, and can be grown and sustained. With cultural mapping and considered policies, an agenda for development can be established.

Such a context of dismissal and denial provides a rationale for the 'Dullsville' tag that has haunted Perth since the *West Australian* newspaper screamed this headline on a front page in November 2000. Andrew Gregory explained that this tag emerged because 'many Perth residents did not travel much, so they did not appreciate the city because they had nothing to compare.'[5] Unmentioned in this article is that Western Australia has the highest proportion of immigrants of any state, confirmed by the 2001 census figures. It is difficult to argue for the monocultural insularity of a state when half the population are either immigrants or the sons and daughters of immigrants. Ironically, when Paul Toohey came to write the next great attack on Perth and its people in a feature article in the *Weekend Australian*, he focused on the racism, insularity, stylistic vulgarity and affluence. Toohey, who left the city aged fourteen and returned only to look down on the place he left, offered advice to those of us who stayed.

> Perth does have a bit of a chip on its shoulder, and it's time to flick it off. Perth has everything but is frightened of losing it. Any city must make its compromise, but Perth is yet to sit at the negotiating table.[6]

The final sentence is an odd one. How an entire city makes compromises is uncertain. He suggests that the city lacks diversity and culture, is insular, inward and arrogant. In rewriting his interpretation with a more positive spin, Perth's citizens are focused, reflexive and confident. It is cheap and easy to live in Perth. Public infrastructure provides trains and buses, there are myriad areas of peace and quiet, and house prices and rents are embarrassingly low. Such an environment can breed inwardness, but it can also create a networked community—a digital fishing village—of culture, economics, education and media. But one of the lessons of this book is that Perth is not isolated. The world has come here, and Perth music goes to the world. The network of cities that includes Perth is formed through a very specific immigration history. Not included in Toohey's article—perhaps because he did not return to the city for a sufficient duration—were the music, dancing, rhythms and passions that punctuate the streets, clubs and pubs.

Perth's weather is light and sunny. Winter days are temperate and the beaches are palettes of bright whites and intense blues. Clichés swim in such environments. It becomes a safe place to raise children, a sporting and leisure capital, and produces a laidback lifestyle. All these mantras may be true, but they miss the mark. To research the music of such a place requires more than hearing The Triffids' 'Bury Me Deep in Love' in every crash of a wave on Cottesloe Beach. The function of isolation is felt not only socially and culturally, but institutionally.

Perth bands, performers and electronica communities are left alone to develop musical styles, honing production, songwriting and live performances. By the time that Sydney music executives 'discover' a Perth band, they have already worked their way through bad venues, aggressive crowds, dodgy PAs and a mixing desk that sounds as if it is below six feet of water. Similarly, DJs and dance producers are freed from the superclubs and insular Sydney 'scenes' to gather their sounds, beats and pulses from further afield. In the global mixing environment, Perth is South Manchester and West Chicago. There is little pressure to homogenise the mixes. House music and its derivatives still thrive in Perth. It is an incubator for a sound and sensibility that may have been lost from a generation of producers eager to conform to the new, fashionable and banal.

MAPPING THE MUSIC

> Why the hell has Manchester got so many fantastic bands? I mean, the thing that amused me about Manchester was that they were saying there was this vanguard of bands from Manchester—the way that Manchester was going to save the world with bands like the Happy Mondays and The Charlatans, Inspiral Carpets, and I used to sit there and think, what is this crap? You look at Joy Division, New Order, The Smiths…But as to why Manchester has so many bands, I've no idea. You could almost be vague enough to say that it must be something to do with the water, because there's no other bloody reason![7]
>
> *Peter Hook*

Something interesting happens in second tier cities, and it is not in the water. Peter Hook, legendary bass player with Joy Division and New Order, expressed the problem well. Why do particular places develop innovative sounds and rhythms, while others do not? Located outside the matrix of global cities (London–Paris–Madrid–Tokyo–Sydney–New York–Auckland), there are advantages in being excluded from the main game. Differences develop and standardisation is avoided. Quirky specificities thrive. But further, the second cities 'talk' to each other, trading differences on the monopoly board of commodified sameness.

Manchester mixes play in Perth clubs. Bristol dub lilts the trance. Dunedin's jangly guitar finds life in suburban pubs. There is a reason why Perth's music is entering a period of visibility. The great music cities—Seattle, Chicago, Manchester, Sheffield, Dunedin, Austin and Liverpool—are not capital cities of their respective nations, but second tier cities. With all the creative, critical, institutional and economic attention focused on London, Los Angeles, New York, Sydney and Melbourne, bands, DJs and producers not resident in these centres can 'hide in the light,' developing a sound, skill base and experience without early pressure.

Research projects, such as the Globalization and World Cities Study Group (GaWC) at Loughborough University in the United Kingdom have attempted to rank world cities into alpha, beta and gamma categories. By their rankings, Sydney is a Beta World City, Melbourne is a Gamma World City, with Brisbane and Adelaide showing some evidence of World City formation. Perth is absent from their lists.[8] Only when looking to their evidential base for such a judgment are the justifications revealed. They judge World City status through the distribution of offices and foreign affiliates for accountancy, advertising, banking and financial services. The creative industries, education institutions and transportation policy and infrastructure are all formations that contribute and facilitate the building of a great city but are left outside of their relevant data collection. To study popular music and its relationship to place requires a mapping of metageographies and the cultural frameworks in which people live. A critical urbanism necessitates more than a functional stock exchange to commence an analysis. The music industry is more difficult to monitor than headquarters of banking services. Particularly if city-region relationships are taken seriously, Perth has enormous natural resources through which to build a sphere of social and economic success.

All cities share particular characteristics, with differences instigated through immigration, landscape and economic concerns.[9] Constructions and mediations of locality are formed around and through cultural sites such as music. Increasingly, as governmental policies aim to develop entrepreneurial rather than social welfare initiatives, cities are sites of marketing and consumption, not collectivised political struggle. The imaging of places has been important to political movements, with Manchester the source for Friedrich Engels' writings about the scars of industrialisation. In a post-industrial age, marketing and government policies advertise the uniqueness of cities utilising the creative industries, tourism and sport to restructure an urban economy.[10] The marketing of place not only sells a city but aims to promote local economic development. These policy initiatives emerged in (post) industrial Blairite Britain, where it has been necessary to re-inscribe the landscape and permit new economic initiatives to develop.[11]

The relationship between music and cities is important, conscious and promotable. Andrew Blake realised that 'we associate music with places, often enough we quite deliberately make music to fit them.'[12] There is a characteristic that links musical cities. Manchester,[13] Austin, Liverpool,[14] Bristol, Sheffield and Perth are sites of large student populations. This base provides a mobile, young and educated group of consumers. Perth, with a population of 1.3 million people, is serviced by five universities creating a broad base for not only musical audiences but academic commentary about the industry, of which this book is an example. Therefore, cities are not only stopovers in a trade route: a musical route can also be tracked. A cartography of music—or a mapping of a beat—offers insight into urban studies. Architects, urban planners, politicians, local governments and engineers all organise space, but an attention to music facilitates an awareness of how cities are lived in, and living.

The rhetoric of globalisation has limitations in the provision of explanations and solutions to social and economic problems. A network of localisms provides a more precise framework for a political economy managing the changes in technology and their impact on the production, distribution and reception of music. For example, for the first time in 2001 the sale of blank discs outstripped pre-recorded compact discs.[15] The purpose and function of record companies in such an environment is unclear. New identities and cultures are forming, and these innovations are ignored if scholars focus on narratives of continuity such as the nation state and musical genres such as rock. The trans-local form of electronica means that these musical formations are rarely visible within national policy networks or infrastructure.[16] It is easier to fund a band through time in a recording studio or tour schedule than to facilitate the development of remixing, electronic commerce and club-mediated events.

Music has been used with great effectiveness to shift the imaging of various cities, and Perth's creative industries policy makers can learn from these examples. Cities embody and perform the health of the economy. Liverpool is an archetype of a beat-led recovery. Paul du Noyer's study of the city has seen the port as 'more than a place where music happens. Liverpool is the reason *why* music happens.'[17] This spatial determinant for musical success is always difficult to prove. But the continual success of Liverpool's music even after the Merseybeat explosion in the 1960s demonstrates that specific social and economic relationships allow innovative music to develop. From Frankie Goes to Hollywood to Echo and the Bunnymen, from Orchestral Manoeuvres in the Dark to Atomic Kitten and the club Cream, the relationship between creativity and commerce has forged an environment for musical production. There are many similarities between Perth and Liverpool. Both are ports[18] and gateways to external musical influences. Both are two cities in one. Liverpool and Birkenhead is paired with Perth and Fremantle. Ports facilitate the movement of people, goods, ideas and records. The disconnectedness of Perth from the rest of the country is similar to the cultural partitioning of Liverpool and London. This distance is not only spatial but cultural, with politicians, business people, media executives and celebrities rarely travelling to the periphery. Further, many bands exist in a small city centre and there are few venues in which to play. Differences do exist: Liverpool has—frequently negative—press coverage about inner-city crime, unemployment and industrial decline. Perth is so ignored by the media that even characters from *Neighbours* rarely end up here. Brisbane is the favoured location when heading for Coventry, in soap-opera speak. Therefore, other cities can offer both insight and assistance in the development of policy initiatives for Perth music.

Probably the finest book written on city music is Barry Shank's *Dissonant Identities: The Rock 'n' Roll Scene in Austin, Texas.*[19] It is comprehensive, ethnographic and sensitive to changing urban and rural relationships. Austin's music is characterised by a desire to work through the ambivalent meanings of Texas and being Texan. As Shank realised,

> the rock 'n' roll scene in Austin, Texas, is characterised by the productive contestation between these two forces: the fierce desire to remake oneself through musical practice, and the equally powerful struggle to affirm the value of that practice in the complexly structured late-capitalist marketplace.[20]

What makes this study so important is that Shank adds new meanings and sites to the study of a music scene, including record stores, nightclubs, rehearsal rooms and streets. He also recognises the crucial role that student consumers play in the music industry. The writers in *Liverpool of the South Seas* have applied this model for a city music industry, while aware of the differences between Austin and Perth, particularly in terms of dance music and culture.[21]

The other great city of applicable interest to the study of musical Perth is Manchester, which suffers through 'London's journalistic reification'[22] in much the same way as Perth's relationship with Sydney-based media. Similarly to Perth's high level of immigration, Manchester's—and particularly Salford's—immigrant cultures initiate diverse musical and stylistic influences. The urgent bass of northern soul alongside the popular groove of funk knitted a network of styles and melodies. Manchester's reimaging is rewriting its social and economic fabric and future. As Dave Haslam realised,

> Manchester, like England, is now re-creating itself, looking for a new role, a life without manufacturing industry. Like a middle-aged man made redundant after a lifetime in a factory, Manchester is either facing years drawing charity, welfare and government

> handouts, or it's going to retrain, reorganise, and find something to keep it occupied.[23]

When leisure becomes a business, the new jobs in entertainment, tourism and the service industries are pivotal to economic survival. Manchester nightclubs pull 15,000 people into the city centre every Saturday night, providing 500 jobs.[24] Manchester is known for its music and football. Both allow a suite of other industries to thrive in design, fashion and hospitality. However, there is a significant social difference. Haslam believed that Mancunians 'have always been haunted by dreams of escape.'[25] In Perth, the dreams are different. A parochial loyalty is what concerns outsiders to the city, perhaps triggered because Perth is a city of immigrants who have lived elsewhere and have decided to settle. There is a simple argument—perpetuated by Sara Cohen and Dave Haslam—that when unemployment is high, music is a viable career option. This is not the case or correlation in Perth. However, because of the geographical isolation, there is a necessity to make entertainment, music and fun without a reliance on other cities and places. Dis-connectedness is a trigger for creativity.

Migration makes a city open to other sounds and visions, creating a bower bird culture, picking and choosing from the shiny, the new and the different. Also immigration cities are aspirational cultures. Some 'immigration' has been forced through exploitation, with lasting musical consequences. Bristol—like Liverpool—was a slave port in the eighteenth century. The street names, such as Whiteladies Road, Blackboy Hill and Jamaica Street, betray this history. The influence of hip hop, punk and reggae cuts through the looping formation that is trip hop, embodied by Massive Attack, Tricky and Portishead. The key development of Bristol's music was the capacity to channel a two-tone musical and social history through world-wide changes in musical technology via the midi interface.[26] Bristol provides an example of how diversity and immigration can shape a city's music.

Like Bristol, Dunedin embodies all the problems and strengths of an identifiable city's sound. Simplified to jangly guitars and a single record label, Flying Nun, Dunedin shows how the focus on 'a scene' or 'a sound' can inhibit the plurality of musics in a city. For example, in 1993, Flying Nun acts toured Australia, under the banner of 'Beyond the Jangle.' The record label's success, so tethered to the sound of The Clean, The Chills and The Verlaines, was marketable, but reified. Dunedin—like Manchester and Bristol—is a university town. It too is isolated, this time in the deep south of the South Island. It is only 20 degrees north of the Antarctic circle and 1,300 kilometres from Auckland. Tony Mitchell believed that 'this isolation contributed to the development of a distinctively local South Island sonic identity.'[27] The impact of isolation—particularly before the proliferation of digital audio tapes and the World Wide Web—means that the main influences on bands are each other. The difficulty is that Flying Nun was circumscribed by genre. By offering and marketing a pastiche of British guitar bands, this style made it difficult to move on or expand musically. Flying Nun transferred to Auckland in 1988 and lost much of its notoriety and fame in the process.[28]

Each of these cities offers insight into Perth and its music, both in terms of how musical success is formed and how creative policies can sustain the industry. There are profound lessons to be learnt from Austin, Liverpool, Manchester, Bristol and Dunedin. Each provides an explanation for the emergence of popular music in a particular time and place. Importantly, many of these musical cities have attracted scholars to conduct research into the night-time economy, music, dancing and city imaging. The possible approaches to popular music are rich and diverse. Many of these methods are included in this collection on Perth. The act of writing about music remains important as it offers a way to mark, judge, connect and theorise space and sound.

WRITING THE DIFFERENCE

Music is important. It is more than a melodic combination of notes, deft turntablism or a probing voice. Writing about music gives rhythm an agenda. Every musical movement requires its enthusiasts to catalogue the experience. Punk had Dick Hebdige.[29] Acid house and techno had Steve Redhead and the Manchester Institute for Popular Culture.[30] At its exciting, passionate best, Cultural Studies writing grasps at the coat tails of fashions. The fame of the best cultural studies scholarship is deserved because the resident scholars wrote about punks or ravers with immediacy and punch. Postgraduate students were dancing and thinking, watching and writing. At this moment a group based within Murdoch University's Popular Culture Collective has explored Perth and its music. *Liverpool of the South Seas* is the first post-scene, post-sound book written about a city's music. The writers featured in this collection were sent out at the same time, to return with a residue of rhythm. As always in these cases, multiple Perths were uncovered, each throbbing with energy, excitement and dark ambivalence suggesting that something—perhaps something big—is happening. The resultant collection is not a work of history or journalism. It is not uniformly ethnographic or musicological, although these approaches leave their tracks on the chapters. Best situated in Cultural Studies, this book is inter-disciplinary and radically presentist, carrying forward the most troubling and exciting parts of the past.

This book is a significant intervention in thinking about music in Australia. The writers are young, conducting ethnographic research as they move through their daily lives. Before they attended university, they were embedded in the scenes they now analyse using the critical and interpretative benefits of their education. They are able to speak and write in a way that captures an adrenalin and energy not possible by academics whose record collection is locked—and lost—in the 1960s. Popular music is the most ephemeral of media, moving and changing at frightening speed. Particularly, this book problematises the notion of a singular 'Perth sound'. Such a phrase makes it easy for recording executives, journalists and academics to pigeonhole the music from a city and then discredit it when a trend or sound is no longer fashionable. Probably, for marketing executives, the 'Perth sound' is currently a combination of a beach beat and jangly Rickenbacker-knock offs. Spencer Tracy's 'Ocean' is probably the closest archetype. But with Little Birdy and The Waifs both gaining chart success,[31] the picture becomes more clouded. The Panics are expansively creative, filling out the extremities of their sonic landscape. Their first album *A House on a Street in the Town I'm From*, pastiches many times and places. Through this diversity, the 'Perth sound' becomes a vague reference point. Add hip hop to the mix, with the pioneering work of Downsyde and Micadelic, who recorded the first acapella hip hop album in the country, and the guitar and drums determinants no longer provide simple answers to difficult questions about space, identity and music. Then there is the Perth dance community, which offers many commodities and collectives, exploding with new genres, mixes and remixes. Probably if this book has a function it is to recognise the long-term and unwritten role that Perth has played in house and drum 'n' bass.

Those writers and record executives who think that Perth's music may be the next big thing have little sense of how big this 'thing' is. From The Waifs' slide guitar to Soundlab's precision loops, from The Bank Holidays' simulacra Beach Boys to Micadelic's beat boxing, Perth's music is delicate and diverse. It has texture, buoyancy, flight and passion: cool guitars and slick rhythms, freaky dancing and famous venues. Perth has always added the jangly guitars to the mix, based on the 1980s performances from the legendary Stems[32] and The Triffids. There is an unwritten history that few mention, composed from smoke and mirrors, cool electronica and hot clubs. Perth may be the new Liverpool of rock, but it remains the Manchester of dance culture.

As a work of cultural mapping, part of the function of the chapters that follow is to reveal the energy of Perth's popular music without excuses. It is a musical map of a city, but like most maps, some features are flattened or absent. Particularly alt-country and metal, with tight and burgeoning musics and audiences, are under-represented. This absence is in itself a strong sign of growth, and demonstrates that no book can be encompassing of all music in a city. Different types of writing were necessary to map diverse communities, identities and music. Drum 'n' bass necessitates different theories and vocabularies to hip hop. The chapters sweep from ethnography to more interpretative work about the night-time economy, multiculturalism, sexuality, gender and dance culture. Attention is placed on post-rock and race. Many e-interviews have been conducted, activating a virtual mode of 'oral' history. As a new tool for research, alternative voices and ideas are created and theorised. These methods have been useful, building a database of material about Perth's music that currently does not exist. The resultant book is not a definitive history, but provides a musical snapshot with a memory and agenda.

The best of music writing is not only 'about' the music, but uses melody and rhythm to commence a critical commentary about society. The obsessional nature of popular music is life affirming, encouraging a plaiting of word play and sound play. Unfortunately, the medium has only rarely been served by great writers. The calibre of Greil Marcus[33] and Paul Morley has overwritten the banality of countless hacks. Music holds a history of magic, excess, power and desire. To write about music transforms emotion into mediated abstraction. There is a need to place in prose what is felt through the feet. Writing about popular music is difficult. It always feels like we are draining the life from the beat, image, fabric or feeling. Because so much of music is non-linguistic, there is a need to translate fashion, rhythm, space and bodies on to the page.

Not a catalogue of great bands, not a narrative of famous record companies, *Liverpool of the South Seas* questions, critiques and researches whether—and then how—Perth's many sounds and scenes are distinctive and innovative. Many books have been written about local and national musics. None have amalgamated dance and rock, success and banality, the big night out and the comedown. By stressing trans-localism and the relationship between cities, new ways of thinking about space, identity and rhythm emerge. While avoiding parochialism, there is a necessity to stress the particular, the specific and the distinctive. Creativity is a social, rather than individual, practice. Creativity always has a place, and emerges from a group of interesting—and interested—people. As Dave Haslam has realised, 'Capital cities have legislators but not innovators.'[34]

The difficulty emerges in connecting innovation with the legislation. Or—put another way by Robert Palmer in *Deep Blues*—'how much history can be communicated by pressure on a guitar string?'[35] Most moments in our lives leave no residue of hopes, desires or fears. Sentiment seems cheap when compared to wider political movements. The aim is to link emotion and politics with colour, light and dynamism. There is no easy tether between landscapes and soundscapes. But by putting pressure on a guitar string, a note reverberates beyond the tone of expectations.

PART I

FRAMING PERTH'S MUSIC

CHAPTER 1

The Wide Open Road—Filling the Potholes

Felicity Cull

> I wake up in the morning,
> Thinking I'm still by your side,
> I reach out just to touch you, then I realise,
> It's a wide open road.[1]
> *'Wide Open Road,' The Triffids*

This chapter investigates the nature of Perth's local music scene through shards of the past—Bon Scott, The Triffids and The Stems. Using these bands and artists as a vector, I track how the Perth scene has been silenced from Australia's music history. I fill in the potholes of Perth's wide open road. It would be impossible to sketch out the bumpy terrain of Perth's music in full, so rather than being a descriptive or general narrative, this chapter looks at snapshots of Perth's music history: Bon Scott's place in Perth's local scene in the 1960s, then moving through two bands with different trajectories from the 1980s—The Triffids and The Stems.

Perth bands seemingly arrive in Melbourne or Sydney as fully fledged performers and the band's history is commenced from their arrival in the Eastern States. The part that Perth played in a band's beginnings is often absent from popular knowledge. Financial backing from a major record company in Sydney has often been a necessity for Perth bands, particularly from the 1960s to the 1980s. But this has led to Perth scenes taking on a unique blend—bands play live, hone their skills and become established before being signed to a label. This process has tended to produce musicians of high calibre and experience. Perhaps the embodiment of this trajectory of remembering and forgetting Perth is the popular memories encircling Bon Scott.

BACK TO THE BON

> 'I met Bon Scott,' he said.
> 'Huh?' I questioned.
> 'Bon Scott. He played here in bands in the 60s when I was playing.'
> 'Bon Scott played in bands in Perth?'
> My father rolls his eyes as if to say 'kids today' and pours more honey on his cereal.

I have never been a huge fan of Bon Scott. I never really get into him until 'TNT' comes on at a drunken party. But I know enough to recognise post-inebriation that the band is Australian. When my father told me that Scott had played a large part in the local scene in the 1960s, releasing singles from Perth before moving to the Eastern States, I was puzzled. If I knew Bon Scott was Australian, then why didn't I know that he had started his musical career in Perth? Bon Scott's place in musical history is assured—but the place Perth occupies within his history is not. Bon Scott spent most of his childhood in Fremantle, and is buried in the Fremantle Cemetery Memorial Garden.[2] He was a part of the musical scene in Perth in the 1960s but this part in his career is barely a footnote of history.

Bon Scott started his musical career in 1966 with the band The Spectors, and soon moved on to The Valentines with Vince Lovegrove.[3] At the time, the local scene encircled 'Stomps' that were organised by radio stations 6KY and 6PR. Three or four bands played a night, and travelled between different gigs. Most of the bands played sets entirely formed by covers of popular songs. If bands wanted to be hired, their play list had to be similar to that of the radio stations. Few working Perth bands at the time composed original material. My father Merv Cull was a member of The Kollection, a band that was advertised as 'The Perth Easybeats.' Bands played a medley of covers from the English Merseybeat sound and original songs from Eastern States groups that had record deals. A youth newspaper at the time wrote of Merv Cull that he 'can make his guitar do anything.'[4] However, despite a high level of skill, the band never played or recorded any original compositions. As Merv Cull states: 'We were like a big jukebox—there wasn't the technology at the time to play records loud enough to fill a club and get everyone dancing, so we played the hits of the time that were playing on the radio. That is what the vast majority of bands in Perth were doing at the time.'[5] The Valentines were an exception to this rule. The band released a single on Perth's Clarion label, which had affiliations with Festival in Australia. 'Every Day I Have to Cry' reached Top 5 on the local charts.[6] Soon after, they released three more songs that were unsuccessful and they moved to Melbourne, eventually disbanding in 1970.[7] Although Bon Scott is considered an Australian artist of note, his beginnings in a Western Australian band are less acknowledged. As Greil Marcus states: 'It's as if parts of history, because they don't fit the story a people wants to tell itself, can survive only as haunts and fairy-tales.'[8] Perth's part in the history of Australian music does not fit into the narratives of Australian popular music which are framed around Sydney and Melbourne. The control of the radio stations in the 1960s meant covers were the norm and because of this, a Perth band wanting work found it hard to obtain a record deal because original songs were required. While having great skill, they were unable to earn a living as a band and be original. As Wayne Hosking, a Perth musician who works in a cover band, states:

> Perth, in general, was known as the cover band capital of Australia. If you were an original band you went to Sydney, Melbourne, any other place, but Perth notoriously had fantastic cover bands.[9]

Because of the economic demands to play covers, Perth's original bands were in a position where they had to relocate. Perth's original musicians have therefore had their origin and locality pruned from accounts of their history.

BURYING THE WEST

> After leaving our hometown we're learning, not learning to love it or anything, but learning to realise what was there, in what seemed like an emptiness.[10]
>
> *David McComb*

The Triffids were a Western Australian band that never played by the rules. They were a group of Perth schoolchildren from relatively affluent families who were connected by a love of music. A band was formed, centred around talented lyricist David McComb. But where Perth bands are supposed to claim either Sydney or Melbourne as their base, The Triffids never buried the West. Their style was distinctive. As a reviewer quipped in 1984, their music was 'resoundingly tuneful and varied—a fact which sets it apart from the bulk of fashionable Australian rock.'[11] While they relocated to the Eastern States and spent much time in Europe, The Triffids let Perth strongly flavour their work and made it almost impossible to forget from where they had hailed. They were a band much maligned and ignored by the Sydney and Melbourne music press, only to be reclaimed by them after David McComb's death. The Triffids did not fit into the established narrative of Oz Rock—their music always accessed a bigger culture. Because of this complexity, the music they left behind has a currency beyond ephemeral chart success.

One of the main reasons The Triffids made a mark on Australian music is that they wrote about the landscape in a new and interesting way. In an interview with Niall Lucy, McComb stated,

> I think it's the great challenge of the moment. To reflect where you came from without degenerating into clichés...in Australia you've got this very daunting, but very inspiring, impossible task to create a new vernacular. Or create something without degenerating into caricature that can reflect, you know, a sense of place.[12]

David McComb's lyrics, particularly in the song 'Wide Open Road,' capture his search for this new vernacular. The metaphor of a wide open road is now established and well used as a particularly Western Australian way to describe emotional desolation. A wide open road, like those roads that take drivers beyond the suburbs of Perth and into rural Western Australia, is the perfect metaphor for the emptiness and isolation felt 'when the one you love is sleeping with someone else.'[13] McComb's use of the landscape is extraordinary and complex. It does not rely on cliché—maybe this is because he is not describing the clichéd landscape of Sydney or Melbourne but the open and sparse spaces of Western Australia. Mike Martin suggests, 'a major influence on the group's sound was their geographical location.'[14] It is an exposed and light Perth landscape that flavours The Triffids. From the aerial photograph of Mandurah in 1961 on the *Born Sandy Devotional* cover to *In the Pines*, which was recorded in a shearing shed in Jerdacuttup, Western Australia never left this band's music, whether or not they were resident in Perth. David McComb told Glenn A. Baker 'we haven't turned our backs on Perth. It still plays quite an important part in our music and our lyrics.'[15]

Despite the strong Western Australian influence in their work, The Triffids' popular history often starts—as with so many other bands—from the moment they left Perth. In an article written in 1984, Stuart Cope writes, 'January 6th 1982 is an important date in the Triffids' saga. This unlikely bunch arrived in Sydney intent on discovering a fortune and maybe some fame as well.'[16] The band's trajectory is measured from the time that they left Perth. Success is assumed to commence in Sydney, rather than when The Triffids were an established band in Perth with regular gigs at The Stoned Crow in Fremantle and The Broadway Tavern in Nedlands. The band was aware that they would 'have to leave Australia to progress.'[17] When they left Perth, the difference and uniqueness the city had imbued in them remained to be heard in their music. For maintaining this allegiance, The Triffids stayed on the periphery of the Australian music business, residing in 'both Sydney and Melbourne and never being accepted in either city.'[18] The song 'Wide Open Road' was popular enough to earn a place for The Triffids in Australian music, and they also played at the Australian Made concert in 1987 with INXS, The Divinyls, The Saints, Mental As Anything and Jimmy Barnes. Tony Barrass notes that they were voted 'best live band in the country' by *Sounds* that year.[19] Often their finest moment is noted as when their song 'Bury Me Deep in Love' was played on *Neighbours*.

Beyond this minor burst of fame, the Sydney and Melbourne music press in the 1980s rarely had praise for The Triffids. Stuart Cope wrote an article in 1984 that commenced with the line 'Almost everything about The Triffids makes me think of Johnny Thunders' line: baby, we were born to lose.'[20] In Cope's eyes, The Triffids were 'out of time'[21] but it may be more correct to say they were out of place. Their music was so Western Australian that it did not translate to the rest of the continent. Stuart Cope went on to write of their album *Treeless Plain* that it would 'no doubt get stacks of critical acclaim and sell about 17 copies. Such is life for a band like The Triffids—never quite hip enough for the inner city, never quite basic enough for the suburbs.'[22] Years after this article was written, this kind of sentiment kept The Triffids unrecognised as one of Australia's finest bands. At the Mushroom 25th Anniversary Concert, despite being part of the label, they were not invited to play. Or so it appears. In a strange moment in the concert, Chris Bailey was joined on stage by Paul Kelly. The latter introduced the duo's performance of 'Wide Open Road' in an odd fashion.

> We'd like to do a song written by Mr David McComb of The Triffids. They can't be—they're not—here today. So we'll sing it for them.[23]

Fifty-two acts performed during the day-long concert, including Christie Allen, Molar and The Ferrets: worthy performers but not, by most criteria, significant. Yet the songwriter who created a new vocabulary for emotion and the landscape, and a band who opened ears to strings, guitars and edgy vocals, was absent. Through this exclusion, The Triffids remained on the very edge of Australia's music history, and would have stayed there, slowly fading from memory.

But then in 1999, David McComb died. The notoriety granted through death has cemented his place in Australian music. As a tribute, Tony Barrass wrote an article about David McComb and The Triffids for the *Australian*. The article commenced with:

> Paul Kelly acknowledges his influence and European rock fans went bananas for his band in the 80s, but former Triffids lead singer and lyricist, David McComb died in Victoria this year to little fanfare in his hometown of Perth.[24]

The Triffids' and McComb's success is measured by the esteem of Paul Kelly rather than any of their own achievements. After decades of ignoring the band and downgrading them in the Sydney and Melbourne music press, it is Perth's music community who are portrayed as the ones who do not understand their importance. Actually, a music community that never really acknowledged his significance during life has reclaimed McComb after death. McComb will remain a testament to the talent that can hail from Perth.

POWER IN THE POP

> They say I'm strange and they think you're crazy
> Don't worry about them
> Don't you worry at all
>
> *'For Always,' The Stems*[25]

The Stems, a band that played 1960s inspired power pop, formed in Perth in 1983 around Dom Mariani. At this time, cover bands still dominated pub gigs. The Stems original compositions led them to lead the original music scene with regular gigs at The Wizbah, and the Shenton Park Hotel.[26] In Perth, The Stems were seriously cool. Rebecca MacGregor, who saw them live at the UWA refectory in the 1980s, remembers 'shamelessly copying their 60s sunglasses and spending a whole weekend screen printing my school bag with "The Stems" in white fabric paint.'[27] The band recorded three songs 'She's a Monster,' 'Make You Mine' and 'Tears Me in Two' in Perth at Shelter Studios in 1984.[28] Then The Stems, like those before them, relocated and made their base in Sydney. The Stems then broke up, re-forming in the 2000s to play live once more.

The Stems occupy a strange place in Australian music history. Their trajectory has not ended—they still play and produce new material. As such, unlike Bon Scott and David McComb they cannot (yet) be canonised into Australian rock history. There is burgeoning recognition of their influence. In 2002, Off The Hip released a tribute compilation, *The Great Stems Hoax.* Their music continues to be played. In a poignant moment in the sleeve notes of the compilation, a Perth-based fan of The Stems tried to capture the band's importance and following in their home city. He concludes his story with a melancholic denouement.

> But this is the point where I should stop. I'm not the one who should speak now. I only saw it bud. Only from afar did I watch it unfold, flower and fold. Anyway, I haven't told you the whole truth here. I've only told you mine. I remember few names and fewer faces, and they won't remember me. There must have been hundreds there—there must have been. But it seems like there was only a handful. Was I there? I don't know. Does it matter? No way![29]

These memories do matter. The thousands of people who saw The Stems at The Stoned Crow or in university courtyards and refectories are now in their thirties and forties, living a life with a soundtrack that needs to be acknowledged and celebrated. Death has led to Scott and McComb having obituaries written about them that track their careers, even the 'humble' beginnings. The Stems have few such articles written about them. The band never set out to leave Perth. Dom Mariani states: 'We set out to record one single and maybe never get out of Perth, but the way the things went the timing was great and we just went with it, and we ended up doing lots of singles and an album, which is more than we ever thought we would do.'[30] Being signed to Citadel meant they were accepted by Sydney's local scene, but they are not a significant part of the Australian music canon. While they achieved some commercial success particularly with their single 'At First Sight,' they are rarely lauded for their innovation. As so many bands erase their history when they leave Perth, the fact that The Stems still play in the city complicates their place in Australian music. Without conscious and active remembering of the sunglasses, the guitars and that incredible voice, their place in the photograph of Western Australian music may fade. It is the role of cultural historians to keep the popular memory thriving and developing.

So many snapshots of Perth's music need to be replaced into Australian music history. In an industry dominated by Sydney and Melbourne, Perth's music can easily be forgotten. Histories that sketch out the role and path of these bands are vital for new Perth musicians and the fans that were there. We need to bring place back to pop.

CHAPTER 2

Selling a Music Landscape

Debbie Hindley

Over three decades ago, 78 Records commenced retailing recorded music to the public of Perth. On 19 June 1971 Geoff 'Hud' Hudson and friends, John 'Scruff' McGregor and John Hood, set up shop on the first floor of the Padbury Building, adjacent to Forrest Place, in the centre of Perth's CBD. Their aim was not to make money, but to satisfy their own and others' interest in the diversity of music that the world had to offer through the recording industry but which was inaccessible via the regular outlets. Their business was founded on passion, an ingredient that has enabled the business to endure the challenges of the retail industry in Perth and changes in the recorded music industry. Before 'cutting edge' and 'niche marketing' were clichés, 78 Records led with Perth's first listening stations to 'try before you buy'. Although national retail music chains use saturation advertising, the business has marketed itself simply through handbills, and word of mouth and those instantly recognisable car bumper stickers with their black on white logo of Blind Lemon Jefferson.

While the philosophy is constant, Hud's business partner is now his wife Sandi, who became involved in the store in 1989 after the departure of McGregor and Hood. Their location has changed four times in the thirty years, first at the Padbury Building and now the Mortlock

FIGURE 1: 78 Records logo

Building in Hay Street, but one element remains faithful—the commitment to music in its myriad of forms and to those patrons who share the passion. 78 Records are integral facilitators of a local music scene and youth cultures. 78 Records offer space and place. The youth of Perth are welcome to be themselves. While politicians and planners ponder how to critique Perth's dull and colourless reputation, its vibrant youth are moved on from department stores, malls and places where only the cashed-up, conventional and suited are acceptable.

There was a time when 78 Records provided space for local bands to perform on Friday afternoons and on weekends at their premises. These gigs were led by Western Australian Youth Jazz Orchestra (WAYJO)—the original in-house resident band for Friday afternoons. Although the Friday afternoon bands no longer perform, 78 Records continue to support local bands by stocking their music and through their website[1] which promotes local bands' recordings to the world. They have also helped maintain the Western Australian Music Industry Association and RTR-FM through sponsorships.

78 Records have served the diverse musical interests of their loyal local customers. The original aim of satisfying complex and plural musical tastes was innovative. Their support for local music over the

years reveals something only recently discovered by journalists and politicians: Perth has a contemporary music industry worth supporting. Yet the proprietors, Hud and Sandi, are self-effacing about their role in sustaining those in the local music scene. They are also critical of 'artificial incentives' offered to fledgling musicians via the creative industries policy, believing in fervour and flair as the genesis for committed and talented artists.

On a wet Sunday September morning I interviewed Hud and Sandi Hudson of 78 Records. We started talking generally about the Perth scene, a prelude to the formal interview.

Sandi: The questions are—are the bands in Perth a little diverse for having been so isolated; and has Perth built up its own culture?
Hud: Yes Perth probably has its own culture. The way it happens in slightly smaller cities is that it is easier to get things organised because the city is not so big. In Sydney young bands have fewer places for them to get gigs because it's just so bloody big.
Sandi: And Sydney has been taken over by pokies in all the pubs.
Hud: Also true of Melbourne and Adelaide.
Sandi: And also they're a step ahead of the rest of the country because they take on the culture of overseas, they are quite heavily into dance music and DJs. So the bands, actual bands, and live music have taken a back seat.
Hud: It makes me wonder sometimes whether if a city is too big it becomes a disadvantage. If you get a city the size of Perth and it's isolated, then there is enough diversity to have a lot of things but it's not too big to water it down.
Sandi: When it gets as big as New York it actually has its sub-cultures.
Hud: It fragments; it has to fragment again, because the city is so big. Whereas Perth is probably the right size. Though in Perth, we definitely suffer a bit of an isolation cringe. I think we are proud of it in some ways. Perth is probably a good size where people with similar interests can still almost get to know each other and play in gigs around the city. It is just that it is so isolated from everything else. When cities get bigger, like Sydney, they're so vast you can't get them all together, you have

all these pockets. Perth can pull it together—it punches above its weight. Whereas in Sydney it is fragmented and that could be a contributing factor for why cities like Perth and Manchester happen more than the Londons and New Yorks. Well, people say it happens. I think it is fashionable to say that these smaller cities can drive it. I think they can organise better because the city is more compact. At the moment you have two bands having a huge amount of success, well internationally, with The Waifs and John Butler.
Sandi: Even more than that you have got The Sleepy Jackson.
Hud: It goes in waves and at the time it happens if there are three or four bands this naturally makes you think 'Oh wow, that's the hotbed of where it is happening.' In the big-time scale of things, it's no more than anywhere else. If you look back over all of the years, it's not as if Perth's been the one constantly pushing out bands. I think that people who are distanced like to say 'We can be as good.' It's the 'home-grown' thing.

What influences did you have to develop an interest in music?

Hud: I was a kid who grew up listening to the radio in the fifties—fifties, early sixties. I can remember listening to the radio in the fifties and all those quirky programs, on Sunday nights. They would have the top ten singles and the hit parade shows, the Ace Drive-In Top Ten on Sunday nights. It was a very different era. I was brought up on radio, listened to the radio all the time. I can always remember my dad had the radio on Sing-along. I guess if the radio had never been on in the house I would have never got interested. I'd listen to the radio and get captivated by the songs, all those corny old songs. And then when I got to my teens it was around the time of the sixties English…the start of The Beatles and that was a pretty exciting time. So if you were at all interested you were really glued to your radio and radio then actually played decent songs. Radio then just wasn't chasing the advertising dollars and demographics, it was playing music like it was discovering it and it was fun, whereas now it is just patter. So radio was really, really, really fun, turned people on to it. It was just a mirror it held it all up and said here it is—here is all this wonderful Liverpool music coming out of England. Previous to that all we heard on the radio was all the white

American middle-class boys, the lovely toothy boys so nobody got near the black music. Then after the English music arrived the radio stations then started playing the black artists that the English had been influenced by. So if you were at all interested in music then I can't see how you couldn't get hooked. Then you start to play guitar badly, do that for a while and then go to bands, muck around after school, always looking for something else, all that sort of caper. I just stayed with it, because I liked it.

Did you have any ambitions to compose music or to perform?

Hud: No not really—not to compose but I played in bands a bit in my late teens. We did some whacky things at work, fringe festival type of things, like the Chainsaw Orchestra. Not as an ongoing thing.
Sandi: Hud is in the National ABC Archives for the Chainsaw Orchestra.
Hud: We just liked doing some whacky things. We actually performed at the Fringe Festival of Perth and Fremantle. It was a bit of a buzz, but I'm not seriously interested in performing. I am more of a collector and listener and watcher of music, a reader. But then again, underneath, secretly, maybe I would have loved to have been one. I am delighted that Christopher[2] is so into music. I get enjoyment out of watching him play. For Christopher, his singing and playing is for now, it's not to create something great, it is the enjoyment of playing for the moment. I find a part of me in him, he sees music as the moment. I guess it is pretty uncanny that he is doing what I would have probably liked to have done, but I enjoy what I have done and am doing in the shop.

As you have now served several Perth generations in 78 Records, what do you believe have been the major changes in music during this time?

Hud: If you're talking about the medium of delivery, then obviously the CD, if you are talking about the change.

What about the sound? Has the sound changed?

Sandi: Kids are always going to look for new sounds but they are all basically working off the same notes.

Hud: It is all the same notes, but what's interesting is the thing that comes to mind, 'The more things change the more that they remain the same.' I don't mean that negatively, it's just the way it is. Of course it changes.

Sandi: I reckon what has changed is that now so many people are making so much music and there are so many sub-genres that people fragment what they listen to more. Before it was like 'This is the sound,' it was the sound of the sixties or the disco of the seventies or the heavy rock or whatever. You either liked the disco or the heavy rock or pop or soul. These days it's just fragmented so much. Too much. To the point where people get heavily into one tiny little thing and as retailers try to keep abreast of all the different areas of music that people are listening to and are passionate about and expect us to know about, it is a nightmare. It's almost got a bit wanky.

Hud: To me it's all music.

Sandi: We pluck bits out of everywhere because we don't really get involved in the style.

Hud: I don't have a style that I necessarily favour.

Sandi: But a lot of people do. Especially the dance scene, the hip hop, trance. Dance music has about ten different genres or more.

Hud: I think there is a bit of wank value about all those names. It's a pity because what it does is to stop people from getting interested in other forms of music and they think that's all they like so won't listen to other music. It's all music, you like it, or not.

Sandi: It's not a new syndrome, there are a lot of people in your vintage who are still stuck in the sixties and don't listen to anything beyond that.

Hud: Yes, but it gets back to radio. These days that's all encompassing. The big companies and the media they have done it for their own benefit, put out so many sub-genres so they can market down to a tiny demographic and milk every vein that they can. Which is sad, but it happens. All those terms, when you think back to it there were enough terms around in the sixties, there was rock, blues and there was jazz and sort of folk and classical and the middle of the road orchestral. Essentially there wasn't too much more than that. Whereas now they hang

every label off it. Struth. A great example is what they call punk today. Now it is just a name. Punk to me, when I think of the word 'Punk' in its first use, I remember Status Quo. I remember using that word for them in the early seventies just because it was a punked out sound but it really was a bruisy sound. But the music industry used 'punk' for that whole English thing, the Sex Pistols. Now if you put those bands in the Punk section—that's not punk. The kids who want punk now, they are into different sorts of bands. The bands who were founded on that word, on that whole English revolution of punk and New York, the Sex Pistols, the New York Dolls, they're not punk—you put them in Rock.
Sandi: It's the same with metal. What we called a metal band in the seventies, they are in Rock and Pop now because now metal is quite different to seventies' metal.
Hud: Darker.
Sandi: Over the years we have had to adjust and move bands into different departments as the times change.
Hud: We also have to reflect what people want.
Sandi: The music from years ago, for the older vintage of people and who are going to walk down that A–Z alphabet, they are more discerning. For the kids who will only listen to punk, it has to go into the Punk area.
Hud: In fact they are less discerning, because they haven't opened their ears. Fashion has driven music into lots of little crevices and while there are good sides about that, it exposes things about the downsides.

78 Records has always been located in Perth's CBD—but its reputation goes much further afield—to those with diverse musical interests and also to many international artists. How has the city of Perth—and the culture of this city—changed what you do?

Sandi: It hasn't changed us at all. We do what we want. We have never been driven by anything apart from our philosophy…Hud has said he always wanted the best record store.
Hud: Never get there.
Sandi: That has always been the dream so we work and work and any profits gained are ploughed back, because we just want the best record store.

Hud: We don't necessarily make good business decisions. You learn to balance it all. We have worked long and hard for a lot of years.
Sandi: We aren't influenced by any culture or anything that is going on. The only thing we are consciously driven by is stocking a diverse lot of music because that excites us and excites the staff. The biggest event of our working month is when an American shipment comes in with a whole bunch of CDs in it and it's like bees to the honey pot. The staff are just so excited by it. There is a long line of CDs at the CD player waiting to be listened to.
Hud: We tend to stay pretty constant, the city changes around us. We have changed a bit, like we said earlier when we have had to move shops. The city itself has also changed. With huge suburban shopping centres fewer people go to the city.
Sandi: One of the things that we do, and other stores do, but we tend to have more than other stores, is the 'in stores'—in store performances, especially with the bigger bands, like a big national band or a signing by an international band. That really does have a culture attached to it, because the kids absolutely love talking about it. It's like when we were young we would reminisce about when we went to Gaslight in Sherwood Court and Alistair Norwood was at the door and he wouldn't let us in, we built it up bigger than it was at the time. Now I hear kids talking 'I went to this in-store at 78 Records' or 'I remember seeing so and so at 78 Records.'
Hud: I think we have stuck around long enough to become a bit of an institution in Perth.
Sandi: Young bands say 'I remember playing up at 78 Records.' It's been part of our evolution, we try and not be stagnant and not stay in our own mindset.
Hud: The core is still the very first thing we talked about, the passion.
Sandi: And we are really patient with people. A lot of places would not be as easy going as we are with people coming in and listening to twenty CDs before they will buy one. We have people we call professional listeners who come in and listen to music but never buy a CD. Then there are the kids who come in and hang around. Sometimes I get really heartened to see some young kid, especially if they are on their

own, not with a pack, choose his CD, buy it and walk out. I get heartened that there are still kids who do want to hear music and I like the excitement of the kids when we do have an in-store. Some kids are there hours and hours before. They are just there, they hang around.
Hud: They are smitten by the excitement where fewer kids are these days.

We touched on this before. Is it accurate to describe Perth music as distinctive, in the way that Liverpool, Seattle, LA, Manchester and Dunedin developed their distinctive sounds?

Hud: A little bit—maybe. I don't necessary agree with that because I reckon it's all similar. Everyone influences everyone else and everyone drinks from the well. I reckon that sort of difference and those cities and those bands come in waves, it becomes 'the thing' for a while. I reckon that's a quirk of fate, a bit of luck, a bit of timing, a bit of the companies that were looking in that direction at that time. I reckon whatever happened in those cities happened in any big city another time and which one gets chosen is a little bit of luck. I don't think their sounds are all that unique; they are all pulling from that same well of inspiration. It gets back to the argument of how original things are and everybody tries to think everything is totally original. I don't think there is anything totally original, it's all been done, it's just how well you put your influences together and how sincere and convincing it is to the listener, listening to it at the time. I can't see what can be totally original.

78 Records would have to have the largest collection of locally produced music. Can you tell me about how you began to support the local musicians?

Hud: It began with cassettes. In the late eighties I began stocking Perth bands without a recording contract. They would come to me saying 'We've made a tape' and ask 'Would you sell it for us?' We started to support them by saying 'Yeah, bloody good idea—why not?' This is the city they come from and even if it's only Mum, Dad and the auntie, at

least they can have somewhere to buy it. We've got stuff they might be interested in too. It was no skin off our nose; it just seemed the logical thing to do. Why wouldn't you?
Sandi: And I guess people came to us because we were known. It became a bigger and bigger thing. Then we highlighted the local music and made sure it was in its own section with its own listening station. We have one staff member, who plays in a band who looks after the local music section. At the moment we have two large wall displays featuring local bands.
Hud: It got to such a stage that there was enough so that you could make a department.
Sandi: Now if a local band has a CD they are in two sections of the shop, they are in the normal Rock, Pop & Jazz and the Perth section, so they can be found easily. Then the website featuring local music started around 1995–96.[3] We decided if we are talking global—what would be unique to our website? We decided we could highlight Perth music to make 78 Records different. So we have always dedicated a large part of our website to local music and we still maintain that. I would suggest that our website has the best database of local Perth music of anything that is available. Everything new that comes out we scan the covers, we put track listings and they can all be bought online. It's as comprehensive as we can make it and we have maintained it over the years, so it is quite extensive now. Even when things are deleted we have left the information there because it's history now.

We sell a lot of local music overseas. Sometimes it is friends of the band, or someone who has heard of the band and word of mouth. They say you can get it from 78 Records online. 78 Records does sell local music to all over the world.
Hud: I think everybody would know this—every city in the world, every city, has just got kids and bands making music and now with the technology they are making albums in their own bedroom, burn it and do it. Then when you have lots of community radio or university radio, they are likely to play anything, play some kid and somebody is going to like it. If that happens you are not likely to find it in any music catalogues. Then where do you go? Where is there a shop that's probably going to sell a band in Perth?

Your support of local music—which is important to the individual and the industry—is not well known. Why do you believe that 78 Records has been left out of most histories and commentaries on the Perth music industry?

Sandi: Because we are a retailer and they see that we are making money from it and that makes us not relevant. It's like the WAMI, Western Australian Music Industry Awards, for years and years and years, we have financially supported WAM, and we support RTR-FM to help keep the radio running so that they can play local music.
Hud: We have always sponsored WAM with money and prizes but I don't care about accolades or kudos. I like being a quiet achiever.
Sandi: While we had upstairs for the 'in-stores' we gave Perth bands a stage, bands that would not have got a gig anywhere else in Perth because the pubs have got to make money. For years we would have two or three bands playing every weekend and all the mums, dads, grandparents would come and watch their kids play their very first gig. It cost the bands nothing, we hired PAs, lighting. It cost us a staff member to run it, to mix their music. We documented it all, we have four volumes of photos and signatures from all of the kids and their bands from those years.

Can you tell me more about the gigs, when did they start, who played, which bands have gone on, what sorts of bands played?

Sandi: The first gig commenced on Saturday 16 March 1996 and they continued until 2000. The first band was Jebediah and they came back for a number of repeat gigs. Over those years hundreds of bands played at these in-stores over Saturdays and Sundays.

Many of the bands who played were straight out of the garage, 78 Records gave them their first gig. In many cases it was their first and only gig because pubs will not employ bands unless they're known. We would get telephone calls asking 'can we play?' As time went on we found that we were becoming a bit more discerning about who played because some were bloody awful and we had to keep the shop's operations going while the bands were playing.

Bands that have gone on that played at 78 Records are John Butler, Jebediah, The Sleepy Jackson, Eskimo Joe, Sodastream, Adam Said Galore, Turnstyle, The Waifs played in December of 1996. Superscope played for years. Spank played for a while and then went overseas. Fourth Floor Collapse—they've been signed by a major label—they cut their teeth at 78 Records. To have 'made it' is to be signed by a major label. Yummy Fur who did well for themselves, went to London where they had to change their name to 6 Mile High.

For safety reasons we had to impose rules that the audience had to sit and watch. And 78 Records was an all-ages venue, many of the kids were under eighteen and couldn't go to pubs.

Hud: I would have loved to keep staging the gigs but it got to the stage where we couldn't because business now just keeps getting tighter and tighter. We could not afford to keep doing it. In an ideal world we would have kept doing it, but it was probably costing us at least $800 a month, just in hiring the PA and the lights.

Sandi: It was really good. The kids loved it. I loved doing it but economics won out in the end and we couldn't afford to run that floor of the shop.

Were you asked for your input into the Ministerial Taskforce on the Western Australian Contemporary Music Industry? What did you say?

Sandi: Yes. It was a phone interview.

Hud: You can imagine what I think about these things. I can see where they are coming from but I just do not know that you need to do these things.

Sandi: They had to determine how to distribute the funds because the Federal Government had set quite a lot of money aside for contemporary music. It had to be decided where it would be best spent and how it would be best spent.

Hud: Any idiot can form a committee in government. Look at great moments in music and they never got any government funding, it just happened.

Sandi: One of the biggest things for me that I cringe at is the amount of people who get government grants to produce music. It's wrong. The reality is that people who have a passion for music will go out and do it anyway and they will always find a way. To be given all that money… having said that we have applied for grants…

Hud: No, not 78 Records.

Sandi: Not the business, the boy's band has applied for grants.

This is The Tigers?

Sandi: The Tigers have received a grant.
Hud: Well, what did you say? 'Bugger it, if they are giving it away…'
Sandi: That's exactly right and we decided that someone is going to get that money and someone is going to go away on the tour, why not The Tigers?
Hud: I disagree with it. There are a lot of social issues the government should be funding.
Sandi: Yes, if music and the arts never got any money you would still have artists and musicians and they would still battle on and do what they are going to do.
Hud: Artists shouldn't be left to struggle, but you open a whole can of worms when governments fund arts, you add another layer of politics that isn't needed. Once you add government grants you add complications. People get chosen for all the wrong reasons.
Sandi: Professional filler-out of forms. Some people are good at filling out forms.
Hud: They could be the least artistic merited people. The person with the most artistic merit could be some bloody left-wing social protest person who can't even be bothered filling out the forms.
Sandi: That is why I was motivated to respond because I wanted to make the point that given that the money is there, it should be channelled into certain areas.
Hud: Talking to Chris, he is dead against it. You should do it because you want to do it. You shouldn't get money to do it. I think he has our same philosophy. Equally there is an argument for doing something, but I don't know, it's a bit Monty Pythonish really, once you get committees and governments…it becomes pear-shaped after a while. I think you should leave this industry to its own devices, it has created wonderful music before and I have a horrible feeling that it could be a dumbing down or homogenising, you could end up with something ordinary. Technically nice but with no soul. We know Bob Dylan can't sing but there is more emotion in his voice than in all these pop idols who get up and 'experts' tell us they can sing.

The interview with Hud and Sandi scratched the surface of their knowledge of the music scene in Perth. Their involvement within Perth music is not just as retailers, several of their employees are musicians, their son is a musician and many of their friends are musicians. They have actively supported the local music industry by dedicating a section of their store to local recordings. Additionally, through their website, they promote local music to the world. In the past, Friday afternoon and weekend gigs provided, literally and metaphorically, a stage for many bands to perform. For some bands it was their one and only gig, while others built on the experience. It is ironic that the Perth music scene has only recently come to the attention of the State Government and journalists when 78 Records have been quietly fostering it for decades.

CHAPTER 3

Party People in the House(s): The Hobos of History

Christina Lee

> History is written as we speak, its borders are mapped long before any of us open our mouths, and written history, which makes the common knowledge out of which our newspapers report the events of the day, creates its own refugees, displaced persons, men and women without a country, cast out of time, the living dead: are you still alive, really?[1]
>
> *Greil Marcus*

History is slippery. It is imperfect and fraught with the dangers of dominant narratives that conveniently erase the stories of the disempowered—the young, the economically challenged, ethnic minorities and the sexually diverse. Add to this the fibre of emotion and the cloth of monolithic history begins to fray at the seams to expose the filaments of supposed 'truths'.

This chapter pays homage to dance culture in Perth by restoring some of its deletions from local history. In doing so, I do not present a complete, irrefutable chronicle of the origins and projection of where this—or any—scene has come from or is going. Dance history is itself an oxymoron. It is impossible to reconcile the experience of nights spent in darkened rooms, drenched with sweat and pulsating to a kicking beat, with directives outlined by the city's Minister for Culture and the Arts. Rather, I revel in a node of time and space that has been largely ignored as a part of the metropolis's cultural and social anatomy. With the glitterati and bright lights that shine from the megalopolises of Sydney and Melbourne as the entertainment capitals of the country, it is seductive to dismiss Perth as 'Dullsville', marinating in backwaters. The burgeoning recognition of The Sleepy Jackson, The Waifs and Eskimo Joe has refocused attention upon Western Australia's music scene, only to ignore dance culture. This chapter grants a mode of representation for the 'faceless many' on crowded club floors who are often relegated to the footnotes of history.[2] Pivotally, my research also arches towards international club studies, offering both a case study and sample for the mix.

When I started research for this project, I would casually ask people: 'Does Perth have a distinctly identifiable dance culture? Tell me about the history of clubbing in the city.' This inquiry would be met with blank stares, or a scratch of the head, or resounding outbursts of 'No!' Unconvinced, I burrowed persistently deeper to find that my respondents were both correct *and* incorrect. The city—like all cities—does not have an indisputable, cohesive dance culture and history. It has always been splintered and fragmented. Its origins are so variegated that it is impossible to clearly delineate beginnings and endings. Perth has no grand master (flash) narrative, no individual place, event and style that has been seared into public consciousness. Devoid of a 'big club' like the Hacienda or Studio 54, Perth's dance history is difficult to track. Instead, traces of this ill-shaped story are summoned through talking to interviewees. The individuals were asked whether Perth has ever had an establishment that was, and is remembered as, the Mecca for weekend dancers. Despite their diverse ages, no consensus is reached in identifying a single venue as ever having been the quintessential meeting point for 'serious' clubbers (by first-hand experience or urban legend).

> The Firm! This is the club that opened up the ears of Perth. When it expanded across the hallway (into the old strip club Tiffany's) it was a dance club on one side and an indie club on the other. It was a symbol of all that was right with Perth in the 90s. Subcultural angst gave way to discernible listening and manic dancing! Also—for me—Berlin and Limbo cannot be ignored—where else could you go for a drink before picking up your map and then heading out into the industrial wasteland for a party!
>
> *[29-year-old teacher]*

> I think Players definitely. Purely because the place changed on different nights. Disco to funk to house to break-beat to doof

> beats. So many different styles, often on the same night. They would bring in the biggest overseas DJs and everyone was there to have a good time. Everybody came to dance, take drugs and love the world. It gave local DJs as much space as international acts, so we'd all go to see our friends play. Plus, everybody loved that bed in the middle of the lounge.
>
> *[30-year-old student and retail assistant]*

> There is no big club in Perth—although most club owners would disagree. The venues are changeable; the organisers of big events do not stick to one venue to house the acts they sell for. All clubs have big nights, but there is no superclub. There is consistency to the kind of events a club will cater for, but no constancy.
>
> *[21-year-old student]*

Without a definitive landmark to act as the anchorage for an era, personal (as opposed to official) histories are constructed through popular memories that, whilst inconsistent and unstable, are no less credible. Although 'the story' of dance culture in Perth defies easy categorisation, it should not be mistaken as being devoid of roots. This becomes evident when back-tracking to the gay glamour of the 1990s.

In the website 'Gay in Perth, Australia,' the authors commented that the scene 'reminded us of the US in the late sixties: unmarked doors and hard to find addresses.'[3]

> The location of gay venues in Perth is very much a representation of the marginalisation of homosexuality in the wider social and cultural consciousness. They all exist on the fringes of Perth's mainstream nightclub area. The Court is hidden behind the Alexander Library, Connections is a non-descript door at the end of a street of popular nightclubs, and Pink is located in The Big Apple—a nightclub in East Perth, far from the Northbridge night scene.
>
> *[26-year-old student]*

This respondent's statement is a telling sign of the position of the gay dance scene outside the centre of dominant culture. With no equivalent to Sydney's Pink Parade—Oxford Street—and lack of archival documentation (with the exception of limited street press such as the free monthly magazine *Shout*), this club culture is kept underground and suppressed in size. However, this interpretation does not convey its significant contribution to the city's nightlife. Perth is home to one of the nation's longest running gay clubs—Connections—which is heading towards its third decade of operation. Still pulling in crowds (the loyal and the curious) on weekends, it is a testament to the sustaining of sexually alternative 'places of pleasure' in a city with a population of just under 1.5 million citizens.

With the phenomenal rise of electronic music and rave culture in the United Kingdom and Europe in the late 1980s, Perth also experienced its own parallel outbreak of patrons who demanded all-nighter clubs where they could, quite simply, dance. With the death of disco, clubbing aficionados demanded spaces where they could be lost in oblivion—which was also partially due to casual use of drugs to reach altered states of (un)consciousness—and which could not be easily found in the straight 'meat markets'. These generic and chemical changes oversaw the migration en masse of straight dancers to gay clubs that were already operating at maximum capacity. Lines around corner blocks and waiting periods of up to an hour became the norm for many of these premises. A 'filtering' of heterosexual customers at the door was not uncommon, to curb numbers and prevent the influx of straight men who were assumed—rightly or wrongly—to bring in 'hostile' behaviour. As one of the interviewees commented:

> DCs in the late 90s certainly had a huge effect on the Perth dance scene—and of course anyone who wanted to be anyone was then trying to get into Connies after that. But puh-lease! The affected drawls that some of the straightest men I knew put on after being at DCs was enough to make you want to eat your own arm.
>
> *[29-year-old teacher]*

While DCs and Connections remained the established oligopolies of the clubbing scene for both heterosexual and homosexual crowds, Perth hosted a multitude of one-night-a-week events that proved hugely successful. These were generally held in straight clubs hired for the evening. They included nights of Passion at Rise Nightclub, Red Lion at The Deen Nightclub (formerly The Aberdeen) and Pink at various locations such as The Big Apple and Rise. One of the most significant in terms of sheer size and flamboyant grandiosity was Trade which operated from August 1996 to 2000. Speaking to James Anthony, the originator and promoter of Trade (and others including Heaven, Camp and the resurrected Pink nights), it is not difficult to see the glint of intense pride and vicarious exuberance he undergoes when recollecting the deep impressions the gay clubbing scene made on the social landscape.

> **James:** If you came to town on a Thursday night, whatever concerts were on, [the performers] used to come up to Trade afterwards because we had a good thing with the record company. We've partied with Jimmy Barnes. He's been up three times to Trade. Marcia Hines, we've partied with. We've had everyone from Bananarama, Newton, Les Girls. The original Les Girls even performed for us...Boy George has been up when he's been in town. I've got a whole photo wall gallery of all these people... That's my idea of a club. Celebrities, star power, the music.

Bananarama? Boy George? As passé as they may be *today*, their presence back *then* would have elicited pandemonium (Milli Vanilli anyone?). What is intriguing in this scenario is where the evidence and records of these occurrences are to be found. If they exist at all, it is in the rapture of reminiscence or a club promoter's personal photo collection. The power of dance culture is its ephemerality—its transience. However, it is also the reason for the consignment of anecdotes and memorabilia to what Greil Marcus terms the dustbin of history, where those rendered invisible and voiceless are deprived of representation and validation.

Gay club culture is not the only community to be made vagrant in time. Despite the barrage of media reports of the rave subculture in the United Kingdom from the late 1980s through to the mid-1990s—vilifying a new generation of folk devils—it is notably missing from the Perth spotlight (although it did receive considerable attention from 1992 to 1994, several years *after* the scene had already been established here). As several respondents were quick to point out, Perth *did* have a prominent rave culture that was not merely a derivative of its eastern cousins. This narrative is often overshadowed by predictable cycles of news broadcasts of illicit drug use at dance parties and the shock-horror antics of young people. I spoke with Simon 'Hutcho' Hutchinson and Barry Mulvaney. Both have been organising parties since 1991 and recall when rave was first introduced to the city.[4] Witnessing (and fostering) its inception and chameleon-like changes over the past decade, they confirmed that Perth—rather than a blip on the map—was a significant player in rave culture. They cited its regular inclusion in *Eternity* magazine after impressing Paul Booth, who ran the publication. *Eternity* was England's largest underground rave magazine in the mid-1990s and was regarded as the Bible for any self-respecting 'twenty-four hour party person'.

> **Barry:** When he found out we had underground rave, he couldn't believe it. He was rapt.
> **Simon:** He made me the Australian correspondent after that for three years until the magazine folded. I was writing for them and doing articles on Perth. Every month, they'd give us one or two pages on the Perth scene which was nice because you knew everyone was reading about the English scene but not many were ever reading about the Australian one, especially internationally.
> **Barry:** And also because the DJs in the UK read that article, they used to come over for raves. They used to love coming here like Scott Brown, Carl Cox, Ratty—the guys from Ratpack.

The Britannia–Australia connection was not arbitrary. Perth, and its surrounding metropolitan zones, is home to a large community of

English-born migrants.[5] English youth were largely responsible for the importing of rave music, fashion and 'lifestyle' to the west coast—or as Hutchinson described, 'boys from the Midlands or London'. Later, the state would be integral in the export of digital music to the east. Whilst the origins of rave culture were transported from overseas, it was hybridised and appropriated in Western Australia to create its own progeny with south of the (equatorial) border characteristics.

> Déjà vu. One of the first big New Year's Eve [parties]. 92. Pretty sure, yeah, 92. That was in the middle of a paddock out Armadale way, I think it was. My memories of that was sitting up on the top of the hill with this girl I'd met, and we were watching over the rave. And because it was, you know, summer and everything, the paddock was all dry, so there was this big dust cloud where everyone was dancing because they were just kicking up heaps of dust everywhere. Probably a couple of thousand, yeah.
>
> *[32-year-old stocktake manager and freelance bouncer]*

In the early 1990s, Perth saw a flood of illegal raves open up in all manner of sites such as abandoned warehouses, mine quarries and empty fields. The scenario was not unlike that occurring in the northern hemisphere (from San Francisco to Sheffield)—day-glo vests, pork-pie hats, whistles, bubble-blowing machines, and the incessant dancing that was only interrupted by the chemically induced hugging of friends and complete strangers.

> [The rave] was in 1997, don't remember what it was called. I remember where it was. In Welshpool, just off Star Street, at a Hellenic centre? Must have been there at least five or six times, but hey, that was years ago. You know how they say drugs affect your memory. Aaarrr—the wonder of ecstasy. I was [dressed as] a bishop...my friend—the Pope—was there along with lots of furry animals. That was my most memorable experience—being dressed up as a bishop, dancing on stage, blessing the crowd of about three to four thousand ravers, and I'm not even religious.
>
> *[30-year-old financial consultant]*

> DJs like Miggy and Big Mac were pumping out the house tunes and we were all having a ball…seeing a handful of people up on the hill, skipping in between trees on the horizon, linking arms, happy to skip the night away together, watching people on the bumper cars cutting sick, the circus set up and the people in costume adding to the theme of 'anything goes'…On our way home we all stopped by McDonalds and my two friends were getting meal deals. I can't remember which one of them said it but I remember one of them looking at their food and saying: 'This is not a meal…this is an adventure!'
>
> *[30-year-old financial planner]*

> There was one I was at that got closed down just after I left, but from what I hear the police went in and they cut the power to the building and told everyone to get out…this girl had actually walked outside to go get some fresh air and then tried to get back in. She'd got through into the building and the police dragged her out by the hair and it caused a riot, because inside the place everyone was making their own music, everyone was stamping their feet, clapping their hands and dancing to that instead. But the place emptied eventually and everyone came outside…I think three police cars got trashed. Someone went up and down the police cars with a can of paint and sprayed them all. Didn't even make the news.
>
> *[32-year-old stocktake manager and freelance bouncer]*

The cryptic maps leading to secret rave locations were metaphoric signs as to how the events would (not) be documented. Rave culture prided itself on leaving little residue, making it as untrackable as possible. The residue of empty drink bottles and the lingering scent of perspiring bodies were the corporeal, tangible evidence that people had been there. Writing about the event is like trying to photograph a shadow that has already moved. The result has been a disorganised tradition of oral histories premised on sensory memories and private collections of paraphernalia—posters, fliers, technicolour garments—hoarded by the 'pack rat' of rave couture.

The impact of this cultural formation inevitably drifted from the hazy fields and ramshackle buildings to permeate the consciousness of those whose days did not start until after dark. The local community radio station RTR-FM 92.1 began to cater for dance music devotees with weekly slots dedicated solely to that genre. Importantly, the station's BPM (Beats Per Minute) is the world's longest running dance music radio program.[6] Suburban clothing boutiques stocked outlandish styles to satisfy the escalating demands of party people. Established venues also began to poach aspects of rave. Even pub-like bars morphed into mini-raves every weekend, with glow sticks, lasers, the embracing of Disco Biscuits and the ethos of being blissed out. This vibrancy and verve were reinforced with a growing populace of DJs who would become the pioneers of a thriving creative industry in the state. Their influence would not stop at the Western Australian border, but would infiltrate the wider national and global markets. Despite this, knowledge of Perth's 'superstar' DJs remains limited mainly to the fans and practitioners of electronic music—possibly by choice, but largely as a by-product of inadequate modes of (re)educating the general public as to the existence and significance of the talent evident in local dance music. Whilst Perth-born Rachel Harvey has attained international recognition and Darren Briais (originally from Queensland but now based in Perth) is one of the country's most sought-after DJs, one would be hard pressed to find any recognition of their achievements and standing in published, authorised documents—past and present.[7] What happens to these figures and experiences—the incredibly fierce energy—when the night is over? How will they be remembered? Who will do the remembering? When the dust of history leaves little or no vestige in the domains of myth, rumour and personal accounts, no truths can be revealed. Only stories can be retold. Are these 'stories' enough?

Wallowing in the past is just as dangerous as never having been written into it in the first place. Holding a midnight vigil over dead and buried beats is a noble cause, but it creates its own displaced citizens in time—those in the present who perpetuate the cycle of historical absence. Fixation on nostalgia means the continuing influence and contribution of Perth DJ culture on national and international circuits are unacknowledged. It creates a blatant disregard of the current 'revival' of gay glamour in one-night-a-week events and 'experimentation' to reinject an old scene with new flavours.[8] It ignores the collaboration of old skool ravers in Perth with young initiates who congregate on a regular basis to relive the music of a bygone 'golden' era, and to explore sounds beyond. Uneasy inscriptions of yesteryear's memories scribble over today's events. What is needed is a negotiation of private memory with accessible forms of history that allow for alternative narratives of people, places and moments to exist—travelling towards a future without forgetting what has been left behind. Change is inevitable—and necessary. After all, who wants to relive the same throbbing bass, in the same room, every Saturday night for the rest of their lives?

Breaking Down Barriers: B-boys and Girls

Leanne McRae

There is an untold history of b-boying in Perth. The young men who have danced their way through youth are scattered among the urban sprawl. Their struggle to find hip hop material, learn new moves and create a community has been erased from the margins. Instead, a culture of extreme games, Donkey Kong and skate-parks market a youth culture to young people. The unique affirmation and empowerment afforded to struggling masculinity through b-boying remains unmarked and untraced.

Through my years of observation on the fringes of hip hop culture I have gained tremendous respect for these dancers. Currently, there is a climate of crisis surrounding masculinity: men are struggling to make sense of themselves and their roles in a ruthlessly corrosive society. Among the b-boys, I see a group of young men generating deep and profound connections with each other. A community of support is formed amongst young men who share a love of dancing.

Rob Maze is the elder statesman of the community. Known as 'Maze 83' (in honour of the year he began breaking) he has been breaking in Perth since he was 15 years old. Through the age of *Flashdance*, *Footloose* and Run DMC's 'It's Like That,' his depth of knowledge about the local scene is staggering. He has seen it all, been to all the battles and danced on all the street corners. Back in the day when everyone knew everyone else (b-boys, DJs and graffiti artists), Forrest Chase was Forrest Place and markets were held there on weekends, Maze remembers scrounging cardboard refrigerator boxes from Retravision to dance on. The Hay Street Mall was off limits to young breakers, as was the Carillon Arcade where a large wooden stage was colonised for as long as the security guards left them alone. Students from almost every high school in Perth, comprising five crews of six people per school, would come and battle in a time when Australia was rated among one of the best b-boy nations in the world.

Maze's own history of b-boying began at a cricket match. Sport has always been a great incubator for Australian masculinity, teaching the values of competition and control. Cricket is a middle-class white man's sport embodying style, strategy and fair play. To find the germination of a traditionally black, working class, hip hop culture in such an unusual cradle forges new connections between men, bodies and community. To move their bodies in a different way, outside of the rules of sport and its regulated masculine identity, made b-boying a node of rupture in respectable middle class society. Hip hop involves a consciousness that works on the fringes of codified culture. B-boying connects music, dance and art. Aggression, expression and politics coexist. Hip hop comprises three spheres—music, dance and art, of which rap, breaking and graffiti are the dominant practices. It does not involve the compliant consciousness of middle-class sporting prowess tethered to a national identity politics.

Maze recalls the indoor cricket match vividly because it was the first time he saw 'a guy' do the moonwalk and the dive. A stereo playing

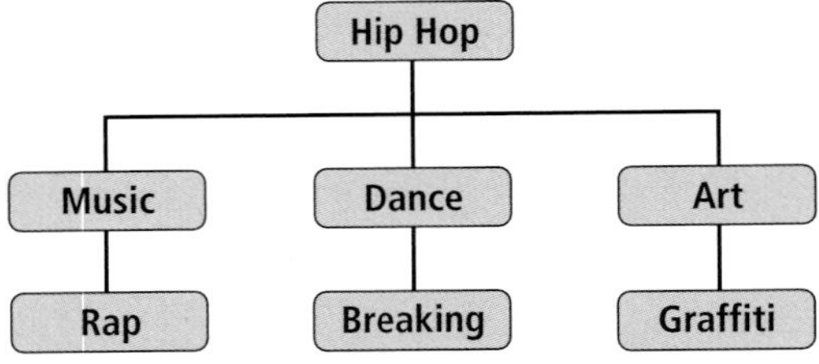

FIGURE 2: Hip hop: A framework

'Freakazoid' by Midnight Star and some 'wild moves' puncture his memory. This experience was common also with older friends who went clubbing where breaking was popular. These older men taught the younger ones some steps, and so the mentoring began. Simultaneously, there was some hint of b-boy culture in North America making it on to Australian screens. But Maze remembers there only being a few film clips from which to learn. No Buffalo Gals, but there was Candy Girl and IOU as influences. The Christmas period in 1983 brought more film clips from the States and a dancing competition on *Countdown* was won by Perth b-boys Steve, and now DJ, Birdie.

Despite the success of Perth breakers, material was hard to find. Videos and films of new moves—like those distributed by K-Tel and performed in *Breakdance USA*—were almost non-existent. The main sources that filtered through were primarily from the UK and US, nothing from Europe or Asia or even (as Maze puts it) from South Australia. Outside of Perth there was little knowledge of what b-boy culture was doing elsewhere in the nation, let alone in other parts of the world.

In terms of music material three record stores, Dada's, 78s and Perth Record Store, were raided regularly. Rap and DJ-ing were not the popular products they are today and it was a challenge finding break tunes. Little was played on the radio in 'pub-rock' Australia during the 1980s. Now Maze has his own RTR timeslot to play old-school hip hop, but back then the material was scarce. Breakers had to be innovative in their approach to accessing the music. American sailors who arrived in port every few months were canvassed for New York radio station tapes, assorted mix-tapes and to share their b-boy skills. This was one of the few ways they were exposed to new ideas, new music and moves. Ports like Liverpool and Fremantle are always gateways to people, ideas, dancing and beats. For the b-boys, Fremantle was a crucial entry into a wider world.

In other parts of Australia, breakdancing was booming with the B-Boy All Stars of Brisbane known for phenomenal power moves in the late 1980s and early 1990s.[1] A key b-boy/graffiti writer named Duel from Melbourne journeyed to California around this time and procured breakdancing videos. The B-Boy All Stars took this material and expanded it, developing new and innovative moves. A hungry breaking community consumed this fresh funk eagerly and the styles began filtering through the b-boy cultural connections.

Perth clubs—Beethovens, Pinocchio's and Jules—held b-boy competitions. Galactic Force (Maze's crew) were banned from entry to Jules in 1984 for the national *Countdown* breakdance competition, because they were too young.[2] The crew that won—Central City Groove—were sponsored by Jules and went to Melbourne where they were judged by the Rock Steady Crew. Outside of this competition, Adidas sponsored Galactic Force and provided yellow tracksuits and boxing boots to the crew. Shows in shopping centres promoted the culture and Telstra's former incarnation—Telecom—paid the crew to pose freeze style, holding new phones.

By the early to mid-1990s the initial mainstream breaking frenzy had passed. The bubbling scene had depleted into one or two crews and individuals breaking for fun. Gangsta rap had become the musical genre of the moment. The politics promoted by Death Row Records and artists like Snoop Dog, Kurupt and Dr Dre made it unpopular among mainstream music mentors. The volatile vocalism in these recordings of 'bitches, gangbanging niggas, killas and "my mind on my money and my money on my mind" '[3] made it increasingly difficult for the genre to be easily acquiesced by radio stations and the corporate consciousness. It was also contrary to the inclusive community spirit of breakdancing.

In Europe, a more socially conscious politics prevailed and in 1991 Germany held the very first Battle of the Year competition.[4] Under the radar of official culture, b-boying continued to embody inclusive politics. In the United States, KRS-One paid homage to b-boys in his album *Criminal Minded*, referencing Rock Steady Crew.[5] Yet the visibility of b-boying had significantly declined. In 1995, Maze was back on the bridge in Forrest Place. It was there that he met and mentored members of the Systematic Crew, who also passed on their skills to others.

Andrew Laver arrived in Perth at precisely the right time. Originally from Melbourne, he was only thirteen years old in 1995 when he made the journey across the Nullarbor. He began breaking two years later in 1997. Despite the successes of the local scene in the early 1980s, the decline of b-boying through the early 1990s made it still largely an unknown community. Andrew affirms that he always wanted to learn, but there was no one to teach him. A crucial meeting came at high school when—as he puts it—a little white dude named Mitch Pollard enrolled and shared his skills with Andrew. Out of this instruction, the Ballajura City Breakers was formed and they performed at small events. By 1998, they were breaking regularly on the bridge at Forrest Place where they had met Maze and many of the other 'old school' dancers who mentored the younger crews.

In 1999 when Andrew finished school, the Systematic Crew was created comprising himself, brothers Rami and Jeffrey, and Beni Benz. This crew entered and won the Street Trial competition held in Forrest Chase in 1999. A young man named Jamie Mills (aka Stormy) who organised this event decided to 'take on' Systematic Crew as a manager, offering to secure them paid gigs and teaching jobs. From these beginnings they began to generate a culture of workshops and community projects devoted to teaching and extending b-boying in Perth.

In 2002, Andrew took over the management of Systematic Crew. They now have an extensive network of contacts and connections throughout the cityscape including Rockingham and Mandurah. They teach at high schools, primary schools and drop-in centres. Shows are performed on the street, in nightclubs and at corporate functions. They have even travelled to Malaysia and Germany to perform. Most surprisingly, this bubbling activity occurs largely unnoticed by the mainstream culture. Andrew maintains that most people know of Systematic purely by word of mouth. They are not listed in the Yellow Pages, they do not advertise outside of specific events, (usually in the form of flyers passed from person to person). They do not have a website. The most frequent form of connection is via the mobile phone. Numbers are passed around and teaching times and events are threaded through the telecommunications network. It is highly effective, and demand is increasing. Andrew is finding it hard to keep up with requests for workshops and shows. The culture of teaching that has always existed through the informal mentoring of b-boy communities has enabled a wider sphere to develop through pedagogy. With the formalised framework, b-boy and b-girl culture is increasingly accessible. Taka Tsuzuki, a relatively new member of the Systematic Crew, is one beneficiary of the teaching timetable.

Originally from Japan, Taka has been in Perth for fifteen years and has been part of the rejuvenation of b-boying in the late 1990s. The alterna-youth marketing frenzy embodied in the turn to Extreme Games in 1995 and X-Games as of 1996 extended the increasingly exhaustive youth market further into fashion, lifestyle and underground sports. This accelerated consumer consciousness bled into the mainstreaming of hip hop music and b-boy/girl culture punctuated by Jason Nevin's remix of Run DMC's 'It's Like That' and its battle film clip in 1998.

Taka's own introduction to b-boys was via music video where he saw swipes and was fascinated. After trying to school himself with little success, he discovered Beni Benz on the bridge in Forrest Place doing a show with Systematic Crew. Taka began attending Beni's class run out of Black American Funk Studios, and followed him when he began teaching at Fresh Dance Studios in 2001. The street culture was supplemented by these classes where b-boying was visible and viable. Within four years, Taka has learnt the gamut of b-boy moves from scratch. By 2001 Taka had developed sufficient skills to enter his first competition where he and partner Tam Dang were knocked out first round, beaten by Leroy and Gaby. But it marked a turning point for him and foregrounded the invitation to join Systematic Crew after a show with Planet X[6] in front of 5,000 people accompanied by television coverage.

> **Taka:** I went into Outbreak 1 coz doing the show I wasn't very confident. I remember with Outbreak I was paired off with Tam. Tam also did the Planet X show. We competed in it and Leroy and Gaby kicked our arses. But, um, I felt like I'm not gonna give up that easily. So I think it came down to I was battling Leroy in power and Tam was battling Gaby in style or whatever it was and

> yeah we didn't give up and we gave a hell of a competition. It was, I think, one of the best battles of the day. It was amazing. I mean we got beaten, but we gave it a good shot. And that was the first time I realised, hey, I'm not backing down, I'm not being thrashed, not yet anyway.[7]

The new generation of Systematic Crew—Taka, Leroy and Gaby—are all respected power movers. It is the new challenge for b-boys and girls in Perth to access and keep up with the aerial acrobatics of the more affluent b-boy scenes over east as well as in Europe, North America, Korea and Japan. They are constantly looking for new material and new challenges to raise the bar of breaking in the state. Taka's respect for his fellow breakers Leroy and Gaby is generated out of their dedication to b-boying and the sacrifices they have made to develop their own abilities and therefore the standing of the Perth scene.

> **Taka:** If there's any b-boy that works harder than anyone it's probably Lee. Coz I think that apart from the fact that he had to give up quite a lot to keep going at breaking. I mean there's a point where you get tired after training and you stop training. You know you're tired and you wanna take a break. But, um, he doesn't stop. He doesn't stop. Even coz he's a labourer during the day and then at night time he just breaks. All the time, breaks, breaks, breaks, breaks. He even breaks through injuries. Like he'll get injured but he still keeps going. So it's like, Oookaay. But that's because so many people envy him and slander him and wanna get better than him.[8]

It is testament to the character of b-boys like Taka, Leroy and Gaby and the Systematic Crew that breaking in Perth is thriving. Their connection and competition with each other has ensured that bigger and better standards of b-boying are being passed through the scene. This community has fostered originality and expression without sponsorship, external funding, press coverage or publicity. It has facilitated an intense rivalry among b-boys.[9] Like all b-boy scenes, they rely on each other to push the boundaries of breaking, and will also conceal new moves and hide choreography. Taka describes this contradictory consciousness.

> **Taka:** B-boys individually and in crews always constantly wanna get better than each other. To the point where people hide their moves from everyone, people hide, people slander, people write things on the Internet…All these things...trying to get against you, tryin' to make you mad…But there's no beef, it's good because breaking makes it breaking. Like it just inspires you to get better. In actual fact that's probably why, um, Lee and Gaby and all of us got really good because we were all against each other. We were always against each other.

This competition is crucial for innovation. The intimacy of the b-boy scene also dictates that there can never be any long-running grudges, precisely because there is a relatively intimate connection to other breakers. Yet a culture of battles prevails. B-boys can be 'called out' to defend their breaking prowess.

> **Taka:** You can like, um, take care of arguments or take care of problems through breaking. You can battle people, you know, you can call 'em out.
>
> *Call them out? How does that work?*
>
> **Taka:** Oh easy, you can just go up to anyone or you can spread the word that you wanna battle someone on this day and if they don't battle you then obviously they were like, they got scared off. Gaby gets battled quite a lot. (laughs) He's getting battled quite a lot. Um me and Leroy…Leroy gets battled a bit but everyone's too scared to battle Leroy, and um, I don't think I've ever been battled or called out. So that's alright.
>
> *What is it about Gaby? Do people just think they can beat Gaby or is he just mouthing off at everyone?*

> **Taka:** Ah, he mouths off quite a bit (laughs). But, um ah, I think a lot of people underestimate Gaby. Like, um, they think they can beat him. Like I personally haven't seen him lose ever. I've never seen him lose. But, um, yeah a lot of people think they can beat Gaby. Like, um, a lot of people get intimidated by me and Leroy when we just like bust big power because when you bust big power, and coz, um, I love freezes as much as power. I love doing freezes. When they see our freezes and our power they get pretty intimidated. But when they see Gaby, because they don't understand style, they only see his power, they think 'Oh I can beat him' when they really can't. They really can't.

B-boys can assert their masculine bravado across the dance floor. This mutual rivalry masks the deep respect b-boys have for each other. The conflict and the collectivity feed off each other. They look to others for diligence and inspiration. Most significantly, these young men value discipline and courage. Getting it wrong is embedded in the breaking. Failing and falling over and over again while attempting even the most fundamental moves is commonplace. The level of discipline a particular b-boy or b-girl displays is directly related to the level of admiration aimed at him or her. These connections are most visible and volatile when b-boys and b-girls gather together to battle or compete.

On 23 November 2003 a local b-boy/b-girl battle competition was held at the Victoria Park Recreation Centre. The small hall was brimming with breakers and spectators numbering almost 200. Special guests from Sydney, Melbourne and Adelaide had come to Perth to compete. The day featured DJ-ing, MC-ing and Beat Box performances. Sixteen three-person battle crews entered, as well as eight individual popping competitors. Many different levels of breaking circulated across the dance floor, from the twists of Leroy to the headspins of Jeff and the six-step, baby-freeze sequences of less experienced breakers. At the end of the day, the final battle was between two Systematic Crews—Andrew (Raz), Leroy and Gaby (El Niño) against Bernie (Third Degree Burns), Taka (Tek 1) and Jeff (the Chef). A magnificent battle ensued with each team trying to outdo each other. Gestures were made, posturing performed, and laughter echoed through the space. In the end it was Andrew, Leroy and Gaby who took out the honours. The depth of b-boying and b-girling witnessed at this event ensures that Perth breaking is flourishing. The spirit of inclusion within this culture is testament to the history of mentoring that began in the early 1980s when Maze was breaking on the bridge. Crews like Systematic continue this tradition and help to create a community full of rivalry and respect.

CHAPTER 5

After Dark: Perth's Night-time Economy

Kathryn Locke

It is late on a Saturday night and the lights of Northbridge are shining bright. Kaleidoscopic rhythms pulsate through the streets. Alfresco diners clutter the pavement, pint-clutching young men spill from Irish pubs, and sweat-soaked clubbers are logging on to their genre of choice. Not all are welcome to take part in this economic and social mélange. Since June 2003, young people have been dislocated from the centre of Perth's music and entertainment district by the *Young People in Northbridge Policy* which has placed a curfew on their participation.[1] The heart of Perth is only now slowly being recognised for its innovative, vibrant and diverse music and entertainment potential. Though regular visitors have always appreciated the district's allure and possibilities, the Gallop Labor Government focused on the profitable promise of Northbridge through the music and entertainment industries.

> WA Labor wants to build on this natural talent to develop a music industry that is vibrant, productive and profitable. We recognise that contemporary music can capture the essence of what it means to be in Australia—even Western Australia—and broadcast this to the rest of the world.[2]

Youth involvement was a clear focus for the proposed *Contemporary Music Direction Statement* and promoted through the recommendations of the Contemporary Music Task Force from the Department of Culture and the Arts. The *Direction Statement* assures that,

> Labor recognises young people's natural passion for music and their serious lack of supervised recreational opportunities. We therefore propose to develop a statewide local youth music program...It is envisaged that under the program, local youth committees—including members aged 14 to 18—will be responsible for organising drug and alcohol free gigs and dance parties for their peers.[3]

Ironically, this proposal has coincided with the implementation of a policy by the state government that forcibly bans youth from Northbridge, Perth's major cultural precinct, at night. The policy issued prohibits all unaccompanied primary school-aged children after dark, and all 13-year-old to 15-year-old children after 10 pm, from entering the Northbridge precinct.[4] At a time when the government has finally recognised the potential of Perth's music and entertainment scene, it must be asked why a whole group within society is being segregated and removed from its heart. The policy was backed by concerns about 'community safety', 'youth anti-social behaviour' and 'the safety and security of children'.[5] Yet an alternative motivation becomes more apparent when considering child welfare legislation has always given police the power to remove children from public areas if they are deemed 'at risk'. The *Young People in Northbridge Policy* reveals a complex economic and social relationship that moves beyond welfare concerns. This chapter investigates the Northbridge curfew as an example of how economic development can affect the role of youth in a community. Drawing on the rationale behind the *Young People in Northbridge Policy*, I illustrate how an emphasis on the creative industries is bringing city imaging to the forefront of governmental initiatives.

The *Contemporary Music Direction Statement* devised by the Office of Minister Sheila McHale followed a growing political impetus, first witnessed in the United Kingdom when Tony Blair decided to harness the possibility for economic advancement through development and administration of the creative industries. With a gradual shift in the economies of wealthier Western nations away from manufacturing and primary industries, alongside the influence of globalisation and changes in leisure consumption,[6] the arts and cultural industries have taken centre stage in governmental planning and management of nations, but more specifically, in the development of cities.[7] These 'engines of economic growth'[8] encompass creative products—such as performance, literature, design and music—and their reproduction as books, magazines, film, radio, sport or fashion. Also included are the activities that promote and distribute creativity—advertising, tourism, galleries, museums and nightclubs.[9] These industries are seen not only as 'growth areas,' but the key to distinguishing the social, cultural and environmental character of the city in a global and competitive world.[10] The emphasis on a city's cultural character results in much more than the development of a music industry or the building of new museums and galleries. As Hubbard explained,

> This type of economic development becomes amalgamated with city imaging. This shift in urban governance has been characterised by the diminishing importance of the local provisions of welfare and services by city governments in favour of a more outward [image] orientated stance designed to foster local development and economic growth.[11]

The construction of an economically productive and internationally attractive cultural sector is sustained by the promotion and (re)imaging of the city. What we are witnessing in Perth is the beginning of this shift with the introduction of policies aimed at supporting economic development, but it is a development that is reliant on a specific city image. What is being articulated here is a predominant trend throughout our history where change in economic strategy transforms the way cities are governed.[12] The shift of focus on the creative industries and subsequent city imaging has social and political repercussions. The *Young People in Northbridge Policy* exemplifies how economic policy is directing a political agenda and moulding current social policy. What needs to be examined is how an economic transformation can be managed in such a way that groups within the community are not ostracised or decentred through this process. When Britain became the first industrialised nation, or when the global recession of 1973 changed economies worldwide, political and social relationships shifted. Both now and in the future, governments must endeavour to employ responsible social management and planning when implementing new economic policy.

Two key strategies released by Perth City Council and the Department of Culture and the Arts have recognised the potential Northbridge, and Western Australia as a whole, holds for the development of a vibrant, economically lucrative and internationally renowned music and entertainment scene.[13] The achievement of this potential is acutely linked to perception. *The Northbridge Action Plan 2003–2007* has clearly identified that the primary hindrance to the economic development of Northbridge is centred in the perception that the area is unsafe.[14] Similarly the *Young People in Northbridge Policy* presents the rationalisation for its implementation as being directly linked with concerns over safety in the Northbridge district. In the opening paragraph of the policy, it states:

> Northbridge is home to the City's largest adult entertainment district and is the State's principal cultural precinct. It is also now subject to a significant urban renewal program that is bringing increasing numbers of permanent residents to the area. In recent years, increasing concern about community safety has affected the vibrancy and viability of much of the precinct and there is now evidence of deterioration in visitation, business performance and community spirit.[15]

What is inherently problematic in both publications is the direct correlation that is drawn between concerns about community safety and the presence of young people on the streets of Northbridge at night. This correlation is even more surprising considering that the number of young people of concern who frequent Northbridge at night is no more than twenty. Chief Executive Officer of the Aboriginal Legal Service, Dennis Eggington, expressed his scepticism of the parallel that was being drawn by the government.

> It must be asked why a handful of antisocial kids in one small street in the whole of the state are taking priority, why they occupy so much of the government's political agenda.[16]

Much further research, which cannot be addressed in a short chapter such as this, is required to ask why 86 per cent of the children picked up by police since the curfew was implemented are Aboriginal.[17] The relationship between a perception of safety and a fear of/for young people seems also to draw a disturbing positive correlation with Aboriginal youth.

> When the Premier announces that he is putting a curfew on young people in Northbridge, and all of us know that it is young Aboriginal kids who are being picked up, it sends a clear message to the general population that there is a problem with young Aboriginal people, that we need to get tough on them. Consequently there is less tolerance and attention paid to the underlying social problems for Aboriginal people, such as the economic, unemployment and educational issues.[18]

When youth curfews are implemented, they are commonly a reaction not to the behaviour of young people, but essentially to their visibility.[19] At night, in an area predominantly regarded as an 'adult entertainment district'[20] young people, especially indigenous young people, are noticeable and this visibility is 'premised on the idea of young people as threats to the community, not valued members of the community.'[21] It is here, in the visibility and perception of youth, where the two spheres—the social and the economic—collide. What the Northbridge curfew fundamentally aims to achieve is the removal of a visible (and perceived threatening) minority group from the very streets on which the development of the creative industries will blossom. Though the government maintains the policy was based upon child welfare concerns as well as a community safety fear,[22] it has also confirmed an apparent relationship between the economic development of the creative industries, city imaging and the removal of youth after dark. Apart from statements released from the Premier's office, the Perth City

Council has acknowledged a similar relationship. Midge Turnbull, Executive Officer of the Youth Affairs Council, explained:

> There is a Northbridge Strategy for 2003 to 2007 and it says virtually that young people affect the amenity of Northbridge. As long as documents like this exist, then young people will never be part of, or feel they are a valid member of society.[23]

Within the plan, the City Council has included the approach of 'encouraging outer metropolitan local governments to increase youth activities near home,' and 'to not attract additional unaccompanied youth at night.'[24] In the plans to develop the creative industries, especially the local music industry, there was no indication that youth exclusion was necessary. Yet both the curfew policy and plans proposed by the Perth City Council indicate that their involvement in Northbridge will inhibit the progress of this industry.

Aside from the discriminatory nature of the *Young People in Northbridge Policy*, many local community groups and theorists have argued that curfews are unnecessary and can create more harm than solutions.[25] In the case of Northbridge, there are several alternative means of combating both genuine and alleged 'problems'. The social issues behind the presence of children in Northbridge late at night must firstly be acknowledged. Whether they are there because of boredom and the obvious lack of youth-based activities within central and outer Perth or because of entrenched welfare and family issues, the right of young people to be in a public space after dark remains. This right may contest assumptions about the position and vulnerability of a child within our society; however, the implementation of curfews can arguably breach 'fundamental liberties of young people to move freely about the community and to participate in various activities.'[26] Both leaders of the Aboriginal Legal Service and the Youth Affairs Council expressed the need for youth activities and events to be established in Northbridge. Midge Turnbull suggests,

> There is absolutely no reason for not providing a youth space in

> Northbridge. If they did, some of the problems would be addressed. People misbehave when they have nothing to do.[27]

Similarly Dennis Eggington revealed past attempts at providing a place for young people to be involved at night have proven successful.

> There needs to be different types of activities that encourage young people's involvement, under 18 dances, blue-light discos etc. If there were specific places and events put on for kids, they would go to those, they would not be hanging around on the streets. An example of this is several years ago the Aboriginal Advancement Council ran a blue light disco. This ran every Friday night, and every Friday night there was not one Aboriginal kid on the streets of Northbridge. It was clear that when these discos stopped the children were back on the streets. There needs to be specific activities for young people and they should be a part of the fabric of Northbridge. How else do you learn to be a part of mainstream adult society if you are not slowly introduced and participate in it?[28]

Theorists have also supported the involvement of youth in 'night economies' by providing spaces for under-age patrons.[29] The provision of facilities for young people has in the past led to decreased antisocial and criminal behaviour while maintaining a youth involvement in the community.[30] The *Young People in Northbridge Policy* was an act of spatial and temporal administration. Underlying its implementation is a politics of time, whereby both government and society consider the night a time belonging to adults. Consistently throughout the curfew debate, the issue of 'correct' usage of time and space in Northbridge has been reiterated in objections to children being in an adult entertainment area, but mostly in their presence being maintained after dark. What the *Young People in Northbridge Policy* is ultimately addressing is the development of an economy in space and time. The government's aim is therefore to control and protect this environment from economically detrimental imaging. The ownership of time (as in the ownership of space) is centred in economic rationalisation. Alongside issues of moral regulation, the economic viability of youth—as both part of the cityscape and as participants within it—is considered redundant if not a hindrance. Yet statistics produced at the Perth Youth Forum in 1997 have suggested that while young people do not have a significant economic or consuming capacity, their contribution as a group is still significant.

> The SKAWA survey indicated that 30 per cent of youth brought less than ten dollars to the city. However considering the frequency of visits and spending power of youth, this represents a significant input into the city's retail and entertainment economy.[31]

Though their contribution to the creative industries may not appear considerable, young people are still active consumers. It should also be taken into account that the youth of today will be the adults who may or may not support the creative sectors tomorrow. The type of relationship fostered with young people will have lasting effects on the way they use, consume and participate in the future market economy.

The issue is not simply the question of whether the curfew placed on young people in Northbridge is appropriate or not. I am interested in a much larger question: how is social justice made a part of city imaging and economic development? This is a question that must be asked of our government, especially at a time of shifting economic strategies. The development of the creative industries in Perth may create a self-sufficient, prosperous and lucrative economy, but the impact it will have on groups within society needs to be investigated. This is especially integral to the welfare and participation of minority or marginalised groups who already lack strong political and economic power. When city imaging and economic growth are the priority, the government must be careful that these interests do not trample the delicate social map on which a city is built.

PART II

PLACING THE BEAT

CHAPTER 6

Heritage and Hard Rock: Silencing the Grosvenor Hotel

Rebecca Bennett

The confrontation between law and popular culture with respect to the Grosvenor Hotel in Perth highlights a history in need of narration. Steve Redhead states:

> there is an urgent need, in my view, to narrate the (hi)story—or indeed more accurately, (hi)stories—of a specific regime of power/knowledge which I have labelled as 'law and popular culture'; in other words, to tell tales of its formation, scope and influence.[1]

Western Australian laws silence not only loud rock music but also the voices and opinions of managers, musicians, bands and fans. Dynamic, ephemeral and experiential venues for original music come and go. The (hi)story missing in the story of the Grosvenor is what went on *inside* its walls. The sounds and stories resonated throughout the city. Legislation that ignores local, national and international interest in Perth's original music, limits the marketing potential in labelling Perth as the next Liverpool, Seattle or Manchester. To reveal Perth's musical identity, emphasis needs to be placed on individuals and local industries who were (and still are) affected by the Act(ions) that silenced the Grosvenor's front room. Conversations between state law and Perth popular culture—such as those ignited by a lone resident's complaints in November 2002—need to be recorded and critiqued if Perth is to secure a place on the national and international musical map.

The Grosvenor Hotel conjures up vivid memories of the taste of Victoria Bitter, sticky pub floors, dim lights, stale cigarette smoke, corduroy pants, pigtails, good friends and loud, live music. It reminds me of a time (not long past) when bands with names like Cinema Prague, Air Ensemble, Beaverloop, Valvolux, Freud's Pillow, Effigy, Sick, Spank, Dirtbag and later Eskimo Joe dominated my CD collection and leisure time. My friends and I—some wannabe musicians and others like myself, adoring fans—would gather three to six nights a week at our favourite venues. We spent our nights in pubs, sat on couches or around tables nodding our heads, sweating in mosh pits or 'indie chicken dancing' (a kind of side-to-side shuffling hopping movement, with heads down and elbows flapping). Our movements depended on the music, our mood and the amount of cheap beer consumed.

From my position within the Perth popular music scene and as a lifelong Perth resident, I was saddened by the removal of amps from the Grosvenor's front room because a piece of my personal and shared history was also disconnected. A feature report in the Australian national music broadcaster Triple J's archives describes the events that led to the sound being turned down:

> 29/11/2002 Grosvenor Hotel
> The Grosvenor Hotel has been issued with a noise-abatement notice by the Perth City Council after complaints from a nearby resident that it's too loud. The pub has had to cancel it's [sic] five nights a week, live band line-up or risk copping a $25,000 fine for exceeding noise limits…This is a big blow to WA's live music scene.[2]

A sole resident moved into a building opposite the Grosvenor, years after the venue had become known for its loud original music, and repeatedly complained about the noise. These complaints resulted in legal and economic pressure for the pub to reduce its decibel levels, even after fitting soundproofing to its windows. Further investigation into the circumstances that led to the removal of amplified music from the Grosvenor's front room suggests the 'blow' to Perth music was not an isolated hit—but a metaphor for the recurring marginalisation of local original Perth-based music in current legislation and state-institutional ideology. Legislative barriers prevent Perth from developing a unique, marketable, meaningful, enjoyable and strong popular music identity in national and international contexts.

The Grosvenor Hotel is documented as being an important historical site in Western Australia. In 1989 the *Daily News* reported that, 'the pub was placed under a demolition order…but historians have been trying to save the building which is one of the last central city pubs.'[3] Historians were successful in their late 1980s endeavour, and the Grosvenor Hotel is secure as an 'authentic,' 'historic,' 'rarity.'[4] Official documentation declares that the building cannot be torn down and the 'two storey brick and iron construction with veranda'[5] is protected as a meaningful historical site. Unfortunately, the Grosvenor's 'integral role in the local original music history for more than ten years,'[6] as outlined in the *Sunday Times*, is not enough justification to preserve popular musical histories reverberating inside the building's walls. The structure is preserved. The sounds are silenced.

Histories of the loud, amplified rock music that shook the Grosvenor's front room for over a decade cannot be found in WA state archives or in formal texts validating Perth's heritage. However, there is a history of the Grosvenor which exists in conversations, websites, local music newspaper articles, national radio station archives and individual memories of the people touched by the local music scene. As Marcus states:

> there are events that are real but they dissolve when one tries to attach them to the monuments, wars, elections, public works projects, universities, laws, prisons—out of which we make our history.[7]

The Grosvenor Hotel, as a loud rock music venue, housed events that felt 'real' for Perth bands and fans. Successful Perth musician Kavian Temperley remembers, 'the front room was where my first band did its CD launch.'[8] Fan turned local band manager Raelene Gill describes how a piece of her meaningful history dissolved when music in the front room was turned down:

> The Grosvenor represented the feel of the Perth scene. Now they just do these quiet gigs in the front room and it is such a shame to see this awesome venue wither like a forgotten grandparent in an old person's home. There is a history that cannot be bought and that is what was lost when we lost the Grosvenor.[9]

Individual and collective musical histories could not attach themselves to the heritage laws that protect the Grosvenor's silent walls. The history of noise, experience and pleasure is governed by a different law in Perth: the *Environmental Protection (Noise Regulations 1997).*[10] This legislation has the power to remove an important monument from Perth's popular music heritage. It reminds Kavian and Raelene that the history they are narrating is not recognised by the city that contextualises their shared past. Complaints from a sole neighbour silenced countless harmonies, riffs, cheers, drum solos, wails and lyrics that filled the Grosvenor's front room for up to six nights a week for nearly fifteen years.

At the time when amplified music was officially removed from the Grosvenor, national music radio station Triple J broadcast the sentiments of local and national original live music scenes. 'Let's hope some quick lobbying can get live music happening again at the Grosvenor.'[11] An online petition was created and political web sites such as *Active Perth*[12] filled their notice boards with angry and disillusioned voices. Disappointment at the final decision to support one resident's voice over live music was widespread throughout the local music scene. 'Quick lobbying' in the Grosvenor's favour did not appear to have enough power to resolve the 'conflict that occurs when pop speed comes up against the inertia of institutions by definition locked in the past.'[13] The removal of amplified music was the trigger for more than nostalgic or sentimental concern. Marginalisation of music and the discourses that support it were addressed online, with no suggestion of how the practice might be changed from within the music community:

> This is certainly not a case of minority overcoming majority. The intolerant jerk who is whingeing about noise is in with a growing majority of inner city residents, who are ushered into their spotless new beige cubes by amnesiac Perth city planners hell bent on systematically razing our civic heritage for $$$ and tightass gentrification.[14]

The decision to empower a resident over a music scene suggests that silent bricks and mortar—whether 'heritage' listed or brand new—are protected by state law. However, Perth's thriving, popular, innovative and acclaimed live music scene is not valued in the same way. Local musicians and fans were reminded that they are vulnerable to attack by any person who objects to live rock music's volume. Perth legislation does not appear to view original music as an important creative industry. Cultural heritage is defined predominantly through artefacts and property, not events or sounds.

As long as Perth's fascination with buildings and real estate is validated over its popular culture, original music born in Perth is not likely to give credence to the city that gave birth to it. The silencing of the Grosvenor reminds Perth musicians and local music audiences that they can be evicted from their favourite venues without negotiation or hesitation by individuals who position themselves 'outside' of the local original music scene. Music is not supported by Perth's dominant institutions in a manner that suggests the city takes responsibility for the industry. A highly regarded original live local music population has evolved largely in spite of prevailing laws.

The State Government's inability to see the full potential in promoting local original music as a valid creative industry is a mistake, according to the executive director of the Western Australian Music Industry Association (WAM), Paul Bodlovich. In a recent telephone interview, he recognised that 'Perth really excels in terms of exporting original music to the rest of Australia and overseas.'[15] Bands like The Sleepy Jackson and Little Birdy have entered the international music market. Other bands such as Eskimo Joe, Jebediah, The John Butler Trio and Halogen have a strong following nationwide. Perth bands pack live venues throughout Australia, get regular national airplay and sell thousands of CDs. Bodlovich labels local music as a 'shining light in our cultural industry.' The problem he faces is getting 'more sympathy for live music as a "cultural" activity and not as entertainment.'[16] His worry is that the separation of local entertainment from city culture denies the economic potential of popular music. To label original Perth music as pure 'entertainment' suggests it is a space of localised experience, hedonism and pleasure, not a potentially lucrative cultural industry. Perth is failing to capitalise on locally produced music that is increasingly being embraced and consumed throughout Australia and overseas.

The current *Liquor Licensing Act 1988*[17] in WA empowers the Department of Liquor Licensing over licensed venues that house live music. Bodlovich explained that the Director of Liquor Licensing has the power to impose and change legal conditions for venue operation, yet is removed from the everyday running of licensed hotels. He fears their job description is to police, rather than support, local licensed venues.[18] Pubs are constructed as potential law-breakers in a legislative discourse. Activities inside licensed venues, such as live music performances, are treated with apprehension by local government bodies, rather than being assessed for their lucrative potential.

Paul Bodlovich said that the Gallop Government's 'Contemporary Music Task Force' (CMTF) has yet to deliver legislative change. He suggested the delay in legislative amendments is due to the CMTF being largely ignored. He laments that 'it is not a ministerial working party; it is made up of "mid-level" public servants speaking to other "mid-level" public servants' that results in 'a lot of talking but not a lot of scope.'[19] While recognising WAM's concerns with the Department of Culture and the Arts, the increase in funding to the organisation by the Gallop Government also needs to be acknowledged and remembered.

A recurring problem with conversations regarding the local music industry in Perth appears to be that those who exist outside the scene have the power to make the ultimate economic and political decisions for local Perth music. Postcolonial theorist Zygmunt Bauman's argument concerning 'local' issues in a 'globalising' world might be applied to those fighting for recognition from within the Perth original music scene. Unless institutions with economic and political power in Western Australia prioritise the concerns of local bands and fans there is little hope for legislative change. As Bauman argues,

> The locals have lost much of their bargaining power; or rather whatever power they may have is of little use [if one side is] free to abandon the negotiating table at will.[20]

Government officials, directors of Liquor Licensing, historians and ministers have the power to influence city law. The apparent inactivity of such individuals and institutions with regard to petitions and future redevelopment plans to support and promote Perth's popular music suggests that such documents are sitting on desks gathering dust. When housing developments sit next to popular live music venues, residents complain. The Grosvenor case does not exist in isolation but similar disputes between residents and venues are being negotiated by local councils over the metropolitan area, with the Norfolk and Clancy's pubs in Fremantle being more recent examples. While at state level old buildings are being heritage listed and the Department of Liquor Licensing hands out fines, local original music is being left on the legislative backburner.

The future for the Perth music scene is not hopeless. Many projects, committees, protests and emerging international acts within the local music industry are slowly chipping away at the outdated and less economically viable institutions masking Perth's full creative potential. Perth popular music is gaining far-reaching support and international acclaim. The present musical climate has created an opportune time to put Perth on the map as a contemporary musical force. One voice should not be able to silence a meaningful and marketable piece of Perth's contemporary music history without scope for negotiation or reflexivity.

Local musician Kavian Temperley looked elsewhere to find his hopes for the future of live music in Perth when reminiscing about the loss of the Grosvenor front room:

> A similar thing was happening in Brisbane. Residents were complaining when they moved into these pretty big bands' (like Powderfinger) stomping grounds. So they passed this bill over there that's like: if the venue existed before the residents then the venue has the right of way...That's *so* what should have happened with the Grosvenor.[21]

Legislation was recently amended to protect live music venues in a popular Brisbane night spot called Fortitude Valley. The 'Valley' has a distinct history of live local music and a high concentration of rock music venues in a relatively confined area. In Perth, live music venues are scattered throughout its widespread urban and suburban sprawl. City planning forms another hurdle that the Perth live music scene may have to overcome. Legislation that was passed for Fortitude Valley would not be relevant to Perth's popular music culture. In many cases individual residents own much of the real estate surrounding pubs that regularly showcase local bands. The awkward positioning of live original music means that laws that encourage negotiation and discussion between residents and venues are necessary. Legislative amendments in Perth need to address Perth's unique cultural and residential needs which are dispersed throughout the urban sprawl with no coherent geographical 'centre' for live original music.

In the contemporary musical climate, local, original Perth-based music is a potential growth industry. The Perth scene appears able to cope with the demands of an MTV consumer culture that celebrates constant stimulation, innovation and change. For such a young and musically vibrant city, Perth clings to its real estate. The potential for a wider tourist market lies in capitalising on Perth's popular culture as well as its official 'heritage' monuments. Geographical isolation allows the city to develop unique urban sounds. Brand argues that the 'future' is an important focus in unstable and ever-changing economic climates:

> If taking thought for the future was essential in steady times, how much more important is it in accelerating times and how much harder? It becomes both crucial and seemingly impossible.[22]

To survive and thrive in accelerating times, Perth needs to validate the history of its popular culture. Current legislation will have to change to cater for the demands of new capitalist enterprises and 'global' demands. Perth should market its popular musical potential by supporting and promoting its local live music culture. Perth is a city that houses the talent and creativity to make it the next Manchester or Liverpool. To develop a distinct and clear Perth music scene, the city needs its Cavern Clubs and Haciendas; its Grosvenors, Rosemounts and Hyde Parks. Live music venues should become popular historical landmarks—not the buildings themselves—but the sounds, smells, tastes, movements and voices inside. Perth's planners need to claim music as a marketable culture, drawing tourists to visit the place that gave birth to their favourite bands.

Current conflicts between law and popular culture block Perth from being a city with a strong, marketable and thriving musical identity. Perth live music should be allowed to formulate a popular musical heritage on its own dynamic, original terms. Dominant heritage and local government discourses need to negotiate with voices of fans, musicians, managers and public servants who are active in the live original music scene. An equitable and profitable way to embrace Perth's popular music culture must be discovered that will benefit both the music and the city. Yet how can Perth music continue to move through international and national borders if the sound is turned down? If the legislation and state-institutional ideology that silenced amplifiers in the Grosvenor front room in November 2002 continues uncontested, Perth music is in danger of not being heard.

CHAPTER  7

The Ass-End of the World: Perth, Music, Venues and Fandom

Carley Smith

Hope I like the life I find
When I leave everything behind
I hope I'm sure I've made my mind to go.
'Leaving Home' Jebediah[1]

While researching this chapter, I found out that Radiohead would be touring Australia. I was absolutely elated, as they have been my favourite band since I was fourteen. I floated on an ecstatic energy for all of thirty seconds. They—or their promoters—decided to visit only Sydney and Melbourne. I resigned myself to the reality that I have seen them before. I also accepted that this happens quite frequently to Perth music fans, be they a fan of local artists who have to leave their home state to make a living from music, or a fan of international acts whose management does not consider us a viable stopover. However, Perth fans are restless in their redundancy. This chapter revels in the voices and energy of popular music's fans who are often excluded from historical documents, journalism or even academic investigations. In the books written on local scenes and sounds around the world, fans are frequently talked about, rather than to. This chapter presents these voices. In essence, this chapter asks why this small, yet lively, city is considered such a backwater.

We do not have a large enough venue left in Perth that would accommodate the kind of crowd an international act like Radiohead can attract. I saw them play in 1998 at the Entertainment Centre—that has since closed down. No pub or club would be large enough to hold a crowd this large, so they could move us to the Burswood Dome, the only benefit for that particular centre being as a venue for the Hopman Cup tennis championship. Even a small stadium like the WACA cricket ground or Subiaco Oval would suffice. In Perth, sporting events raise stadiums while music demolishes them. Equally, the 'revamping' of music venues is robbing a new generation of Perth music fans from experiencing our eclectic local scene. I am a rock and pop fan who has also become a dance music devotee in the last five years. Save for hokey country music, I will listen to anything. I like music for what it is and not from where it is sourced. I must admit to paying more attention when I like something and I know the act is from Perth. I liken music fandom to supporting a sporting team—we go for the home team or the underdog. Perth acts are both.

For a centre that is supposedly about to 'burst' with ripe talent, local acts have little opportunity to remain in Perth. For local talent to be considered 'successful' there is a familiar narrative and trajectory that is repeated endlessly: they have to first make it 'over East' and then overseas. To make this success a little less impossible, they usually relocate to Sydney or Melbourne, only reinforcing the lack of opportunity for them here. There is a stigma, instilled so deeply in our culture that we do not question its presence anymore, that Perth is the ass-end of the world. I wanted to get a broader view of what other fans thought of the 'scene'—or even if there was one. I interviewed fans who mostly grew up in Perth. They are not famous and they are not in the music industry, but they are fans—expressive, passionate, opinionated and informed. They have something to say about Perth's disappearing venues and lack of consideration nationally and internationally. They come from a wide range of backgrounds and have very different tastes in music. All but two grew up in Perth, and all spent their teenage years here.

What did you grow up listening to? Where did you go? Who did you see?

Erika: We went to many a gig; mostly Australian stuff as there was a boom then...Jebediah, Red Jezebel and other local acts, it was when these people were just getting popular. [I] mostly went to festivals like the Big Day Out, Mudslinger, in-stores at 78s and occasionally afternoon all-ages gigs at Greenwich and Grosvenor backroom. Mostly 'indie' Oz rock, and international bands like Ben Folds Five, Weezer, Radiohead, Blur, and Beck.[2]

Do you prefer pub rock, concerts or going out to dance events?

Mary: Considering that there are hardly any good venues for live music any more (the Grosvenor) dance events are better, but there is nothing like seeing a good band on a Sunday arvo![3]
Derek: I like the laid-back atmosphere of events held at pubs, although I've noticed that international acts tend to play at larger venues. Unfortunately I dance like a chimpanzee with Parkinson's disease so dance events are out of the question for me.[4]

I spent most of my time in Fremantle and Perth when I was a teenager. I went to the City if any of the clubs there were hosting afternoon gigs for under-eighteens and there were always decent local bands playing in Fremantle on the weekend. The Fremantle Passenger Terminal used to host small events and many pubs and clubs had all-age afternoon shows. The music is still there now for adults, but there are not many places kids can go to see local talent. I have to, and still do, find out about upcoming tours in the street newspaper *X-Press* or on Triple J. The broad coverage in *X-Press* includes the useful 'Gig Guide' and 'Clubbers Guide.' If it was not for their extensive exposure of local talent, most of us would be sitting at home wondering why yet another international act was passing us by or mourning the loss or 'renovation' of another fine venue.

Where did you/do you find out about bands/events that you want to see?

Erika: *X-Press* primarily, also through friends and through fliers/advertising at other gigs. Occasionally radio, but they didn't cover underage gigs that much (and never do now as they are non-existent).[5]

Do you go out a lot, or do you prefer to buy music and listen to it at home?

Jemima: I have so many CDs—so I definitely love to listen to music at home. I would say that whilst I enjoy going out and listening to live music, I mostly listen to it at home. Especially if there are hefty cover charges (i.e. international bands) and, being a student, I just can't afford it sometimes. Case in point—The Eels. Why, oh why, did those tix have to be so damn expensive?[6]

Isolation leads to fan depression. Our local talent gets pilfered by the East, and international rock and pop acts quite often skip us when touring. The only scene that actually comes here, rather than leaves, is dance culture. This culture still captures the energies of resistance, aligning young people and class. Now, through Ministry of Sound and Gatecrasher events and compilations, Perth is regarded as commercially viable. Dancing is profitable. That is why the stalwart hosts of the dance music industry rarely skip Perth when holding events.

Do you think the transportation of dance events, especially through Ministry of Sound from the UK to Perth in particular, has transformed dance music, as a scene, from a working-class sound into a highly marketable middle-class sound and experience?

Mary: Yes, I think it has. It is now more expensive and has become a little exclusive.[7]
Erika: I think it's not so much to do with the transportation of it than the saleability of it (and the transportation of it comes into this too, as it becomes profitable to do so). Dance and drug culture is very marketable.[8]
Stacey: No, but I think it seems like that because the working-class/middle-class distinction has changed; the working-class are

becoming more upwardly mobile. It has definitely become a marketing thing where people who would never have been involved before are being attracted to these events. However, I believe the experience is still pretty working-class.[9]
Jemima: It seems as though the whole scene has been co-opted somewhat. You only have to take a look at all the dance compilation CDs out in the market to judge how commercialised and commodified the dance scene has become. I can't help but think the politics has been removed from it and that…many people would be unaware of its history as a response to conservatism.[10]
Kirsty: I like to think of it as a 'groupie' like following; people see it as 'cool' to be seen at these events, as it's highly sophisticated to be caught in the actual club in London.[11]

I do not begrudge anyone making money from music. But if we had adequate venues and gave local acts the ability to promote themselves they would be reticent to leave. There are hard-working, signed and unsigned local acts that are playing the small circuit in Perth but most are simply biding their time until fame, fortune or break-up comes along. When I was a teenager the 'scene' seemed sufficient. Bands had appropriate venues in which to play, there was the summer festival circuit, and dance and hip hop events were gaining an audience. Now there are few all-age gigs to accompany the over-eighteen sessions, the summer rock festival circuit has a new 'commercial radio' feel to it and a lot of venues have been 'revamped' or closed down. There are very few spaces left for fans to go and listen to local acts. Hardcore fans flock to the places that remain, but their devotion has not managed to keep venues from closure.

The Perth scene is exploding at the moment. Do you feel a certain amount of pride/'ownership' listening to/going to see Perth acts?

Jemima: I enjoy acts for who they are, but I don't actually feel any ownership or 'pride' in the fact that they come from Perth. I love Perth and I enjoy the vibrant, fresh, innovative scene that has developed here over the years, but I am not really patriotic about it.[12]

Derek: I do feel a slight sense of pride when going to see Australian and Perth acts. This is substantially influenced by the fact that I have been disillusioned by a lot of what is in the charts at the moment. It seems to me that to have your songs played repeatedly on the radio you must have a socially acceptable body shape and lots of tattoos (if you are male) or cleavage/booty (if you are female)…If it was the other way around I would have a top ten hit on my hands (or under my clothes as is the case).[13]

Erika: No. All the great bands leave Perth for the east coast as there is no way they can fulfil their potential [in Perth]. The great venues that we have in Perth are gone or they have evolved in to something else. The Grosvenor was *the home* of live music just four years ago, and now there is no one there but yuppies luncheoning and old men drinking beer. Mojos has become some sort of cocktail bar, and the good venues that we do have now are not regular band venues…[T]hey have advertised gigs there, but there is no longer anywhere (central) to go to 'see who's playing.' I don't know why the east coast is jumping for Perth music, when Perth people barely have a chance to hear the music that's being made there anymore…Being in Melbourne it actually makes me kind of sad to hear [people] talk about the great music that's coming out of Perth, because all I can think about is how great it used to be.[14]

I loved going to rock events like the Big Day Out and Mudslinger and more recently to Delirium events. The same process is repeated at all of these events though. The international or east coast act plays the main stage and people flock to see them because they think they should. Meanwhile an admirable Perth act plays their hearts out to a devoted bunch of fans on some stuffy stage behind the port-a-loos. We are so far away from what is considered Australia's 'centre'. What has to be dealt with is the distance between Perth and the centre of the Australian music industry in Sydney and Melbourne. Overcoming the preconceived attitudes of music industry leaders about Perth will remove, or at the very least problematise, social stigmas attached to our isolation. The centre cannot sell what the centre cannot see. It is a very long journey across the Nullarbor. Studies into the musical culture that exists here allow for a more considered recognition of the unbelievable talent that exists in Perth and will provide local artists with the ability to grow and prosper *here*.

CHAPTER 8

Home-Grown: Music from the Backyard

Rebecca Bennett

> There's a garage in Fremantle lovingly dubbed 'The Hit Factory.' From this remote shed have blasted some killer riffs, delicious melodies and thoroughly original music.[1]

'The Hit Factory' is in musician-producer Rodney Aravena's backyard. A registered business, 'The Hit Factory' is called Debaser during office hours (which usually spans from after midday until closing time when the beer runs out). Debaser records 'demos' for selected original Perth bands who hope to enter the local and national market. It has achieved moderate success and notoriety, being mentioned on national music radio station Triple J. It has helped Perth bands such as Eskimo Joe, Little Birdy and The Fergusons hone their skills, circulate their music and get signed to established record labels.

Rodney Aravena has been involved in the Perth local original music scene since he moved from Adelaide in 1991 at age fourteen. His experience of original music in Perth began as an underage punter in local music venues and as a guitarist in high school bands who never made it out of their garages. By 2001, Rodney's commitment to the local scene led him on to the stage as a member of popular Australian and internationally recognised band The Sleepy Jackson.[2] Rodney left The Sleepy Jackson just after their 2002 UK tour to return to his garage in Fremantle. His vision was to pursue what made him happy: playing guitar in his 'other' band End of Fashion, and making Perth 'backyard' music visible and marketable in local, national and hopefully international original music scenes.

I spoke to Rodney Aravena on his shady Fremantle back veranda. Our backing track comprised faint vocal harmonies and keyboard and guitar melodies escaping from a semi-unhinged, paint-chipped garage door flapping in the afternoon breeze.

What's happening in your backyard right now?

We've been doing some recording. Funnily enough it's the 'Eskys'[3] of all people. I run a studio out the back of my house with Joel Quartermain [Eskimo Joe] and Andy Lawson called Debaser—and yeah, we've been recording many bands' demos and releases for the past few years.

How did you get involved in the Perth music scene?

It was pretty simple, really. As a young kid I was a punter. I loved going to gigs. I came from a family that really enjoyed playing music and listening to music and it was just a logical extension. I really wanted to play music for a long, long time. When I was old enough to go out—even when I was not old enough to go out—I'd go to pubs and see bands play. At first I never made it a priority that I went out and played music. I really enjoyed watching bands and (later) recording bands. When it came to actually playing in bands, I tried to start a few but it never happened. I didn't get into playing music live until pretty late in my years—not that I'm that old. So yeah, since then I've played in a few bands. In my recent history, it's been End of Fashion and The Sleepy Jackson and Adora. Adora is the band that really set the wheels going of getting me into the scene as a musician—as opposed to a punter. For many years I've also been helping bands do recordings and stuff. Probably the main one is Eskimo Joe. They were my mates and I did them a favour for free.

How did you start producing music?

I've always really enjoyed the whole technical aspect of recording. I started doing it when I was a kid. I remember my brother and myself got tape machines when we were about ten years old. We used to record insulting songs to each other. Another embarrassing thing we did was record love songs for these girls who we liked on ukuleles, which was hilarious. The recording kept going and we got little four tracks and started recording friends. I learned—pretty much by trial and error—the process of recording and how to get a nice sound. When I finally felt that I was confident enough to do so, I approached other bands about doing demos for them. With Debaser we've worked really hard just on our skills of working. We don't merely record bands we also give them advice on their song writing and stuff so that puts a bit of an edge on our work. That's why people are interested in working with us—even though it's in the back of a shed.

Are you a certified business?

We are a business but due to the nature of the people running it—like Andy and myself who work in the industry in other guises—the business sometimes doesn't run. A lot of times we're touring over East so [Debaser] doesn't run for several months at a time.

How does living in Perth affect your business?

Living in Perth is a boon for us. It's just the nature of the environment of being in Perth. It's relaxed, it's cheap and you get to work on many projects without being too disturbed.

Can you name some popular local bands that emerged from your back shed?

The first band we did was The Fergusons.[4] We recorded the drums in the lounge room; we mixed it on an eight track, put it on to computer and burned it on to CD. The mixing was done in about two hours late at night because we had to go to a gig first. Yeah, and they've [The Fergusons] just kept coming back to us and they've been signed to a label called Due Process. The second band we did was Gyroscope,[5] and again they've been coming back to us. They've also recorded in the lounge room, the shed, everywhere and, yeah, they've been signed as well. Little Birdy[6] also got signed. A few bands have been signed by us so we've been pretty lucky that we've had, you know, great bands to work with.

How has the recording studio affected your own bands?

The reason the whole thing [Debaser] started was so we could work on the songs of our bands. We worked twice as hard. Before we took our songs to our studios we'd go through the recording process ourselves feeling what was good or bad about the songs and what could be improved. Once we've done a recording we can analyse it. It is a luxury we have that we decided to share with others.

Can you describe an average working week in your life?

Well, I sleep a lot. Nothing's ever really that constant. Being in bands you often find out that plans change at the last minute. Sometimes you'll be set to stay at home and you'll be sent touring. The next time you think you'll be travelling and you end up staying at home. There is, of course, doing shows and recording. In my schedule a lot of bands come and work in my house. They record at my house so I've got to make allowances for that and for rehearsals with my own band. In general my work is a mish-mash of parts of the industry.

Are you kept busy?

Busyish. As busy as a musician in Perth can get.

How do you keep up both of your roles as a musician and producer without compromising either Debaser or End of Fashion?

I think to try and maintain a career in music in this day and age you have to adapt to many different roles. I mean there's no guarantee that anybody can live off music by itself—no matter who you are or where you live. Perth especially is just not the environment to earn a stable income—even if you are, say a session musician. In order to survive in the Perth original music scene you have to adapt to a lot of different roles and be very business minded about what you do.

You were a member of The Sleepy Jackson. You joined the band at the time that they really took off internationally. UK's NME magazine said The

Sleepy Jackson: Lovers would be an 'Album of the Year contender'[7] *in 2003. The Sleepy Jackson was invited to play some big rock festivals such as Reading and Leeds. Why did you return to the Perth scene?*

I came back because in any job you do, you have to be happy. The environment that you work in has to be good. It doesn't matter what job it is, it could be that you're a garbage cleaner or a doctor. With any position that you're in you have to be happy in yourself and be happy with the direction that you're taking. I had my time there [in the UK] and I think I really enjoyed what I did. I just decided that I had other projects that I wanted to move on to; projects that I really enjoyed doing and had a greater compulsion for. I'm a bit of a gambler and I like to take chances with things. I see things—I'm probably a bit of a dreamer—I see great things in small things and like to take a chance and give it a go.

What is it about Perth that made it the city where you decided to take a chance at making small things great?

Perth has got a great support base for local music. People are very passionate about it. It's sometimes a bit of a clique, but it's because people love what they love. Perth bands would like to share their passions with a lot more people I think.

What are your favourite things about making music in Perth?

Number one is the isolation. You can work here without any problem. There's no record company looking over your shoulder finding out what you're doing every second. There are also not many temptations to continuously go out and have a good time that big cities have. Sydney and Melbourne are big places; they've got 24-hour everything.

But, more than anything else, my favourite thing [about Perth] is definitely the people within the environment. In the scene that I work in we've started a community of musicians. It's really good. Everyone helps each other with their projects that they do. We're very inclusive. We don't hire session musicians. If we need extra musicians to play on our tracks the first people we go to are our friends. We give them a shot because if we can help them then it helps us as well—as a community. We just love the ideas that each person has to give within this community and it's worked out in many ways. It's very interconnected. In this music scene people really put a lot of time in—mostly unpaid—to make the scene work.

What are the limitations of the Perth music scene?

Ironically, number one is the isolation. The sheer cost of travelling carrying only members of a band—let alone a road crew—to the Eastern States and coming back again is very difficult. This means we have less access to larger markets. Eastern States bands can travel up and down the East Coast in a battered van quite easily and cheaply. This means they keep up a profile in live venues, playing lots of different pubs and stuff. In Perth it's a lot more difficult to promote our live music. With The Sleepy Jackson we had to stay in Sydney as a base because we couldn't afford to keep on flying back into Perth every time we needed to tour.

In your experience, how does the Perth scene compare to larger Australian capital cities like Melbourne and Sydney?

I'd say Perth's definitely better than Sydney in the sense of live music and the variety of live music. It's quite odd, but the live original music scene in Sydney is quite small and not very organised for such a big city. Western Australia has got the advantage of having a highly organised structure. It's got the WAMIs [Western Australian Music Industry Awards][8] and Arts WA does a lot of good jobs for live original music. There is a strong structure within Perth that you don't necessarily see in the bigger cities. But Melbourne definitely has a great pub culture—very parochial—but a great pub culture. You can go out and see lots of bands play. Last New Year's, at the Espy I saw Jet, Dan Kelly and Perth band The Local Pricks playing. There were heaps of bands playing at this gig that was packed. It was great!

Perth is, at the end of the day a very nice, quiet city. It's so suburban. The isolation makes us more passionate but we're such a young city that we don't have the cultural aspects of New York, London, Paris, Barcelona…or any city in Europe. Even over East has more culture, you know. When you play to larger markets there is always heaps of people there which is a better way to sustain a career in music. The original music scene can expand within the Australian environment. Not just in Perth but in the Eastern States too. Perth just doesn't have a long history of generations creating its musical environment. It's brand new and we've got to try and give a bit of…a bit more culture to the city. More people could be interested going to a pub and seeing a band play.

How do you think the Perth original music scene might be improved?

I definitely think licensing hours can be changed. Compared to other places in this country and definitely overseas, we've got very restrictive laws. Perth has a very conservative way of looking at society. We have so few venues that are open late. Licensing requirements mean most hotels have to shut at midnight and earlier on Sundays. Also venues can be shut down because of noise restrictions and complaints.

Engaging the public—maintaining and supporting their interest in live music—is also important. Ten years ago there were so many people who grew up going and seeing live bands play. I remember when I was travelling in Rome I met an Australian at this backpacker hostel. He was a schoolteacher but he'd got into teaching after playing live music for ten years. He'd been playing in pubs in Sydney. [His band] never got huge but the culture of live music in Sydney at the time, meant that they could play original music to packed out venues six nights a week. He said that the hardest thing in his job was trying to write new songs every week to keep an edge on the public. I was astounded that such a thing could exist. This couldn't happen now, there's no…the culture's not there. So many interests are taking up people's time. We have to try and make people want to go to original gigs.

Hypothetically, what would make your life in the Perth music industry ideal?

I think just a guarantee that we can promote our own music. That's the biggest thing for Perth in general. You don't want to spend money going over East without the support of national stations like Triple J or local music stations in other cities. You don't want to go anywhere without that guarantee. There's that story of The Beatles not going to America because of the humiliation that other British acts had over there if they didn't have a number one. The Beatles could afford the tour because they had such a strong following in Europe. It was an intelligent decision to not go anywhere as a complete unknown. The biggest things that I'd ask for Perth music are promotion and publicity.

Where would you like to see the Perth original local music scene in ten years?

I would like a healthier live music environment, that's all. When people play they should have an opportunity to show what they're doing. If it was my scene...if it was up to me...there would be more venues, more people going out and more opportunities for bands to play and earn a living. There are opportunities developing now for a lot of bands. You don't necessarily have to be signed to a record label to release albums. Since the Internet, communication is opening in Perth. You can send a disc or an MP3 of something overseas rapidly and have it shown to people but at the end of the day we still need the networks and the contacts.

If you're in a new band, live venues are so concentrated that getting a gig is a difficult thing. Once you start getting gigs and getting people to turn up means that you get other gigs. It is slow steps up a ladder. To go from playing some shitty pub somewhere in the suburbs to big original pubs in the city to eventually playing festivals and stuff is very difficult. In Perth you have to work really hard or get really lucky to get that kind of attention.

Where would you like to be in ten years, both musically and geographically?

I'd love to still be living in Perth. I've always been a big fan of bands and musicians just giving it a go. I've been very lucky I've recorded very talented songwriters and musicians. I think that if there are such talented people already here in Perth, there's bound to be more kids out there who I haven't seen. I'd definitely like to keep recording and helping promote the things that we do here. I think that live original music is an important cultural environment in every city and Perth musicians should be heard.

CHAPTER 9

Mapping Perth

Amanda Evans

Flying, in more senses than one, is a 'trip,' involving a shift in both geographical and existential co-ordinates; we go to an 'other' place, but eventually we also go home. The journey acquires its final shape and sense only once we have returned to the familiar textures of our world.[1]
Iain Chambers

A remembrance is in very large measure a reconstruction of the past achieved with data borrowed from the present.[2]
Maurice Halbwachs

The position of nightclubs in the history and cultural identity of a city is inherently political. When families retreat to their suburban enclaves, the night envelops the city and a redistribution of social power is activated. It is these dynamic spaces that are explored in this chapter, through a filter of collective memory and composition. The struggle over meaning in these creative industries exposes the social power of a subordinated group: youth. To affirm the rights and roles of young people, the value of these social spaces needs to be marked, acknowledged and remembered.

This chapter focuses on the spectacle of Perth's night-time identity. This investigation resides between the textual landscape of Chambers and Halbwachs—the space that exists between remembering and constructing. My words are intended to act as a filter of the past to inform the present. It is not intended to be read as a whining cry of despair that clubs in the 1990s were better than today—quite the opposite.[3] This journey then, seeks to assess and illustrate the cultural significance of particular clubs and their traces on the present scene. It demonstrates the constant reinvention of Perth clubs through the past fifteen years and illustrates the fact that each scene kills the club it loves.

ALL ABOARD THE NIGHT TRAIN

Let me take you on a journey—a passage into the night-time economy of Perth in the 1990s. Let us enter the clubs. The composition of this trip may seem limiting at first, but by narrowing the investigative area, the social growth and experiential consumption of these social spaces in Perth can be seen with clarity. The Perth club renaissance in the 1990s was partly due to the America's Cup yacht race that was defended in Fremantle in 1987. Licensing laws in the city were relaxed so that hospitality/cabaret venues could 'cash-in' on the internationally attended yacht race. At that time, Perth had the most liberal licensing laws in Australia. Cabaret licensed venues therefore could remain open until 6 am as opposed to the previous closing time of 2 am.

This expedition is—and must be—by nature experiential and should not be read as definitive—it is a bluffer's guide to the clubs of the 1990s. I would like to defend this angle. My words do not assert that these were the *only* clubs on the Perth landscape, nor were they the *coolest* venues. Secondly, it is the *spaces* that are of interest here, the sites that enveloped the music, rather than DJs, people, drugs, events and scenes. I am also very aware of the pitfalls of nostalgia. The practice of 'composure'[4]—the past mixing with the present—has undeniably impacted on these recollections. One of the most difficult aspects of any discussion of the past is the intersection of memory with spatial surroundings. Time and space occupy a complicated place in the history of any club. Our memories are often reliant upon the ongoing relationship with our tangible environment. In other words,

> Collective memory unfolds within a spatial framework…space is a reality that endures. Since our impressions rush by, one after another…we can understand how we recapture the past only by understanding how it is, in effect, preserved by our physical surroundings.[5]

A journey back in time is always reconstructed and never authentic because the past is shaped by the truths and changes in the present. All that remains is the flash of insight filtered through prior utterances, bodies on dance floors and mornings after. The composition of these feelings and spaces do not stand alone. Reflecting upon the past, I sat and talked with many people and these discussions served to remind me of how individuals become part of a community. That is, the history of these social spaces often echoes not one voice but the voices of many in the reconstruction of time and space. More importantly, private memories often require the framework of the collective to be seen as credible. Individually and collectively we 'compose' memories that cut away the pain—we reconstruct and rewrite to find comfort. It is this comfort that will inevitably be (re)presented in this analysis and this journey. These spaces are sifted through the memories of a 5'6" brunette who had the temporary pleasure to reside in these spaces and inevitably leave lipstick traces on the dance floors of all of these clubs.

All that remains now is to grab a map and sit back and enjoy the ride.

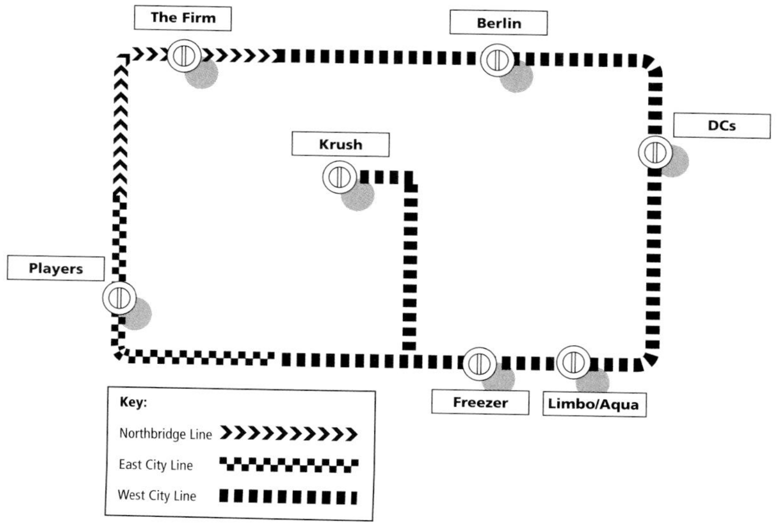

FIGURE 3: Club underground map

THE FIRM[6]

Located in the Old Melbourne Hotel, on the corner of Hay and Milligan Streets in the city, The Firm originally was a one-room club accessed by a rickety steel staircase. On busy nights, the stairs were packed with people who stood to the right, allowing for people to exit on the left. In the club, booths were located on the right and a pool table to the left. The bar extended the length of the dance floor and the DJ booth was elevated. The booth was so small that only the DJ and their records could fit. If anyone wanted to request a song it was either by shouting up to the DJ or attempting to get up the stairs through the women's toilets.

The Firm was a very dark and small space that activated the diversity of subcultures that inhabited the city. Most Friday nights were filled with students and diverse tunes pumped out from the Happy Mondays, Northside, James and The Stone Roses, punctuated with northern soul, disco, Nick Cave, Cabaret Voltaire, Joy Division and Dead Can Dance. Saturday nights were often more 'up' in tempo and a catalogue of acid house tunes were mixed.

The first few years that The Firm was open, a strip club—Tiffany's—operated next door. You could not access Tiffany's from The Firm, though many tried, as the two clubs had separate entry points. Upon the closure of Tiffany's, The Firm expanded across the hallway and what was colloquially known as Firm II opened. Firm II arrived when acid house began to impact on the Perth scene. The old steel staircase was closed and both areas of The Firm were accessed through the main entrance of the Old Melbourne—up a Heritage Trust-listed wooden staircase. At the top of the stairs, a decision was thrust upon the punter—turn left to go into the old Firm or right to enter Firm II. Most nights this was an easy decision—right first to get the night started, then left to get a hit of more alternative tunes, then right again to end the night.

The Firm remains one of the most innovative clubs in recent Perth history. It not only catered for an alternative club set, but was one of the first, and perhaps the only club to fuse together the dance and indie scenes successfully. There was much lamenting on its closure, but due to fickle clubbers, its tenure ended in the mid-1990s. The Firm also became a victim of its geography—the majority of Perth clubs were located in Northbridge, an area positioned across the railway tracks from the city. The most easily accessible route for clubbers to get to The Firm from Northbridge was across the tracks near The Berlin. This passage was closed and replaced with a footbridge that seemed more hassle than it was worth. The Firm was also a casualty of its time, as raves became more popular in the mid-1990s and many Firm-clubbers trekked out to industrial areas for their weekend entertainment. The Firm no longer exists as a club or venue. The space that housed The Firm is now rooms in the new improved Melbourne Hotel—one of Perth's first boutique hotels.

My favourite Firm memory is the night when an underage girl found an innovative entry point into the club. I was at the bar in Firm II one Saturday night when I noticed the huge, round air conditioning vent attached to the roof had begun to sway. I pointed it out to my friends and we thought that the air conditioning was just overworked. We started dancing and suddenly a girl popped out and on to the dance floor—out of the vent. She was covered in dust and spider webs, but hit the floor, literally, and started to dance madly. In shock we stared and laughed. Within seconds two huge bouncers appeared and dragged her off—she had been stopped from coming in about twenty minutes earlier. The club was packed and everyone started shouting to leave her alone. Offers were made of an ID trade, but to no avail.

THE BERLIN

Unlike the eclectic nature of The Firm, Berlin was a club firmly rooted in dance music—more precisely techno. You could feel the bass before you turned the corner of James Street into Milligan. But like The Firm, Berlin was cavernous and dark upon entry and had corners for escape when the dance floor got too much. Berlin was a huge room with one long bar to the left and a back bar off the dance floor. Dancers dominated the space. The Berlin became the blueprint for all hardcore/techno clubs in Perth. It was one of the first clubs to directly combat the house-dominated environment of the city.

I can honestly admit that it was only on odd occasions that I would stay at Berlin for longer than two hours. At times it felt like the music was too much, my jeans weren't baggy enough, my hair wasn't short and blonde enough and I did not have a boyfriend with a French Crop. It was however, a place that was worth going to for an hour or so, as a reminder why Vicks VapoRub was for a chesty cold and not an industrial mask; why classical music with a throbbing bass line and accelerated BPM was dodgy; and that gurning faces and clenched jaws are funny on all faces, whether twenty or eighty years old.

DCs (DUAL CONTROL)

Located on Francis Street near Russell Square in Northbridge, DCs[7] was originally set up to offer an alternative to Perth's premier gay club—Connections. DCs was an oddly shaped venue—it occupied the front area of a larger complex and the back large room that joined it was filled by various techno/jungle/drum 'n' bass clubs. As you entered the club there were bars to the left and right, with the latter infinitely more popular (and considered the main bar) due to its proximity to the dance floor. If you did not veer off to the dance floor upon entry you entered a long corridor. This area contained pinball machines and seating areas, alongside a space not cluttered with anything. Towards the end of the corridor was the second toilet and an outside courtyard with a limited bar and seating.

DCs was a club that was founded on tolerance and was active in the dissolution of stereotyping in the Perth club scene. Unlike other clubs that had signs outlining their dress code upon entry, DCs had a moral code where intolerant clubbers were encouraged to go elsewhere. The atmosphere was carnivalesque—with blissed out 'hets' mixing it up with camp homeboys and gals, and fabulous drag queens feeding off the chemical-induced egotism of the club. One of the most popular aspects of the venue was its long corridor (where the second entry door of jungle/drum 'n' bass club, Gravity, was located) and the small outdoor area. It was here that you caught up with weekend friends and rehydrated after two solid hours on the dance floor. DCs performed the energetic Perth house scene at its climax—it educated the scene and at the same time showed it a damn good time.

One night while getting a drink at the main bar, I noticed a very 'het' guy ordering a VB. I originally thought he looked a little lost and that when he realised where he was his attitude might change from bewildered to angry. Talk about stereotyping. I was pleasantly proved wrong later in the night when I saw the guy cutting up the dance floor, blissfully reaching for the lights and partying with some of the resident drag queens and shop-girls. It was a moment that reminded me of how unifying not only dance music was, but also DCs. To this day it remains a club that makes me smile when I remember it. It was social justice to syncopation.

AQUA

The previous name of the club that occupied the William Street site before Aqua was scene-setting Limbo. It was innovative and a true pioneer of dance clubs in Perth. It was one of the first venues to break from the irritating Top 40 club format that had dominated Perth throughout the 1980s. It was also the venue that launched the first 'official' rave. To acquire the map to the rave, the prospective punter had to meet at Limbo and sit through the 1992 FA Cup final. This was an interesting test of Englishness. After the demise of Limbo, house venues became very popular—Network, Berlin, Firm II and James St.

Aqua took over the site and kept alive the tradition of Limbo. Brilliantly simple in layout and energy, Aqua was entered from a street level staircase. Once at the top of the stairs you were thrust into the music and on to the dance floor. Originally there was only one bar—to the left of the stairs—and it was surrounded by high tables and bar stools. As its popularity grew, a second bar was added to the right at the back of the space near the women's toilets. Aqua remained popular for longer than most house clubs in Perth. This can probably be attributed to its handbag/hard house energy. This was also part of its downfall: once the lay-dees with the bags moved west to Krush, the lads obediently followed. Ironically it is now a site that is occupied by a strip club and the gents have returned—minus the handbags.

One of the many interesting spatial facets about Perth clubs is that many of them are located above ground level and therefore have to be accessed by stairs. The stairs leading into Aqua were quite steep and formidable, even when sober. My experience of these stairs had been fairly amicable up until the night I decided to go down them on my face. Not one of my better social moments. While talking to a friend at the top of the stairs—he was leaving—I realised that I had over-estimated my social dexterity—laughing, drinking and standing in platforms heels all at the same time. As I laughed, I threw my head back—or what I had anticipated to be my head—and my body followed. I rolled down the entire staircase, but somehow managed to right myself and land on my feet at the very end. I then threw my hands in the air to signal the end of my routine and skulked back up the stairs—uninjured.

THE FREEZER

Located next door to Aqua, The Freezer was musically similar to its neighbour. The obvious difference between these two clubs was its regulars. The Freezer appeared more exclusive, but played the same cheesy house tunes to attract the handbags looking for eligible wallets. Perhaps my least favourite club of the time, but it rates a mention for its staying power and the laughs it provided for the more knowing clubber. While Aqua was the preferred club it was always fun to go next door when it got too crowded on the dance floor. The layout of The Freezer was very generic and it appeared that not much thought had gone into its design—door, door bitch, door, room length bar, dance floor, tables, toilets. The dance floor was the most fascinating place—it was very small and appropriately resembled a gym weights area—mirrors everywhere. I can only conclude that the reason this 'tasteful' décor was that dancers could watch themselves being watched by others in the club. The lighting differed from most clubs whose design was dark and unobtrusive—like a comfortable mist to allow the dancer to be anonymous and lose inhibitions. The Freezer was awash with pale blue lighting to reflect not only the name of the club, but also to feed the voyeuristic tendencies of its clubbers. The Freezer—like Aqua—became a victim of clubber-induced blasé-ness and shut its doors to make room for the 'stylings' of Orsini's.[8]

Remembering The Freezer is not always pleasant—one of my freakiest and scariest clubbing memories is associated with this place. Whilst watching the spectacle in the club my friend and I noticed a group of lads backslapping and reassuring a short and agitated young man. It obviously did not work—minutes later the 'angry man' broke free of his friends and produced a gun and threatened another guy further down the bar. For what seemed like forever—nobody around him moved, the bass kept throbbing and people at the front of the club remained blissfully unaware of the pseudo gang-star—the guy stood there pointing the gun and ranting. Finally, a bouncer and the manager approached the guy and his friends and quietly subdued him—and then bought them all a round of drinks. The two guys who were previously involved in the ridiculous standoff shook hands and went on as if nothing had happened.

KRUSH

The heir apparent to Aqua was a small club located on James Street above a Spanish restaurant. Like Aqua, Krush was accessed by a staircase. The dance floor was revealed upon entry. The DJ booths in both clubs were on the dance floor and easily accessible—the Krush booth was at leaning height. The similarities between Aqua and Krush were quite unnerving. Even the Aqua DJs seemed to move to the decks at Krush. The club was popular and always full. It seemed to attract serious clubbers and students alike. Its appeal was a relaxed atmosphere and lack of pretentious posers who frequented The Freezer. While a success, it seemed too burdened by a lack of vision—and when it closed and reopened as Geisha it reached the climax that it deserved. It is this capacity for transformation that makes it an influential club of the 1990s.

One night a posse went out to Krush with a friend of a friend. Pete was a little out of his depth and not really socially astute—he also had a short fuse. A little later in the night, Pete had been chatting to two girls and had gone off to buy them drinks. I saw him twenty minutes later with a beer for himself, and two other drinks that were obviously for his newfound friends. After forty minutes he conceded that they were not coming back and went looking for them near the dance floor. He stood near the DJ booth and placed the drinks on the bench atop the decks. The DJ was frantically looking for records and accidentally knocked over Pete's drinks—Pete snapped and lunged for the DJ. He missed, but managed to knock the needle off the record playing (insert needle scratching record sound here). The whole club stopped. We all watched in silence as Pete grappled for the DJ, but was pummelled for his efforts. Then the bouncers arrived and poor Pete was escorted from the club black and red-faced.

PLAYERS

Players was, after The Firm, my favourite Perth club. There are a number of factors for this—its location: it was as far away from Northbridge as possible. The people: clubbers and staff alike were knowing and literate in club etiquette. The layout and design were stylish, located down a carpeted staircase decked out with fish tanks, couches—even a bed—and the dance floor was located away from the chill-out area so you never got stomped on by those who were in a frenzy. The bar was a horseshoe design that serviced all areas; so getting a drink was convenient.

Players was as comfortable a club as Perth could imagine in the 1990s. It was also the club that adopted and promoted a dramatic generic shift in dance music—break beat. International DJs and acts were booked often, but local DJs were never treated as second best and some of the more memorable nights were when local DJs and acts were featured. Its closure was premature and it was a long time before a club took over its mantle—perhaps Ambar and the newly invigorated Mount Lawley enclave are the logical choices.

Players was a great 'must visit' place most weekends, particularly when an 'event' was on—Soundlab, the Ku-Ling Brothers, Waterslide, Fat Boy Slim, Adam Freeland and The People Under The Stairs were all riveting, apocalyptic moments at Players. For me Players signalled a site of personal change—not only when I was on the dance floor but also when I took those moments home with me. It was at this club that I realised that I was in a hideous relationship and needed to get out. It was also the place where I fell in love with the man I am going to marry. And you really can't ask more from a club than that. I know that this final memory is less pointed than the others, but it does illustrate the influence of the spaces we occupy in our everyday lives. Dancing, through its history, has facilitated how generations of people meet, move and fall in love. Nightclubs house and perpetuate these stories.

The impact of these clubs on the present dance scene in Perth is undeniable, perhaps not sonically, but certainly through design, management and the literacy of contemporary clubbers. Each of these past venues is silently carried forward to dance floors in the new millennium. New clubs are easily replaced by a new generation in months or years to come. No club outstays its welcome—in Perth or anywhere in the world. It is a respect and acknowledgement of the past that maps out a possible future for the dynamic and enduring Perth club scene.

CHAPTER 10

Tuesday Night at the Hydey

Angela Jones

'What *is* this pink building?' was my main question when I first visited the Hyde Park Hotel front bar on a Tuesday night in 1999. The doors were covered in gig posters of local artists and muffled, bassy, electronic music seeped on to the pavement. We entered the dark pub. There were pool tables located in a sunken area to the right, a bar in front and an array of coloured tables, bar stools and booths to the left. In the left-hand corner, a lone DJ bent over two turntables, mixing something dark. This night was my first introduction to drum and bass. It was the first of many new musical experiences that I was to have at the Hyde Park Hotel.

It was during the First World War that the Commonwealth Hotel changed its name to the Hyde Park. The lounge bar was established in 1972 and the Higgins family took over ownership and management in 1979. It is formally known as the Higgins Hyde Park Hotel, but to the locals it is simply referred to as 'The Hydey'. This hotel, situated on the corner of Bulwer and Fitzgerald Streets in West Perth, Western Australia, encourages diverse expectations for different patrons. It is a place to play pool, eat a pub meal and listen to an array of music genres. From the fondly remembered Precision drum and bass night in the front bar, to the Perth Jazz Society meetings held in the lounge bar, the Hyde Park is one of Perth's musical hubs. As the Hyde Park Hotel has gigs in both bars almost every evening of the week, the main focus of this chapter will be on jazz and electronic music. The many 'nights' held at the Hyde Park Hotel have evolved and changed with the tastes of organisers and patrons, but the hotel continues to be a key player in the music scene in Perth.

The Hyde Park Hotel has been the home of the Perth Jazz Society for twenty-three of its thirty years of existence. It is internationally renowned as Perth's home of jazz and the Society holds its meetings in the lounge bar every Monday evening. In the Perth Jazz Society's 30th anniversary editorial, Peter Kanyon, the Chair of Jazz WA stated,

> It is not an obvious place for a world-class jazz venue and program. But on any Monday night at the Hyde Park Hotel in Perth on the fringes of the City as it blurs into suburbia, the Perth Jazz Society presents jazz that would be at home (and often is!) at the great jazz clubs of the world.[1]

The ageing surrounds of the Hydey are an evocative backdrop for a swinging jazz scene. As Kanyon remarks, it is the hotel's location, bordering on city and suburbia that makes this place so important. The Higgins family has made it more than a hotel, particularly for the jazz community. Eve Arnold states,

> The Higgins Family, owners of the venue and avid supporters of the Perth music scene, may be the only publicans in Australia who actively support a jazz organisation and who have made it a priority to make the hotel a suitable venue.[2]

Paul Higgins is the current owner/manager of the hotel and it is easy to see the family's love and support for the Perth music scene is still intact. In a telephone and email interview with Higgins, I questioned him on the scene in Perth, and the role of his hotel.

What are your opinions of the music scene in Perth?

My opinion of the music scene is that generally it is very healthy but in need of venues. There is no shortage of quality acts from all genres of music. As a venue that runs two rooms with either live bands or DJs seven nights a week I see how strong the quality is. We have everything from modern and Dixieland jazz to country rock, stand-up comedy, cabaret bands, tribute bands and orchestras to indie rock and pop, punk, acoustic, thrash and everything in between. It is as diverse a range of styles possible in the one venue. This is one of the reasons for its success in that they all draw from a quite different customer base.

Perth also has a very strong indie scene. The success of RTR-FM and JJJ is testimony to that. This breeds a very active and somewhat underground music scene, but one that continues to thrive.

I also see the success of the Conservatorium of Music in Mount Lawley having a major impact on the quality of musicians in the Perth scene. These musicians cross over into many styles of music and take their musicianship with them. There have in recent times been many of these graduates that have gone on to national and international fame.

How do you think the Hydey has contributed to this scene locally, nationally and internationally?

As far as the Hyde Park Hotel contributing to the Perth music scene, I think that we have offered a quality venue that can seat 500 and can offer the artists very good acoustics and surroundings. Often artists cannot fill a concert hall but are able to fill a venue our size. Again our diversity has contributed in that as we cater for such a diverse array of music we have attracted many international and national artists to Perth because there is a vibrant scene in that style of music in Perth. We have always taken our live entertainment very seriously and as such have always tried to use acoustic engineers whenever we have done any renovations and the best equipment whenever supplying anything.

From Paul Higgins' testimony, it is clear why the hotel, with its array of music, televisions, lounges, tables, food and beverages, feels like a home to its patrons. The relaxed environment enables the eclectic music to blend with the rhythms and patterns of everyday life. It may also be why the Hydey has become the base for so many 'nights'.

As well as being the home of jazz in Perth, the Hydey is also the home of Signal to Noise, an original electro night, and Precision, Perth's longest running drum 'n' bass night. Signal to Noise, started by Vince Valentini and Mike O'Brien, was held on a Thursday night. Valentini had long been involved in electro-industrial music and had several releases under the name Crimson Boy. O'Brien is a longstanding member of the Perth industrial community fronting such bands as Heratech and Biomekanik. Signal to Noise was created to coincide with the release of a local alternative electronic CD. It quickly turned into a popular dance music evening attracting Perth's top DJs and live electronic acts such as Modular, Cambion, Cell7, Choice, Jayd and Jogy, Big Mac, Lilly and Dirty Den, and some special appearances from international guests. The night was eventually taken over by Jayd and Choice (of Awarehouse) and for two years confirmed the strength of local support. Many of the musicians and DJs who began and/or stabilised their names at this gig have gone on to play larger events and venues. Signal to Noise is now run on a Wednesday evening by Ivor Lee and Ben Przywolnick. When I questioned the audience about their opinions of Signal To Noise and the venue Louisa Davin—long-time supporter of the original and current night—stated,

> Because the Hydey is a small venue it forces people to know and recognise each other and is an alternative to the larger trendy venues. The Hyde Park has been less about the fashion and more about the music. Signal to Noise is now diverse, ranging from breaks to techno, with people appreciating the craftsmanship of the sets as well as the choice of tracks.

It has evolved from a night dedicated to local electro talent with an equal mix of musicians and DJs, into its current form of DJ mixes of anything from break-beat to electroclash. It remains an influential space for new DJs and artists to test, trial and perfect. Along with the less generic kinds of dance music, the drum 'n' bass community also benefited from this 'evolutionary' contribution that the Hyde Park makes to the local scene.

Precision Drum and Bass, started by Dave Cutbush in 1999, was held in the front bar on Tuesday nights. It was passed over to Krank when Cutbush left Perth, and ended in May 2003. Precision provided the audience with a mix of progressive drum 'n' bass, and dark breaks, along with the occasional incoherent utterance of MC Braindred. In an email interview, Krank remarked, 'the Hydey was the first successful weekly D 'n' B night in Perth—many current artists such as elhornet from pendulum, shuey, uisce, Ajm and more had their first residencies there.' Precision provided a regular evening for Perth DJs to perform their skills and allowed an eager crowd to gain and build local drum and bass talent.

Initially a small but devoted audience frequented the night. This included DJs such as Greg Packer, Adrian Sardi, Mystique and Krank, organiser Dave Cutbush and the regular drum 'n' bass supporters. It often looked like a club, where the audience would perform the familiar 'running dance' in front of the DJ. The atmosphere was fresh and exciting, where both DJ and audience were on the same social level. Songs were requested: DJs would play them. More recently, the dancing was replaced with a relaxed, lounge style set-up. The audience sat and watched the DJs' technique, listened to the tunes and debated whether their head went back or forward on the snare. As the popularity of drum 'n' bass grew outside of the Hydey, its audience grew within—along with DJ worship. Tuesday nights became absolutely packed. People stood and nodded to the beats, primarily because there was no open space in which to sit, and the 18-year-old Gatecrasher-kids murmured about how long they had been into 'D&B', and when they were leaving for London. This lasted for a couple of months and when the younger crowd dissipated, the old audience remained. Tuesday nights at the Hydey, like Signal to Noise, offered a midweek musical interlude. The Hydey provided a space for local supporters to hear their favourite styles midweek. Whether the crowd is club size or just the regulars drinking beer, the night continued.

ROAR hardcore techno, run by longstanding electronic music citizen Hutcho, is the latest offering on a Tuesday night. I decided that, even though hardcore techno is not my genre of choice, I would investigate the newest transformation of this space and place. On opening the door to the pink building, I was pleasantly surprised to hear some hard breaks. I sat on a stool for an hour, watched and listened. It was mostly hard techno but the night evoked the freshness of Precision. The audience was small but dedicated to these local DJs who are veterans of the scene. This is what makes the Hyde Park Hotel so special. In one room, there is swinging jazz. In another, there is oldskool hardcore techno and tomorrow there will be a new DJ mixing up fresh tracks that the next style of electronic music conveys.

The Perth electronic music scene is fickle. The popularity of a style can die quickly and those in charge of gigs change constantly. DJs and audience alike often stray to other venues like the Rosemount and the Velvet Lounge, but when the popularity of a night dies there is always something else at the Hydey. The support of the ownership, audience and the relaxed 'homely' atmosphere have contributed to the success of the Hyde Park as one of Perth's major electronic music hubs.

CHAPTER 11

DIY D'n'B

Felicity Cull

If you don't know who I mean, then you could be one of them: those people dressed in party clothes swarming Northbridge after dark. The women totter on impossibly high heels. Tight clothing seems to stay on their bodies only because it laces up. The men wear tight T-shirts that say 'Busted' or 'Ian Hard,' hold water bottles in their sweaty hands and spike their hair like the Bell Tower. When at the age of eighteen I first started to frequent clubs in Northbridge like Rise and The Church, these men and women were everywhere, and so was a name for them—House Sluts. When I stood on the dance floor at these clubs in my sneakers and jeans unencumbered by their tight clothes and high heels—watching these House Sluts move in sweaty beauty—perfectly applied makeup glistening—I knew I could never be one of them. I cannot apply makeup with that level of skill and cannot execute dance moves in high heels without taking an embarrassing tumble off the podium and into the crowds below.

The House Sluts and I had a rocky relationship right from the start. I never belonged, no matter how much time I spent on the top level of The Church or on the balcony at Rise. Soon the House beats got repetitive, and I started to look for blacker haunts on the weekends. Searching, I started to enter the smallest rooms at events and heard music that was fast and dark: drum 'n' bass. I found a new place to be every weekend through this music, The Drum Club every Friday night, and then later Saturday nights at Heat. At these nights, there was just as much sweat but fewer high heels. I could not be a House Slut in my clothing, but I have become a follower of drum 'n' bass.

There is a subtle divide in Perth's dance scene between those affiliated with the two most popular dance genres. Perth is known as House central, and these scenes and venues are still thriving. As popular Perth DJ Adam Kelly asserts: 'most clubs/events always promote some form of house music.'[1] But on the (high) heels of House's popularity, Perth's drum 'n' bass scene is starting to gather a huge following, Perth's producers and DJs have a large fan base and popular international drum 'n' bass DJs such as Grooverider, Total Science or Ray Keith play clubs here at least once a month. Regular events organised by Loaded Dice and Delirium pack clubs full of sweaty bodies.

One of the most popular nights of the year in Perth is the annual Two Tribes event. It unites the two factions of Perth's dance fans for one night. Event organisers coordinate two clubs at different sides of the city with DJs playing two styles of music and link them by a bus that takes revellers between The Globe on Murray Street and Metros on Roe Street. In 2002 this event joined two of the most established promoters and was arguably 'the best show of the year'.[2] The event demonstrated how the geography of Perth as a city can be cut up by the different dance styles that compete for popularity. After dark, Northbridge becomes Perth's city centre. While drum 'n' bass clubs remain on the periphery of the night-time city, house and techno clubs usually lie in the heart of Northbridge. At Two Tribes, the dance fans stay on their sides of the city but have the ability to pass from one 'tribe' to the other. Dancers are divided by the style of the beats and by Wellington Street; but a bus, a bridge and chemicals connect them. While traditionally house events stay close to the city centre, there has been a change in recent years. At a recent Two Tribes event, after packing the smaller Globe to an uncomfortable capacity the year before, drum 'n' bass moved to Metros and closer to the city centre. That year, the House Sluts with their heels and water bottles moved further away from the centre of Perth. This spatial movement is tracking changes to popular culture. The scale of the drum 'n' bass community is growing, and Two

Tribes, Heat Nightclub and the packed drum 'n' bass events are the visible proof. Adam Kelly, when asked what was the most popular genre in Perth, replied that 'It would have to be drum 'n' bass.'[3] This chapter follows one of the two dance 'tribes' in Perth, looking at the role that technology has played in its popularity, and how it has allowed Perth to become a major player in drum 'n' bass, instead of a minor partner doomed to remain in a musical backwater.

Original guitar-based bands still encounter some difficulties living in Perth and getting noticed. However, technological advances have allowed the electronic dance scene to leap over these problems. Perth's DJs and producers use technology to produce their own sound and style. CD turntables, CD burners and software that can be downloaded from the Internet have allowed this scene to become based on music made in Perth, rather than records from the UK. While overseas records still get played, they are not the only sounds to be heard. Producers like Greg Packer and Echoic have become internationally recognised in their own right and Perth's drum 'n' bass is thriving in the mix.

Perth is doubly marginalised. Journalistic attacks confirm that 'Perth in Australia is like Australia on the globe—insignificant to the whole.'[4] With the proliferation of such press, technology that cuts through geography is important. The drum 'n' bass scene in Perth relies on this technology, and 'those who don't jump on the technological bandwagon will, I fear, soon fall off altogether.'[5] Despite the fact that technology can have the positive effect of defying geography, some advances in gear are criticised or ignored as many argue that these technologies destroy creativity in music. For example, Jeremy Gilbert and Ewan Pearson state:

> Many discourses around music consider the presence of certain technologies in negative terms; as a marker of the elimination of human agency from the production of music, the 'murder' of music as a living creature.[6]

Turntables, synthesisers and mixers are demonised and their use is attached to an idea that the music they produce is without human agency and creative input by a 'true' musician. But this kind of technology has pulled Perth out of musical isolation and into a pre-eminent role internationally in the drum 'n' bass scene. Internationally and nationwide, Perth is no longer on the periphery. Original producers need only a PC with an Internet connection and the right contacts (which can also be established through the Internet) to have their material distributed by major labels.

The Internet now plays a large part in getting involved in 'the scene', to become noticed and involved. Perth's Pendulum is quick to cite the Internet's influence in interviews. El Hornet states: 'the Internet is handy promotion wise but we can't do without it for getting tunes and talking to people…We'd be isolated without it.'[7] In the realm of electronic music, the Internet has dissolved boundaries that have kept Perth's music in a cone of silence for years. As Adam Kelly states: 'the Internet has meant we can contact anyone, artists labels, promoters etc.'[8] Internet fora and email are of major importance in Perth's drum 'n' bass scene. The Internet allows software and samples to be downloaded, which means for a relatively small outlay, drum 'n' bass tracks can be made from scratch. Online fora allow news to be circulated. Atmoceanic Magazine, which is handed out at clubs and music stores free, is peppered with advice on how to use technology to further the punter as a DJ or producer. Twisted Individual tips 'get yourself a 512k (or faster) broadband connection so you can download software or samples.'[9] Programs like Fruity Loops and Reason provide the user with beats and samples and can be downloaded from the Internet, and they are widely used. The accessibility of programs like this has allowed complex, creative, diverse and different soundscapes to emerge from Perth's drum 'n' bass producers. Perth is not a groupie to the overseas scenes but an incubator of new sounds. DJ Infinite Detail is yet to play any major drum 'n' bass nights in Perth, and states that technology is going to play a role in allowing him to get involved in Perth's scene. He states: 'I downloaded the program I produce on from the Internet. The Internet keeps you in new samples, lets you know what's being released and who is playing where.'[10] On this program, he has produced about thirty original tracks, and now, after purchasing a set of CD turntables he can play a set entirely of his own tunes rather than vinyl from overseas. Greg Packer, arguably Perth's most prominent drum 'n' bass DJ who has been internationally recognised with twenty-seven individual tracks signed,[11] uses CD turntables regularly in his sets. At a Perth Producers night, Greg Packer used them to play his own burned CDs.[12] He played a set using CD turntables with his own new material. Infinite Detail states:

> I got my Technics when I was seventeen and spent every cent on vinyl but I always wanted to create in my own right. CD Turntables and my burner let me do it. Burning my own tracks on CD has let me get my own original sounds heard—I pass them around to mates who also produce and we give each other tips. At least half of the drum 'n' bass we listen to we created.[13]

Perth's drum 'n' bass scene has become self-sufficient, confident and expansive: outside influences are not as needed as they once were to create a unique scene with a unique sound.

Perth is no backwater for drum 'n' bass, despite its geographical isolation. In a short space of time, Perth has become a place of note in the drum 'n' bass spectrum. Technological proliferation, and the burgeoning fan following in Perth, has meant that producers and DJs do not need to leave Western Australia for Sydney or Melbourne to get recognition. Perth can boast that in Australia, this city is the drum 'n' bass capital.

CHAPTER 12

He's Electric: How Perth's Electronic Musicians Gear Up

Angela Jones

LIVEJOURNAL is a worldwide web community that differs from general interest chat rooms. It is a step beyond the 'invitation only' Internet Relay Chat. To join this forum the user must obtain a code from a current member, and current members can only obtain one code every few months. It is in the 'old skool' chat rooms of IRC and on the message boards of tech-geek forums in such communities as LIVEJOURNAL[1] where the friendly information, pertaining to selection of gear and software, flows. A search on this website for electronic music produced 123 available message boards. Discussions, such as the one in this chapter, are intertwined with links to eBay gear sales as well as reminders about what is (legal) and is not (illegal) allowed to be discussed within the forum. Message boards and chat rooms are the informational link between the world's electronic musicians. They allow for technical and musical expertise to be swapped in a matter of minutes. But when the Internet was not yet common, how did an electro muso write a tune? They got hardware. Original 808s and 303s are rare due to Perth's size and geography. They are hard to locate and ship. So how does a Perth electronic musician get their gear and fit out a studio?

Ben Jones was born into a musical family on 3 November 1978. His mother and her brothers spent much of their youth singing in the

(who's afraid of) (barkis) wrote in musictech,
@ 2003-06-01 22:42:00

My brother has made an offer to me to upgrade my computer for my birthday. I told him I really just needed a new hard drive, but he started talking soundcard too. Sound Blaster Audigy 2, to be exact.

Now that my motif 8 is (almost) paid for, my next step is to buy a mixer and start running keyboards into my comp (PC) and use protools for recording. Will that Soundblaster card work for me, or should I direct his natal generosity elsewhere?

acidbathlove
2003-06-01 21:42 (link)

free stuff is good.
...try to get receipt maybe?

the audigy 2 is a solid card, and it supports everything you'll need (other than maybe ample MIDI support.. probably only 1X1), but if my memory serves me right that card is at least 48khz/24bit compatible, maybe even higher. theres definitely some nicer stuff out there than SoundBlaster, but you'll pay for it. so.. try out the card. worst case scenario, you hat ethe card, have no receipt to return it, and you sell it on ebay. ::shrug::

good luck!

(Reply to this)

prof_landslide
2003-06-03 14:50 (link)

I have the use of a pute with an audigy mk1 in it, plus the socket thingy that goes in the front (which is fab & has midi ports) and it's pretty good, by my standards... It plays back at 96khz, but 'only' records at 48. (personally i'm a big fan on 32khz... sounds like vinyl...) The new one records at 96 though. (Get a BIG harddrive) I don;t think pro-tools likes soundblasters... The free one definitely doesn't. It comes with cubasis, which doesn't allow you to record on more than one track at the same time, but is ok apart from that... The synth module on the audigy 1 is fab for 80's synth pop. The drums are poo though.

(Reply to this)

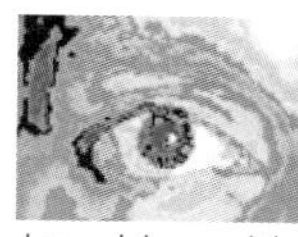

deharmonic
2003-06-04 00:41 (link)

I would go with an m-audio device if you could.
http://www.m-audio.com/products/m-audio/audiophile.php
24 bit / 96khz - midi, dig in/out (believe you can do surround sound using the dig), analog l+r in/out
Around $120 on eBay

(Reply to this) (Thread)

orbisan
2003-06-18 14:54 (link)

agreed. soundblaster stuff is not meant for recording and the D/A converters are shit. get a delta 44 or even teh 1010 if you need something more. just make sure you have breakout box with DAC or you'll encounter some line noise.

(Reply to this) (Parent)

FIGURE 4: Extract from LIVEJOURNAL

church choir. His uncles are all musicians, from strumming guitarists to plucking banjo-mandolins. His father is a music teacher and performer. With the saturation of music in the house, it seemed normal to start a musical career at five learning how to play classical guitar. He excelled on classical, electric and bass guitar as well as on piano and drums, and many musical doors have opened. After being a member of amateur garage bands, in his mid-teens he swapped the guitar for a turntable. His involvement in the electronic music scene had begun. Ben's other loves in life were computers and electronics. He was always pulling keyboards and other electronic devices apart to see how they worked (and never putting them back together). After a few years of trying his hand at mixing, he turned to making his own music using computer, synthesisers and other instruments. From 1995 Ben and his 'electro mates' bought, sold, swapped and made electronic hardware and software to cater to their musical requirements. In an email interview, he explained how he and his friends circumvented the problems of minimum wages and minimal equipment to achieve sounds and mix solutions. He also discusses the value of gear, software and musical expertise in Perth's contemporary electronic world.

When you first started using computers and synths to make music what kind of equipment was available around Perth?

There was a lot of gear available from the time I first started looking (mainly in the second-hand department...); however, there was not always a wide range. There were the favourites like the TB303, 606 and 909 tone generators which are renowned for their unique analogue sounds. The AKAI-2000 series samplers were popular too as they were 'reasonably' priced compared to similar units. There was always a plethora of early and late model middle-of-the-range synths in the paper—all of which made pretty much the same sound, but with different user interfaces (known as 'bread'n'butter' synths). The 'creamware' at the time was the new style of digital 'analogue' synths that were appearing, these had all the bells and whistles (effects, multi outputs and digital wavetables) and a price tag to suit.

What were you doing at the time?

I was working as an Apprentice Instrument (not the musical kind) Electrical Technician. My wage was $180 per week.

Do you think there is a typical member of the 'electro' community?

There is definitely a predominance of tech geeks in the scene. It's pretty much a prerequisite as you need to be a tech head to figure out your gear and get it up and running. An affinity with 'the abstract' is quite common too.

As you and your friends had limited funds and were only in your late teens and early twenties how did you get funds and where did you get them from?

As far as financing gear went, my mate Al and I formed a syndicate, each contributing half toward most of our purchases…As far as finding gear we mainly searched in the papers and at the local Cash Converters. It was not uncommon for us to pay off a lay-by after being paid on a Thursday and take the Friday off because we had stayed up all night playing with our new toy.

How important is this 'gear getting' to music production?

Well the gear that you have defines the music that you make, so if you have dodgy gear the chances of getting any kind of good sounds is minimal. So in order to make good tunes that can have both musical and tonal qualities you need to know what equipment does what, so the choosing of your kit is very important. Once you know what you want you then have to hope that it is available in Perth (or Australia if you're desperate)…If it is not then you go back to step A and hope that you do not spend all your money on beer before you find what you are looking for.

Do you think the role of gear has changed over the last few years?

The role of acquiring gear has changed a great deal over the last few years. Now that the average home PC has more than enough grunt to power software synthesis engines ('soft-synths') the traditional hardware synth/sampler/FX units are no longer a necessary part in the electronic artist's inventory. Soft-synths are capable of producing all of the sounds and effects of their hardware equivalents and more, whilst taking up no more space than the hard disk they reside on. A late model computer with a good quality sound card and a decent pair of monitor speakers coupled with a few good soft-synths and samples is all an electronic muso will need to write the next chart topper, should they have the talent and desire to do so.

So how much do you need to know about software and programming to make a tune?

For starters you need to be familiar with the PC as well as naturally technically minded, otherwise you will be spending a crapload on tech support before you record your first note of music. Then you have to learn a sequencer package (electro muso's equivalent of a canvas). The sequencer is where you compose your song. Generally the more features a package has the harder it is to learn so this can take the user a while to master. The sequencer can be used to play third party soft-synth plug-ins as well as hardware synths (via MIDI), and can also route sound through third party effects plug-ins. These all take some time and patience to master. As well as these skills you need to be able to adapt your thinking to conform with less-than-intuitive hardware interfaces which make up the majority of interfaces.

Would you say then, that software is part of a more world wide electronic community?

Yes...There is a large software development community which provides thousands of software products ranging through soft-synths, effects, sequencers, soft-samplers. There are big bucks to be made in this business as the popularity of PC music production is growing rapidly. Then there are the warez-headz, hanging out in the dark IRC backstreets sharing pirate versions of the latest software. There are various hacking syndicates who provide a steady stream of copy protection-free software versions to couriers who distribute these files via IRC FServs [domestic file servers]. These releases are known as 0day releases (0 days old). People who initially make available 0day releases are well respected and considered high up in the Warez scene hierarchy, they are seen to have links to the mysterious hacking syndicates, of whose members are considered l33t (elite).

A few years back an international electronic community existed where if an overseas musician came to Perth they would do the ring around to see what kind of equipment they could get hold of. How do you believe this community is functioning today?

I'm sure this kind of thing still happens regularly as there are many hardware collectors who seek out rare and vintage hardware. There is also a lot to be said for having a dedicated interface for your hardware as opposed to the often finicky interfaces provided by modern day soft-synths/effects processors and soft-samplers. Many purists also still argue that a computer will never truly replicate the complex tonal qualities of the old school solid-state synths.

Does Perth play a large part in this community?

I'm sure it still plays some part in this community, but I cannot say how big or small a part for sure...

Is there anything specific about Perth-based electro?

It's fickle. Given that Perth is small and the electronica community is smaller still, every seasoned producer has probably come into contact with the majority of other Perth producers at some stage or another. How far you are able to take your music can often depend on who you know rather than the quality of your tunes. Those crews who hold the monopoly on venues and air time will generally guard these assets closely as this allows them to dictate who hears what, and ultimately who gets promoted and who gets forgotten. This has caused rivalries among many producers and has made the scene quite political.

So what is your current studio set up?

I have a PC which runs my sequencer and many third-party soft-synths/effects and samplers and a PC controller keyboard to play interface with the soft-synths. All the audio is routed through an 8-out 2-in sound card into a Fostex 8-channel 4-bus mixdown desk. I have a pair of $800 reference monitors which I picked up from Cashies [Cash Converters] for a steal at $250. I also have some hardware synths, samplers and effects units but these are used far less than the PC due to the ease of the all-in-one solution which the PC provides.

If there was one piece of gear that you could have, what would it be?

Probably a pair of Mackie reference monitors. They allow you to hear a standardised representation of your music so you can hear all the tonal interactions present in your mixes. This means that your finished product will sound better on a wider array of listening devices and allow people to hear your music the way you intended it to be heard.

Not a TB303?

That would be nice!! But that's more a collector's item than a practical studio tool. All the sounds of a TB303 can be successfully emulated with soft-synths.

Do you think that your skills as a non-electronic musician, make it easier to write software that caters to your electronic music requirements?

In some respects, however, many rules of musical theory are broken regularly in the composition of modern electronic music, so sometimes I find it hard to break traditional constraints learnt in my musical training. This has caused me much frustration in the past.

Finally as you said most electro musicians now have soft-synths in their possession. With this in mind, do you believe that writing envy has replaced gear envy?

Yes, I think that is an accurate statement. Due to the availability of pirate soft-synths and accessibility of powerful computers it is no longer necessary to have rooms full of expensive gear to produce electronic masterpieces. This opens up a door for people with talent but no money to compete for recognition alongside those who in the past could hide their mediocrity behind elaborate rows of knobs and pretty flashing lights. I think this is a good thing.

CHAPTER 13

'It's Not My Fault You Hate My Band': Perth Art-Rock

Adam Trainer

In an accelerated, media-literate age where academic inquiry attempts to transform the ways in which we negotiate with cultural artefacts, it is easy to affirm the redundancy of cultural elitism. Endless postulations can be made that the binaries of high art versus low-grade entertainment no longer exist and all culture is equivalent. Nevertheless, when confronted with the reality of subcultural collectives and popular music, there are arguments and debates to be made about quality, currency and relevance.

The plethora of rock bands that play and find success in Perth is staggering. There are scenes of all descriptions. In such a small, isolated city, almost any type of Anglo-centric popular music is present in at least some form, making for an eclectic and diverse local music industry. However, the various scenes that thrive in Perth are almost exclusively independent from the others. Although different scenes share venues, the bands that play within them attract different crowds on different nights. For instance, over four nights at the Rosemount Hotel in North Perth, audiences may see indie rock bands or the occasional *first past the post* zine launch on a Wednesday, drum 'n' bass DJs on a Thursday, punk bands on a Friday and an international or interstate touring act on a Saturday. The audiences for these shows are almost always different each night. There may be a slight spill from one scene to the next, but largely there seems to be in existence at any time, a number of vibrant and healthy scenes which operate in almost complete independence. This is where notions of cultural elitism still thrive. Not that it is often even vocalised or manifested in anything other than a predilection towards a particular aesthetic or political pre-occupation. Usually there is a vague understanding of which bands might be popularising a particular scene, but often there is merely a lack of interest in anything that does not concern a specific individual's aesthetic predispositions. The notion of community and the feeling of belonging that people gain from their involvement in a particular form of music is where the cultural hierarchies of particular subcultural formations become relevant to how particular groups express themselves.

Although it is always pointless to argue that all members of a collective interpret in the same way with cultural forces around them, cultural elitism—whether a concern for some individuals or not, is assumed in particular forms of cultural expression. For those involved in the Perth local music scene, there are specific clusters of bands that represent exclusive forms of musical expression. Of course, generic classification is the arch-enemy of any self-respecting band operating within the unavoidable postmodern paradigm of contemporary culture, but there are several terms that are generally bandied about to classify the scene in Perth that fosters a brand of rock bands characterised by a complex and adventurous aesthetic palette. There are a number of potential labels for such music: avant-rock, space rock, math rock and progressive rock are all popular terms that carry with them specific nuances. The major label of the last few years under which much of this type of music has been grouped is post-rock, which can be classified as 'avant-garde eclecticism with a strong bias towards the instrumental'.[1] However this description does not accurately encapsulate the mélange of Perth bands successfully trading in soundscapes and complex textural combinations. The label post-rock became unfashionable the moment the music it describes became the cutting edge of cool. Tim Gane of Stereolab:

> I think that, as for any name that people give to a type of music, it's a truism that once a term is established to encapsulate some-

> thing it's immediately broken. 'Post-Rock' is an eggshell and the beast that it may have once contained has long-since expanded beyond it.[2]

In defining post-rock, there are certain characteristics of the bands operating within a specific contemporary Perth local music cluster. An affinity for either jazz or droning krautrock rhythms often drives the music, sometimes both at the same time. There is also sometimes the use of multiple instruments, as particular acts attempt to cultivate a diversity of sounds by employing anything from a theremin to a glockenspiel, to samples and looped effects.

For all its supposed aesthetic and structural freedom, post-rock is still a term that constrains. Not all Perth bands that operate under such terms can be so easily defined and it is perhaps more fitting to locate this form of expression as belonging to a blander, less specific label. Art-rock is almost a musical genus as opposed to a species: a more generic way of referring to those bands that carry similar characteristics without becoming a specific label. Art-rock has been associated with genres as diverse as post-punk and progressive-rock, carrying with it an assumption that the music operating within it carries a certain affinity towards artistic merit as opposed to populist sentiment regardless of political rhetoric. This labelling lends itself to culturally elitist notions of art versus entertainment binaries, which seem to have become unavoidable in terms of contemporary popular expression.

This cultural elitism is reinforced as much from exterior sources as from within the scene. The relative popularity and commercial viability of other genres of organic rock music grants an appeal to disparate audiences, larger venues and often more press. With the commercialisation of grunge and 'alternative' music late last century, the nature of popular musical expression changed dramatically. Pop music once referred to the material in the charts, with most organic forms of rock music being classified as 'alternative' because it was written and performed by individuals operating seemingly outside of the economically deterministic demands of the pop industry. The line between pop and alternative has blurred. With the burgeoning success and commercial viability of supposedly alternative music within the pop charts, the configuration of music according to a political stance as opposed to aestheticism has become more important to the establishment of sub-culture. It is for this reason that those creating music that operates in a more experimental fashion, as opposed to being lumped under the genre of 'indie,' are in this instance referred to as art-rock.

The diversity of sounds on offer within the Perth art-rock scene is impressive. From the sonic theatrics of Polaroid Ghost to the subdued yet similarly galvanising Gata Negra to the almighty racket of Ten Speed Racer, there is something specifically Perth about all of them, yet it would appear to manifest itself differently for each band. Bands such as Adam Said Galore, The Tigers and Tucker Bs have arguably been instrumental in establishing an aesthetic backbone through which the Perth art-rock sound can be characterised. Complex, often intricate melodic patterns jostle for attention over shifting rhythms. Alternately, there is the use of droning, melodic and rhythmic repetition, out of which subtle textural shifts may emerge or an intense crescendo may be built out of layers of feedback and distortion. Sudden pauses in the flow of a particular track are not uncommon, as song structure does not always follow the standard verse, chorus, bridge structure of traditional rock music. This is the most obvious touchstone through which to witness the influence of jazz on more experimental, progressive forms of rock music. It would appear that since punk's anarchism changed the political nature of youth and music as self-expression in the mid to late 1970s, that the term 'progressive' has become particularly unfashionable. Nevertheless, the influence of progressive-rock is undoubtedly evident in genres such as post-rock and other experimental forms of music. However the contemporary Perth scene is filtered through the political sensibilities of punk's DIY preoccupations, the similar political rhetoric of grunge and especially the lo-fi aesthetic of indie.

Arguably the most successful of the current swag of Perth art-rockers, Adam Said Galore have been playing locally since the mid-1990s and their position within the Perth scene certainly reflects their long-standing lustre. Always well-respected for their melodies and interesting, if subtle aesthetic nuances, their debut, 1997's *Domino Comfort* was released to significant acclaim from the local music community. In 1998 Adam Said Galore brought prolific US post-rock act Tortoise to Perth in order to play with them at the now defunct Players Lounge and as a result their second release, *The Driver Is Red*, recorded in 1999, was produced by sometime Tortoise engineer Casey Rice.

The reaction garnered by *The Driver Is Red* propelled Adam Said Galore into the major leagues in Australian indie rock. They scored both local support slots for the Scottish post-rock outfit Mogwai in 1999 and 2002, as well as other support slots such as that for Iceland's Mum. In 2002, the band released *Of Lost Roads*, which showed a diversity that allowed them to unleash rock tracks such as the quasi-single 'Bent Like Christmas' and the album opener 'Drive-In Scene' as well as more plaintive, languid material such as 'Must Sleep Now' and 'Travelling Record Collector', both featuring mellotron by former ASG guitarist Michael Lake. He had left the band after the recording of *The Driver Is Red* to pursue his other band Mukaizake, and was replaced by fellow-Mukaizake member Geoff Symons.

Adam Said Galore's intricate, constantly shifting music benefits from songwriting brought to the fore by energetic and unpredictable playing, where the guitars bounce so tightly off one another that it is hard to determine who is playing what. The mixture of pop culture references, from Pavement to The Kinks and Star Wars, makes for an intriguing landscape of cultural inquiry and observations on the contemporary urban condition. As stalwarts of the local scene Adam Said Galore lead the field in terms of organic, guitar-based post-rock in Perth.

Since 1993, the Tucker Bs have always been a solid local act, receiving something of a rebirth in popularity in the years surrounding the release of their second album, 2002's *Bish Bosh II: The Bosh Bosh*. Taking the loose swagger of alt-country and injecting it with distorted guitar noise, shifting melodic and rhythmic textures and a dose of shouting, the Tucker Bs have survived several line-up changes to become arguably the most respected of the Perth indie rock fraternity. Several interstate tours have seen them play with east-coast bands such as Sealife Park and Love of Diagrams as well as a Melbourne support for

US post-punk outfit Interpol. In early 2004 they toured the US for the South By Southwest festival in Texas. Their combination of the playful, the absurd and the serene have made them a popular band on the live scene, whilst an exemplary knack for melodic and textural diversity has ensured that their following has maintained its vitality both in the live scene and in popular media consciousness, receiving considerable airplay on local radio institution RTR.

Mockingly self-proclaimed 'thinking man's band', The Tigers have always impressed and continue to reinvent themselves in odd and interesting ways. Before the release of their first album, 1999's Space Coyote, The Tigers had been named best-unsigned band in the country. It took the song that arguably got them there, 'Slayerbells' another few years to make it on to an album, 2002's *Christmas Album*. In between, *And With That The Audience Disappeared In A Flash Just Like In The Movies* EP was released, containing two untitled songs that stretched over twenty-five minutes, gaining the band a significant cult following.

The Tigers shift melodically from off-kilter atmospherics to full-on guitar bile: often within the same track, piling layers of noise over a jazzy, meandering rhythm section. Their songs are capable of stretching between minimalist drones and extremely noisy and cluttered chaos, often changing tack in a second. With a double remix album released by Melbourne-based distributor Sensory Projects and a further EP, the six-tracker *It Hath Been Falsely Supposed That All Tigers Be Female And That They Engender In Copulation With The Winde*, itself remixed by various Perth experimentalists, The Tigers have amassed a colourful and individualistic career, that has become the stuff of local music legend and can certainly be considered a definitive high point of the Perth art-rock scene.

It was arguably the reputation of the more established bands such as The Tigers and Adam Said Galore that led to the growth and expansion of a thriving art rock collective in Perth. Along with the now defunct slowcore act Blue Tile Lounge, the sporadically gigging Tucker Bs and others such as Mukaizake and the cyclical shoegaze of Cypher, these bands provided a base for the emergence of a number of others playing experimental rock music in Perth. In the early to mid-1990s

Wooden Fische's dark, brooding, masculine take on indie rock was a galvanising and resonant blast of clanging guitars, shuffling rhythms and embittered prose. Their sound can arguably be heard in the almost dissonant, impressively hook-laden work of Adam Said Galore and Tucker Bs. Local record label Veeline was particularly important in terms of establishing a solid indie rock collective in Perth with the release of their sampler Signals. Featuring tracks from The Spinsters, Emmerson International, The Panics and Still amongst others, the Signals compilation provided a glimpse at the range of indie rock talent existent in Perth at the turn of the new millennium.

The emergence of other bands trading in the slightly abstract, considered atmospherics of the post-rock and art-rock sound has increased the vibrancy and vitality of the scene. Polaroid Ghost, with the melodic synthesis of their twin guitar drone, sparse drumming and sampled loops have established themselves as an impressive space-rock trio. Winners of the 2003 Next Big Thing competition, Snowman have been described as 'Bizarre, dark, eerie music for the borderline insane.'[3] Front man Andy alternates between emotive crooning and bizarre falsetto, backed up by the band's jazzy, atmospheric might, with viola making a special appearance on several tracks.

Sharing songwriting duties and instruments between four members, Radarmaker attempt a sense of diversity as a constant in their music, employing guitars, keys, glockenspiel, screwdrivers, e-bows and feedback as best they can to create a mélange of sounds and shifting timbres, and attempting always to tread the fine line between cyclical repetition and structural invention. Recently others such as the terse post-punk of And Your Youth Will Punish You Like A Milkless Fridge, the balminess of Maple, and the all-girl team of Trash Band 1987 have made an impression on a scene that continues to diversify. There are a number of bands such as Ten Speed Racer, The Stickfigures, Rickety and Airport City Shuffle who create guitar-based music that is in turn both structurally and aurally frenetic and untraditionally emotive, whilst firmly grounded in the indie rock platform.

Sodastream provide the antithesis of the noisy antics of Perth art-rock's aesthetic foundations. Emerging out of Thermos Cardy,

Sodastream's stripped back acoustic guitar and double bass was a new direction that brought Karl Smith and Pete Cohen first interstate success, then international exposure thanks to John Peel. Their line-up expanded on recordings to include horns, strings and percussion, adding a depth of texture and melodic richness to the duo's beautifully affecting compositions in order to create some of the most sublime contemporary chamber music on offer. The EP *Practical Footwear* and the albums *Looks Like a Russian* and *The Hill for Company* were released on Tugboat Records, before the band was out of contract. The third album *A Minor Revival* was produced independently. Residing in London, Melbourne and Perth, Sodastream always receive strong support when returning to tour. Wistful, reflective and autumnal, their sound has no doubt been more than influential locally and can be heard in a number of Perth musicians who choose something of a pastoral approach to their craft and often include either acoustic guitar or strings.

Amongst the collection of Perth bands trading in vaguely chamber-oriented music are the guitar, cello and drums combination of Mitey Ko, whose indie pop songs are injected with a warmth and beauty. Earnest, literate and intimate, Benedict Moleta is arguably the most well-respected solo artist on the contemporary Perth indie rock scene. With gentle, bittersweet songs of simple beauty, Moleta's soothing voice plays the delicate balancing act of complementing his pastoral guitar pluckings, whilst creating a warm, soothing texture of its own. In 2003, Benedict fronted Whitepaper, which collected various individuals from the local scene on accompanying instruments. Gata Negra utilise a brooding, almost minimal approach to their music, balancing Cat Hope's sparse vocals against the warm, resonant tones of bass and cello. Melancholy and nocturnal, Gata Negra have released two albums on Hope's label Bloodstar, *Cage of Stars* in 1999 and *Saint Dymphnae* in 2002. Hope's other project is Lux Mammoth, a studio-based avant-garde duo, who produce structureless noisescapes of bizarre and fascinating textures. Schvendes have also received considerable attention for their genre-bending antics, utilising the disparate melodic approaches of cello, keys and slide guitar, backed up by an unwavering rhythm section and topped off by Rachael Dease's breathy, intense vocals.

The art-rock scene in Perth facilitates the coexistence of electronic and organic musics. Chrism + Fenris, Elemental and Gate have arguably lead a number of other acts in establishing a constantly growing live electronica scene. There are significant links between various bands and their remixers, the obligatory studio projects and home-computer composers operating everywhere in Perth. In no other context can live bands be seen alongside electronic musicians. Live electronica is certainly a realm of music creation likely to confuse and baffle the uninitiated. Samples and loops are plucked from within the bowels of the machine, uploaded and manipulated live, forming a mix of a track that is completely improvised and unlike any that may have come before it. The results may be disorienting, but for those willing to focus on the structure of the music as opposed to its danceability, the experience can be particularly exhilarating.

As with any subcultural formation, the nature of the community extends beyond the music. The music does not limit or generically label the aesthetic and political predispositions of a collective of people, rather it presents a frame of reference, the spaces and events that make tangible the circuitry of community. In Perth there is a healthy Internet community that is intrinsically linked to the music, where web journals provide people with the opportunity to impart their opinions on their favourite local bands, chat about their weekend and plan meetings. The website www.perthbands.com provides an invaluable resource for those involved in the industry as either a fan or an artist to communicate with each other and create conversations that revolve around the music and other topics of conversation. The music, the bands and the events: the gigs, parties and meetings are the tangible manifestation of these connections, whereby the popular histories of a scene can be made, created, lived.

PART III

HEARING THE DIFFERENCE

CHAPTER 14

Writing the Perth Music Scene

Carrie Kilpin

John O'Donnell, managing director at EMI Australia, visited Perth early in 2003 with a flurry of other company representatives keen to check out the local talent in Western Australia. Having attended the Little Birdy residency at the Amplifier, he remarked to Simon Collins, music editor of the *West Australian*, that Perth's isolation had harvested a form of 'scenius.' This term was first coined by Brian Eno connoting a rich interplay of 'scene' and 'genius.' Perth's reputation as a backwater city is being challenged by the musicians, DJs, producers and publicists emerging from Perth's clubs and pubs.

The music press in Western Australia has been cataloguing the events surrounding this scenius. I spoke to two of Perth's most prolific music journalists about the process of writing for a scene. Julian Tompkin was the local music editor for Perth's street press magazine *X-Press* and Simon Collins is music editor at the *West Australian* newspaper. Both spend their time monitoring CD launches, checking out new bands and interviewing musicians. Their views of music journalism in Perth and the success of the local scene are significant. Music is always mediated, and journalism is a pivotal site for the translation of music into written form.

The importance of journalism to music is paramount. The reviewing of albums, provision of gig information and exchange of ideas about style and taste form a significant contribution to the development of local music. The perspectives music journalists offer play a large part in forming the success or downfall of musical groups. In fact, Ed Needham, formally an editor at *FHM* and now of *Rolling Stone*, declared that 'Music establishes a profound emotional connection: more than movies or TV. But I considered the writers the equals, if not the superiors, of the people they were writing about.'[1] Journalists create a vocabulary and literacy for discussing and debating this 'profound emotional connection'. The ability to transform an aural sensation into a written expression is a pivotal skill employed by journalists in writing song and album reviews.

Music journalism in Western Australia maintains a distinctive voice through *X-Press*. It has been running for twenty years and is Australia's largest street press magazine, with a distribution of 40,000 copies each week and a readership of 80,000. It is as much a part of the Perth music scene as the Grosvenor Hotel or Mojo's in Fremantle. Julian Tompkin remarks upon this phenomenon: 'Whether you're eighteen or forty, people on a Thursday morning on their way to work pick up an *X-Press*. It's become a very important part of Perth society and I think it will remain that way simply because people have grown up with it.'[2] *X-Press* provides information about gigs, venues, clubbing and interviews with popular international and local musicians.

Another source of music journalism, which slots alongside wider discussions of news and current affairs, is found in the *West Australian*, Perth's only daily newspaper. Within its *Today* lift out section,[3] Simon Collins manages the music editorial which incorporates articles ranging in subjects from the Williams Brothers to Dizzy Rascal. Collins identifies the limitations in writing for a wide demographic: 'I try not to be too esoteric in that I'm not writing for a music publication. I've got to appeal to people who might have stumbled across our article whilst looking for something on fishing.'[4] The music section of the *West Australian* comprises articles about recent album releases, concert tours and interviews with musicians.

In writing about music, both journalists agree that subjectivity saturates the field. Tompkin admitted that,

> At the base of the music press, there is no real structure. I think that's why people become music journalists—you get a platform to say what you want. Whoever I write for, be it the *Australian* newspaper, the *West Australian* newspaper, *X-Press* or the other number of magazines I write for, you get told you have 300 words to say whatever you want to say. I don't think, okay I'm writing for the *Australian* now, I've got to put on my serious reporter voice. You just write what you want to write because people are asking for your opinion. It's that simple.[5]

Having the freedom to write informally is an advantage music journalists enjoy over their colleagues who may specialise in finance, hard news or politics. Music journalists frequently have more in common with each other—regardless of their publication—than the writers within their own newspaper. A music review in a Perth newspaper is analogous in tone to that of a street press magazine in Sydney or Melbourne.

There is, however, a difference between the styles of writing in specialist or general publications. The *West*'s articles appeal to a wide audience, while *X-Press*'s informal style is directed at younger readers. In an article about Australia's music press, Craig Mathieson stated that,

> The music press is also competing with the broader media. The field they specialise in, popular music, is now an integral part of daily newspapers and broader interest periodicals, with the copy being penned by music press graduates.[6]

Simon Collins is a clear example of this tendency. He started in journalism by writing for his university newspaper before attaining his job at the *West Australian*. In considering the writing in each publication, he discusses the more relaxed and knowing style that *X-Press* encompasses:

> They're pure music. Some of their writing is a little bit rougher than ours—without being disrespectful to them. They are a street paper. We've got limits as well. We don't like to put swear words in

> there. We'll put in a few because a lot of it is in the actual interviews. Obviously we're thinking about an audience that ranges up to eighty-year-olds plus, so [there are] a lot of conservative readers we have to be conscious about.[7]

The two perspectives in the *West* and *X-Press* exemplify the range of music journalism in Perth. It is influenced by a youth discourse in the street press, while a more conservative voice is presented in the *West*.

Compared to larger centres of music production in Australia, Perth's smaller population means that the competition between music publications is not particularly fierce. However, the city is unique in having such a successful publication as *X-Press* commenting on its music scene. A significant reason for this, Tompkin notes, is because of Perth's location:

> Because we're so isolated, maybe we take a more holistic view. In Sydney and Melbourne they have levels. You have underground journalists and then more professional journalists. There's a hierarchy. Whereas in Perth, because we are so small, we're an amalgamation of all levels.[8]

This amalgamation of genre and style means that within the one publication, writers are covering bands from alternative acts to the mainstream pop world. In comparison to larger cities, Perth music journalism is limited in its range of topics.

The two journalists' opinions about the Perth music scene provide important insight into its development. The recent success that Perth's bands have experienced is chronicled by Tompkin. His perspective as commentator shows the influence of the music press in the bands' achievements:

> A period in time a few years ago really stands out. I'm writing a story and an A&R Person [*Artist and Repertoire*] who's responsible for signing bands to major record companies will phone and go, 'I read that story. Who's this band?' So slowly you feel the

> momentum start to build and it was obvious when The Fergusons and Gyroscope, The Panics and Fourth Floor Collapse really started to garner national interest and also a bit of international interest. When all those people became interested, that's when End of Fashion, Little Birdy, and The Hampdens popped up—all these bands who people are really talking about. Now we're at a level where we're at the highest point we've ever been as a city. It's phenomenal. All of a sudden we've got a handful of bands signed to major record companies. Then we've got a handful of bands who are making it independently [such as] John Butler and The Waifs. We have this immense scene. It is the biggest Perth has ever been and it's the focus of the country.[9]

The 'discovery' of these bands by large record companies in the past few years has put a spotlight on Perth as a city being harvested for new talent. The success of these bands has helped promote interest in other musical acts, and contributed to Perth's current position as a city gaining a reputation as a musical capital.

As a diverse city, both in its multicultural and international influences, Perth music does not unify into a single sound. However there exists a particular *style* which is observable in all of the successful Perth bands being recently signed to major record labels. Having observed the scene for some time, Tompkin elaborates: 'The base of the successful Perth sound is pop. Perth was famous in the 1990s for its power-pop with Ammonia and Jebediah who are very pop oriented. Now our sound is pop, but it's a distortion. It's pop with a touch of the avant garde.'[10] Collins agrees with Tompkin that Perth's bands are producing a style that oscillates around pop:

> There was a big power-pop sound of the eighties and nineties, like The Stems and The Neptunes and those sorts of bands coming through. You could hear that in bands like Effigy who put a goth spin on it. Jebediah have that sort of sound, and also Ammonia. There was a kind of indie pop punkish sound. Now it's gone another way. Bands are doing their own thing.[11]

This twist upon a 'pop' style is a significant reason for Perth bands' recent success. Rather than conforming to a mainstream, conventional sound which is epitomised in bands produced from larger cities, Perth musicians are developing distinctive modes that twist genres through a distinct type of urbanity.

Due to Perth's size and distance from other capital cities, it is tempting to place the city into a generic category defined by a particular sound. This occurred in the 1990s when journalists labelled cities like Seattle and Manchester with distinguishing genres of music. Perth music does not emulate the categorically distinctive sounds these cities produced. The variations between Perth bands are too broad. As Collins elucidates,

> The joke was going around—was Perth the next Seattle? Or Manchester? And the answer was of course 'no' because Seattle threw up a genre specific movement in grunge and Manchester also had the Madchester sound with Stone Roses and Happy Mondays and all those bands. [Looking at Perth's best bands], you've got The Sleepy Jackson and The Panics, who are pop and rock, and you've got Little Birdy who are pop rock but all sort of different as well. Downsyde who are hip hop. Gyroscope who are pop punk. End of Fashion who are kind of pop, sort of rock, sort of Jeff Buckley vocals. The Waifs who are folk. John Butler who is folk-rock. It's all different genres. It's not as if all these bands have been playing gigs supporting each other.[12]

The Perth music scene does not encompass a particular *sound.* As Collins noted, there are too many diverse genres to weave a distinctive sonic resonance. Nevertheless, the pop base underlying Perth's bands demonstrates that they share a common style. Tompkin evaluates this distinction:

> The Perth sound, at the end of the day, is indescribable. There is no specific Perth sound. Yet if you had to describe it as anything, it's our knack for being able to create bands that have an underlying sense of melody. They know how to work the melody in an

> interesting way. Bands like Little Birdy are all over the radio. They're not straight-down-the-line pop. They're accessible, yet interesting: they can be embraced by the straightforward, commercial pop-loving world, and also by people on the leftfield who like something a bit stranger.[13]

The alternative approach to these standards ensures that the music appeals to a wider audience through the familiarity of 'pop'. Perth bands also appeal to niche audiences in the manner through which they create individual and unconventional angles in their music's composition.

Although Perth musicians do not share a common sound, there is nevertheless a difference between the types of music produced in Perth compared to much larger cities like New York or London. Perth's location is an important factor in how contemporary music is developed and written about by journalists. In an article about The Whitlams and the influence of cultural geography, authors Jessica Carroll and John Connell noted an important point about Australian music studies:

> A number of studies have begun to explore the connections between music, place and identity in efforts to trace the role of the 'popular'—and popular music—in the creation of geographical knowledge…though only exceptionally do these consider Australia, and then with particular reference to indigenous issues.[14]

Very little cultural research and mapping has been published about the contemporary Perth music scene. The connection between music, place and identity is a significant consideration in writing about sound. The city's isolation from the rest of the world marks it as unique due to its distance from the influences of major record company offices in larger cities. Perth bands have an opportunity to develop independently of large organisations and fine-tune their own musical style.

This paradigm is also recognisable in other parts of the world. The sound produced in smaller locations is much more culturally distinctive than the music from larger centres. Tompkin agrees with this:

> In Melbourne and Sydney, you're part of the same world that New York and LA and London and Paris are a part of. At that top level, half the time you couldn't tell New York bands, Sydney bands and Melbourne bands apart. Whereas in Perth, we don't see ourselves as being one of those big cities. You could generally tell a Perth band apart from a Munich band, or one from Lyons, or from Dublin, because we all have our own identity.[15]

This identity is as much geographical as cultural. Being located away from the large centres of music production means that bands in smaller cities are less influenced by the pressure to produce a copycat song of last week's chart success. Perth's isolation actually contributes to a freedom in style for its musicians. They have the ability to develop a sound in an environment that is not as crowded with large company representatives and writers eager to box them into particular categories.

Another advantage of Perth's isolated location concerns its potential to become well known as a city for its unique music production—as occurred in Seattle and Manchester. Tompkin remarks that, 'In Manchester, when the bands broke out of there, they created an industry in itself. The Manchester scene became phenomenal, and Manchester became known itself for that. Sydney or London are not known for their music.'[16] Bands playing in smaller scenes, such as Seattle, Perth or Dublin, are much more likely to be natives of the region, and thus contribute to a localised identity. This distinctiveness adds to the city's economic development, encouraging further interest extending to levels in the government. As Tompkin explains: 'Perth could very well become known for its music because it is a small city. If our music becomes big, the councils become interested, and the government becomes interested, and everyone wants a part of it which creates a really healthy scene.'[17] An active involvement of government and council departments encourages the creation of a substantial creative industries project in Western Australia. With bands such as The Waifs and Downsyde acquiring considerable success in the Australian music industry, Perth is building a reputation as a centre noteworthy for its musical achievements. This spotlight is drawing attention to lesser-known bands and contributing to a growing interest in Perth as a source of talented musicians.

Perth's recent development as a home to many successful bands has made being a writer of music an exciting job for those in the industry. As Collins notes: 'It's been a fun year to be a music editor. It's been great to have these local bands in front of you and actually like them. As a music lover you keep a list of your favourites for the year and in my top four there's going to be The Sleepy Jackson and The Panics and they're both Perth bands.' The enthusiasm shown by Tompkin and Collins in discussing recent developments demonstrates the Perth music industry's ability to foster an exciting and active community. The contributions made by the music press are pivotal in maintaining this interest, and in encouraging further development in the future.

CHAPTER 15

Breaking with Beni Benz

Leanne McRae

Beni Benz greets me warmly as I step through the door to the King Street Dance Studios.[1] He is in the middle of a class and has left a young dancer mid six-step (a fundamental breakdance move) to grasp my hand. To any experienced pedagogue Beni's classes appear to have no structure or syllabus. But to those who have experienced it, there is an intimate knowledge that Beni's teaching style of relaxed ambiguity masks the intense one-on-one encouragement that characterises the sessions. In a flash, Beni returns to his student and congratulates her on a clumsy crawl that has the beginnings of six-step mastery.

As I scan the room, I immediately recognise the grouping of individuals—the beginners cling to each other warily, the slightly more experienced learners lean against the wall occasionally practising locking or a sequence of footwork, while the hard-core b-boys diligently practise flares, twists, and assorted breathtaking moves.

The unique structure of this collectivity betrays more nuanced relationships. To the outsider, it appears that a hierarchy is clearly in place, and to an extent this is correct. But a more intense examination reveals a dynamic fluidity to the organisation. The groupings are necessary for rehearsal. B-boying[2] requires continuous practice to master even the basic steps. Staying with those at your level is a way to support and generate connection in the practice and failure of the moves. On a larger scale, there is an unspoken code in operation whereby any breaker—just beginning or experienced—can approach a more experienced b-boy for assistance in achieving a move. These young men do not hesitate in offering advice to anyone who requests it.

As I observe, the room is continually moving. An intermediate-level breaker walks over to the b-boys and strikes up a conversation. Within minutes they are on the floor going through a move step by step. Simultaneously Bernie,[3] a member of the Systematic Crew, saunters across the room and spots a newbie having difficulty. Without hesitating, Bernie gestures to him to help correct the move. The newbie gets the message and continues while Bernie looks back and nods with approval.

The subtle nature of the structures and relationships in the class reveals a great deal about the manner in which b-boying has been fostered in this state. The support and sense of community these young men have created has generated a rich and vibrant breakdancing culture. The Systematic Crew are the core group who have, through their own energy and dedication, fostered a unique b-boy/girl collectivity in Western Australia.

I have known Beni Benz for a number of years. We both taught dance classes at the same studio. He started b-boying over eight years ago while a refugee from the Bosnian war in Germany. In Munich he joined a Crew called 'Step to Diz' and was mentored by local breakdance legend—Storm. When he arrived in Perth, b-boying was found predominantly on the bridge in Forrest Place. Beni and three other young men—Rami, Andrew and Jeffrey—hooked up and formed the Systematic Crew. In 1999 they entered a b-boy street trial competition. They won. Their legacy continues to grow. Perth now has at least seven crews with eight members each.

The day of the interview, Beni is not happy. The crew had returned from the Battle of the Year heats where for the second year in a row they were runners up.[4] He is sure they should have won and claims that even the crew that succeeded were startled by the result. He smiles ruefully and shrugs off the disappointment. The entire crew—facilitated by Beni's laid-back attitude—have dedicated themselves to furthering the b-boying and b-girling community. They have represented Australia nationally and internationally with good humour and integrity.

When did you start breaking Beni?

I started breaking eight years ago in Germany through a video clip for headache tablets, with Storm on it. And, yeah pretty much got into a dance school after that with the crew 'Step to Diz.' And got taught by Swep there teaching me some rocking and some basic breaking and stuff like this. From there on I just, I just pretty much hung out with all the 'Step to Diz' crew, I joined their crew and yeah we pretty much had the crew and we trained together and yeah that's pretty much it.

And you came to Perth about eight years ago?

That's correct, oh nah, about five or six years ago now. And I wanted to build up a crew here so we started a crew. I met a couple of guys, Andrew, Rami and Jeffrey, and we started the Systematic Crew especially for the Street Trial—Street Trial 1. We made up a routine and it all worked out together and we won the competition and that's where and how Systematic Crew got started. Through the years we just kept going. We added our second generation with Bernie and Crisco and Ringo and the third generation with Leroy, Taka and Gaby.

How do you think breakdancing has changed in Perth over the years that you've been here?

OK, well I think that from approximately twenty people to three hundred is a big change. I think it's probably workshops and it's shows and it's media exposure and it's just a breaking thing that's really happening lately that you've seen everywhere around. So I think us also doing workshops getting people involved—boys and girls—we do a lot of workshops around the place, like schools. We also get asked, people call us up, it's mainly word of mouth advertising, that's where we get all our jobs from, pretty much.

How many paying jobs are you able to get?

Oh it depends. Sometimes, I think probably a year we probably do around forty shows, that's like about every second week we do maybe a show definitely. And there's workshops regularly like every Saturday here and there's other workshops at the schools which every member has their own kinda workshops and that's where it's built from—their own kinda little swarms of people, you know? And tryin' to get crews together and stuff and I think from back then I came here and there was just maybe one crew here. I think it's expanded to seven crews now and there's eight people each and it's going crazy.

And do you all get on with each other?

Yeah yeah yeah especially in the Perth scene and the Western Australian scene is just big because people are just friendlier to each other. If you go over east across to Sydney or somewhere else there's a lot of beef between people—they don't like each other and there's always battles and it gets, you know, messy. It's not in a way physical or whatever, just people are just like blah blah blah and blah blah blah. I think in Perth everything is cool and people are still kind of with each other. That's why I liked it from the start because when we built up Systematic first I said to the guys 'Look, you know you have to start teach people to make friends with each other and try and make this whole thing bigger and not just try and like, you know, beef up with people.'

Do you think it's because Perth is small or that it's this isolation that makes it such a good scene?

It could be. That's a positive and a negative thing about the isolation. But I'm not sure. I just think it's the people, and you know there's not too much politics involved and everyone knows each other, kinda thing. It's just like people are just more friendlier to each other. I don't know. But that's just my opinion.

What kind of relationship do you guys have with local musicians?

We did a couple of gigs with a couple of Perth hip hop acts and all that stuff and also we did the Big Day Out with Resin Dogs. There's lots of stuff. Yeah, I think it would be better though if the local whole hip hop scene would work a bit more better together because then it would have such a big market created for itself basically for anything. Like, you know, it could just make up a big jam with [graffiti] writers and MCs and DJs and b-boys you know. But the main thing is here that it's happening, everyone is trying to keep it to themselves. B-boys are making their own jams, well it's not so much the b-boys, but let's say the MCs are making their own jams and the DJs, you know, and it's all a bit separated. But like Germany's not like this man. When you go to Germany everybody is just like at the same place. Everybody is jamming together. You can have the writers. The jam goes for the whole day. It starts probably around 3ish, the writers just big walls, like all legal stuff, of course. You have the MCs, the stage and you have your b-boys and DJs. It's just like a big festival kinda thing, you know. You get people from international and nationally, you know. I would like to see something like that in Perth, you know.

So how does Perth breakdancing compare to over east and overseas?

I think Perth through these years, it's gone up, because if you just have a look at the latest, like, competitions for the last four years probably since we started going to the X-Games 1 in Melbourne. That was like straight out of nowhere we came out and there was like, from around twelve crews I think it was back then that entered, we came third. The following year after we also came third at the X-Games in Sydney and then the year after it was at the Sydney Battle of the Year, we came second and this year [2003] second. So it's basically like going up and they know this too and I think we're pretty well respected over east, I'd say, yeah. But, of course, we have love for these guys too because they are also very good dancers and especially a couple of people from Melbourne. Yeah, I think ah there is just a lot of respect going. The standard of breaking you see, like, I think it's gone up really really really high. Everything has just gone, lately especially last year, just gone through the roof. The moves we're really doing alright some people over there they dream about it. (laughs) Anyway…nothing bad on them, I mean you know.

We keep coming second, which is really impressive for such an isolated out of the way state. I mean, obviously you're going to win eventually. Why do you think that we're so successful in the national breakdancing competition?

I think it's just the crew that's going over basically, our Systematic Crew, because we've got every aspect of the dance covered. From popping to locking to power moves and footwork and freezes and blow-ups we're pretty much all-rounders. So, yeah, that's the good part about it. I think, yeah—who knows?—maybe next year it's our turn.

Have you guys been really conscious about developing all these aspects of breakdancing?

Yeah, from the start. For me, I'm pretty all-round, I do pretty much everything. I think a lot of the guys in the crew they also see, like breaking on itself as in b-boying developed through these years that you're better off doing everything and not just going, yeah, I wanna just do power moves, you know.

It used to be quite like that…

Yeah it used to be just power moves, but like people started to realise that b-boying is not about that, it's about dancing to the beat, about trying to be more innovative, and trying to be creative with your own style, own flavour. You have the basic steps, the six-step and a couple of baby freezes, chair freeze and stuff like this—that's the basics, that's the foundation of breaking but you build up moves on top of that. The dancers know what's going on, which is you would show someone else what's going on and people are just gonna go 'Ooo, that's a head spin,' 'He's spinning on his head,' that's when it's good, but footwork at some times counts definitely more than head spins or anything like that.

What is the future of breakdancing in Perth?

Well I wanna try and get into organising events, trying to get um… organising maybe some little comps for people. Yeah just that's for me, that's my perspective, I wanna go more that way, just reaching people, like. Because we're so isolated and stuff like this but Systematic Crew has a chance to go overseas and go internationally so we can bring whatever we get, pretty much, we can bring here and teach people. So that's what I want, I think, in workshops, trying to organise events, trying to get international people over, trying to make the whole scene a bit bigger and a bit more, like, involved, you know. So people actually see what it's about, when you're really into it, is really really interesting to anyone, seriously, coz I just think it's amazing.

Do you get asked a lot to go over East?

Yeah, we did a tour just recently with a car show. We did Melbourne and Sydney. We did Perth, Melbourne and Sydney with that. It was the saloon car exhibition. So we did shows with them and we did Battle of the Year. We have an invite for that.

So these people who organise this, they just send out an invite?

Pretty much. If you wanna try an audition you can send them a tape, maybe. But it's a limit and in Australia there is almost no more than fifty crews—that's the limit.

So are you guys the only ones to get an invite from over here?

Yeah, we're pretty much the only ones from Western Australia. So that's pretty cool. We went down, we were invited down to b-boy camp in Munich in Germany. There was two of us. Only me and Rami did that.

How was that?

That was excellent. Good experience. We went together because b-boy camp is this big free youth event that's organised by the city of Munich but it's all about b-boying basically and it's just about people getting together, jamming together, doing workshops, teaching from each other, learning and stuff like this. You can get all these big heads there like from LA and everywhere. From France, people from Russia there, there's people from everywhere. You learn heaps and you get to meet people and hang out and stuff.

What's the short-term plan for you? What have you got on, what are you doing?

Next up we got Rock Steady Crew, we're doing a free show there for them and we are doing a couple of other things. We just got sponsored by Adidas, actually. And we got that sorted out. Yeah, just trying to get into, like, trying to get our video finished. It's just a short promo video we can send out to people. Just so we can get jobs and stuff like this. Coz basically for us it's the flights that we get to go overseas. A lot of it we pay for, that's why we wanna do workshops stuff like this so we are able to go. Yeah, that's getting a bit hard because you need jobs to be able to get money to be able to fly. But it's all good, like you know, we're working on it. Everything's cool, everybody's doing workshops and saving money, yeah.

Would you like to breakdance full time, if you had your own way?

Ah, I don't think so. I don't know. I'm a full-time dental technician and I'm pretty happy about that. Good job, good fun. But, I dunno. Maybe, maybe not. I've been on holidays and sometimes you get sick of it—24/7, you know. Just breathing and, you know, breaking, sometimes it gets too much. Yeah I dunno. I wouldn't mind trying it out some time. But I'm pretty happy like it is. Sometimes on the weekend then two three times during the week practice—it's all good.

CHAPTER 16

A Crooked Crooked Reign

Adam Trainer

When I was fifteen I went to my first local gig at Planet Nightclub on Charles Street in North Perth. Like many suburban teenagers on weekends, my mate and I had ended up in the city, milling about in record stores when we spotted a poster for a local band with which we were vaguely familiar. We ended up there half an hour before anyone else, wandered round the back to a sound check, got a burger up the road and returned some time later to a slowly growing army in khaki pants and cardigans neatly lined up on the kerb the way only underage indie kids can be. What happened over the next five hours shaped me in a way I have never really thought about, but have felt inherently ever since: the smoky smell of the club—the sticky beer-soaked floor—the blackness during the day. The sweaty mosh pit, the sea of Nirvana shirts, the dyed hair and facial piercings are images I have carried with me into adulthood with reflexive humour and much fondness. These consummate individuals, flocking together in respite from the rest of society, were strangers at a glance and companions for the rest of the afternoon. Much has changed. I now live no more than three blocks from that club, which has become a strip joint. The venues have changed and so has the attitude. No matter how amazing the performance, the crowd never seems as excited or liberated as they were without the alcohol. None of the bands I saw that day are still together. Just as the venues have been replaced with new ones, so have the bands been usurped by fresh faces and new sounds. But the rationale remains the same. There is a genuine feeling that we are doing this because this is what we want to do.

It would appear that more than ever, the cultural currency for upwardly mobile youth is the media. For those with nothing better to do than surf cable channels and Internet bandwidth, the media is, as opposed to an outlet, an inlet for information and cultural capital which is constantly utilised and challenged. For the middle class, the decision to articulate oneself creatively through music is not born any less out of a frustration with the media, but carries a different rhetoric to those cultures for which it is a political necessity. The term 'indie-cred' is often used with reference to youth culture. Indie music often presents itself as an 'alternative' to homogenised youth culture.

The socially disempowered often have the discourses of class and race to work through in terms of the cultural statements they wish to make. All middle-class youth really have to rebel against is homogenised mass culture. However, indie rock attempts to operate outside of corporatised pop, rather than opposed to it. The ways in which middle-class youth 'create images of themselves that interrupt, invert or at least answer the ways in which they are defined by those in power'[1] double back to define an identity through lack and difference, not struggle and social change. According to the assumed ideological position of mass culture, network television and commercial radio adequately articulate the concerns and contemporary preoccupations of youth. Much has been made of the ways in which disempowered groups utilise the popular cultural sites that hold the most relevance to them in order to articulate and negotiate their social position. However, when the cultural group in question is made up of white, middle-class, suburban kids whose parents bought them a Marshall stack or Pearl kit in an attempt to nurture their creative spirit, the paradigm shifts slightly. Cultural appropriation is arguably a constant process and it would seem there are few avenues that are not at some point mined by the mainstream for their own purposes. This occurred in the 1970s with the punk movement and again in the 1990s with the rise of both rave culture and grunge.

Indie rock does not have the racial or working-class credibility of hip hop or metal respectively and is often characterised by sensitive, skinny white boys whingeing about not getting laid. Hip hop culture in particular offers a plethora of outlets for creative expression such as graphing, beat boxing, DJing and breaking. Metal too, can arguably be seen to have a predisposition towards a particular brand of working-class masculinity, which often utilises a discourse of violence in order to articulate its rage. But indie kids have arguably never had a common struggle for either social position or racial acceptance. Lipsitz argues, 'People resisting domination can only fight in the arenas open to them.'[2] However, often the arenas open to the middle class are particularly diverse. In middle-class indie rock, the protagonist is less likely to be a downtrodden member of a culturally insubordinate social group and more likely to be someone who has lived in an affluent suburb all his/her life, received music lessons throughout childhood and in the teens decided to utilise his/her musical knowledge as an avenue for personal expression.

This lived experience does not make the music less culturally valid, less 'authentic' or less galvanising. However, it does change the way in which music operates around subculture and the formation of communities. Hip hop is the genre often cited because of its plethora of activities linked to the one subcultural formation, often viewed by those in positions of authority as being antisocial or politically resistant. Middle-class youth rarely have their identities called into question by those in positions of power. They are usually privileged with the opportunity to pursue whatever choices they might like to make in terms of a career as well as leisure activities. Many study at tertiary institutions and are privileged with the opportunity to perpetuate or even improve upon their middle-class social standing. Dominant cultural models can be challenged in indie rock. Arguably dominant tropes of Australian gender roles are subverted by the long-haired, corduroy-wearing, sensitive, semi-sophisticated boys who frequent the scene. There is very much a notion that young men, 'by playing rock, are allowed to display feelings of weakness, tenderness, intimacy, sorrow and frustration which would be otherwise stifled.'[3] This is also an acceptable mode of communication for females involved in local music. Segregation via gender is arguably not an issue in the Perth indie rock scene.

Amid the loud guitars and corduroy, youth take solace in music that articulates their dissatisfaction with the seemingly insuperable economic determinism of the popular cultural landscape. In the local indie rock scene youth are presented with an articulation of their situation. These are not rock idols gazed upon in magazines: these are kids only a few years older than them who grew up in the suburb next to theirs. I remember once being ushered backstage at an underage gig at the UWA refectory because my friend had passed out in the mosh pit, and having Jebediah frontman Kevin Mitchell poke his head out after their set to make sure he was OK. Kevin grew up in Leeming. I grew up one suburb north in Bateman. We did not know each other: he was just concerned. Local scenes certainly give the impression of being communities, but often those within them, particularly in indie rock, see themselves as a collection of disparate individuals with only the music in common. However, the transitory nature of local music is what makes a scene unique, vibrant and appealing to those who can think of nothing they would rather do than watch their friends make a lot of noise on stage or in the corner of a room.

So how does this socio-political situation manifest itself musically? Historically there has been a constant slew of innovative and talented rock musicians emanating from Perth. From The Scientists in the late 1970s to the occasional group trickling through national consciousness in the early to mid-1990s such as Ammonia or Effigy, Perth has had consistent musical representation in terms of nationally and internationally recognised acts. However, in terms of a contemporary indie rock sound, the breadth of the local scene can be understood through the success of two bands: Jebediah and Sodastream. These two acts characterise the polarity of the local scene, the former leading the catchy pop entourage and the latter garnering attention for a supposedly artier aesthetic with their tranquil, articulate songs. Karl Smith's first band Thermos Cardy was part of the catchy indie pop fraternity that made it possible for acts such as Jebediah to gain recognition in a national capacity. However, when Thermos Cardy disbanded and Sodastream was born, an art-rock tangent in local music was seemingly revitalised. Sodastream relocated to Melbourne and then to the UK where they courted John Peel and made some fine records. Meanwhile others such as Wooden Fische, Tucker Bs and Adam Said Galore were banging around the venues making galvanising, considered art-rock that never produced radio hits but made for a captivating live scene. For those willing to shrug off the seemingly vacuous power pop that has eternally characterised Perth music for a wider audience, the music of these bands appeared not to be striving so much for popularity as opposed to musical gravity.

For a few years it would appear to anyone unfamiliar with the plethora of talent in Perth, the local scene was all about Jebediah. Long-time pin-ups of Perth indie music throughout the late 1990s, they led a thriving Perth scene. However, Jebediah arguably had more in common with the previous phase of Australian indie rock that came largely out of Brisbane. 'Brisvegas' as it came to be known, spawned the likes of Powderfinger, arguably the most successful band in recent Australian history, as well as others such as Regurgitator and Spiderbait. Whilst Jebediah's sound was undoubtedly reminiscent of the Perth power pop sound, they toured with these Queensland bands and other acts such as Something For Kate and Bluebottle Kiss and received national and international attention largely at the same time as them, as documented in *Dead Set*,[4] which despite being little more than a starry-eyed imitation of Doug Pray's grunge documentary *Hype!*,[5] had significant points to make about the nature of playing rock music in Australia.

For a while, especially to underagers, Jebediah were the coolest band on the block. They were influenced by an American indie band that only the really cool kids had even heard of (Archers of Loaf), released a song about smoking pot ('Jerks of Attention') and put a picture of that big spaceship-looking sculpture that used to be on Leach Highway in Rossmoyne on their debut album sleeve. However, Jebediah are significant for another reason. As arguably the most influential local band of their time, they hold a key to the way in which the Perth indie rock sound developed towards the end of the last century and the beginning of this one. The influence of the Jebs on other varyingly successful Perth bands such as Eskimo Joe, The Fergusons and Cartman cannot be denied. All these bands arguably share catchy guitar hooks, backed up by a solid, undeniably grungy rhythm section and somewhat playful, higher register male vocals. The Perth indie-rock sound as characterised by these bands is undeniably listener-friendly. The chiming guitar melodies recall the Flying Nun era, the rhythm section is usually recycled grunge, crunchy enough to gain the band indie-cred with those punters wanting something to jump around to, and the vocals are delivered in either a high register whine or a pleasant boy-next-door charm with lyrics mostly concerning girls, drugs and the usual cornucopia of youthful suburban angst. Bands such as Jebediah and Eskimo Joe certainly gained national recognition for a Perth scene, albeit one characterised by seemingly lightweight but catchy guitar-based pop music.

Like any local scene, the only constant is change. When national youth broadcaster Triple J unearthed Perth in 2002 everyone in the popular musical landscape had been turned on to the garage/roots revival and it was The Fuzz, hailing from Bunbury, who took most of the glory. Whilst there has always been a thriving heavy-rock scene in Perth, it would seem that it took the international attention placed on guitar-heavy cod and punk influenced rock that kick-started a more readily recognised scene in Perth. Whilst Capital City had been doing it for years, in 2002 the hard and heavy antics of Jed Whitey made national and even international ripples, garnering split releases with US heavy rock acts and even a government sponsored anti-speeding campaign for Australian television.

Longtime local favourites The Sleepy Jackson and The Panics have taken their particular brand of jangly Euro-centric pop music to a much wider audience and are finding success. The Sleepy Jackson has garnered four-star reviews in British music publications *Uncut* and *Bang* for their self-titled mini album and full-length debut *Lovers* respectively. It is always intriguing to see a local band gain success interstate or overseas. I remember going to the now-defunct Grosvenor to see The Panics play with the likes of The Tigers and Halogen. These gigs were reasonably low-key affairs. Much like any local scene, it was very much a bunch of friends standing around watching each other's bands.

Others have also succeeded with their own interpretations of the Perth guitar-rock sound. Halogen and Fourth Floor Collapse have gained considerable interstate attention with their melodically intriguing alternative rock sound that subverts the traditional power pop sound associated with Perth for a denser, atmospheric take on indie rock. Spencer Tracy and End of Fashion were each signed to the same label on the strength of one gig at Amplifier. Others such as Grand Central would appear to be releasing music with commercial viability whilst relying on their local followings and chipping steadily away at the Triple J interstate market.

Both Little Birdy and The Hampdens gained rapid success through considerable backing from the local press and great commercial potential and appeal. No more than a few months after their arrival on the Perth scene, Little Birdy were headlining a Thursday residency at the Amplifier and lead singer, Katie Steele was featured on the cover of the birthday edition of local street music paper *X-Press*.

Such is the nature of community. Perth is large and diverse enough to harbour talent and innovation in a myriad of musical styles. Under the umbrella of what could be termed guitar-based rock and pop music there are thriving scenes in many different genres. In terms of indie pop, bands such as Fighting for Alaska, Josivac and Triple J Unearthed winner Yunyu are all contributing to a thriving scene. The rebirth of punk and its angsty offspring emo have seen bands such as Gyroscope and Times Up garner considerable attention from out-of-state sources. In the hard rock sphere, there are a number of bands such as Heavy Weight Champ and El Horizonte, hailing from Geraldton, who are taking the genre into new realms of recognition and popularity with an exciting stage presence and urgent, frantic resonance.

In terms of a definable Perth sound, there is a plethora of guitar-based indie rock bands that could be seen to be of influence or importance. The transitory nature of local scenes ensures that oral history and popular memory are the only way to remember what has made our musical experiences worthwhile. The nature of a local music community is ephemeral. It comes and goes with bands, scenes, venues and even friendships. In a city as isolated as Perth, all these links, the personal, the experiential and the sociological, have manifested in a vibrant and interesting fashion. Whether or not Perth has a live band scene to rival other cities is—in the end—irrelevant. The most significant recognition is that there is a strong community of local musicians and local music fans who make the gigs worth attending and the scene worth investigating. Through this acknowledgment, we discover a similar motivation to what I experienced all those years ago: we are doing this because it is what we want to do.

CHAPTER 17

A Seychelles Rhythm

Rachel Shave

> I feel that it is important that you don't lose your roots, your sense of grounding, because it does give you a sense of identity and 'being' as well. But also, it gives you something where it acts as your springboard so that you can actually acquire other cultures and get also a sense of respect for others and also be able to share what you already have.
>
> *Giovana Neves, Manager of Seychelles Rhythms*[1]

The Queens Park Recreation Centre in Cannington epitomises 1970s blocky, light-brick public buildings. Some thirty years after this architecture's heyday, on a mid-October evening, its car park is filled to overflowing. Inside, half of the hall is decked out with forty tables, each with a cream or burgundy tablecloth and a centrepiece of candles and miniature red or white balloons. A few people sit at the tables, some with small children in their laps. But the majority are packed on the dance floor, hips swaying to the traditional moutya beat. Ages range from mid-teens to those of sufficient years to acquire grey hair. Many of the people originate from the Seychelles, but people from South Africa, East Timor and Samoa, as well as a few of Anglo-Celtic origin, are also present. Onstage, the well-known Seychelles performer Jean-Marc Volcy is singing the Creole song, 'Vandredi Sen,' in his rich, mellifluous voice. He is backed by Seychelles Rhythms, a group of young people who have come together to enjoy their culture and bring it to the wider community. Welcome to multicultural Perth.

This chapter is not an overview of Perth's multicultural music. Rather it embarks on an excursion through complex rhythms, sounds, languages and identities by focusing on one group, Seychelles Rhythms. The aim is to explore the challenges for migrants in retaining place, space and self while simultaneously embracing Australian citizenry and citizenship. From its inception, Seychelles Rhythms has consciously sought to address these issues of home, origin and belonging. While each band and performer has unique experiences, these can resonate for others, enabling self-awareness and collective insight.

Music permeates all aspects of life for the Seychellois. Its roots are in the rhythms of Africa, the Caribbean and the Indian Ocean but it also incorporates European, primarily French, influences. These intertwining contexts, origins and sounds are directly linked to geography. The Seychelles is an archipelago of 115 islands in the Indian Ocean, just 4° south of the equator. The islands, still covered in lush, tropical vegetation and surrounded by broad, white, sandy beaches, were uninhabited until the French landed there in 1742 and formally claimed them in 1756. The population grew from the original French colonists, deportees from France and large numbers of African slaves who were initially brought in to work the land. After the Napoleonic wars, the colony was ceded to the British and remained under their influence until granted independence in 1976. The following year, a coup d'état formed a republic that continues to this day. Through the years, Asian influences arrived along with migrants from India, China, and Malaya. Widespread intermarriage has resulted in a people of mixed descent who are open to a wide variety of cultural inflections, dialogues and translations.

Today African, Caribbean, Indian and European elements continue to shape the music which spans traditional, hip hop, electronica, jazz, blues and pop. When Seychelles Rhythms perform, they use keyboards to reproduce the French influenced sounds of accordion and violins. They draw on the African soukous and the moutya, a traditional song originating with the African slaves in the Seychelles, which survives through a bedrock drumbeat. The band can then segue into the sega, a very fast, up-tempo rhythm, incorporating both Indian and Portuguese influences. Both the sega and the moutya have been translated into a contemporary context and instrumentation, with the use of electric instruments. The band also plays segae, where sega is blended into reggae, softening it into a more mellow, lilting sound. Similar to the sega, but with an even faster pace, is a Caribbean zouk, which is

Creole-based and inflected with Brazilian rhythms. Very rhythmic and with a 4/4 beat, it compels dancing and movement. Seychelles Rhythms also incorporate their own beats, blending them with others encountered in Australia. The lead singer, Grace, clarifies the rationale for this diversity: 'If it's catchy and creates a good vibe, a good mood, a good beat, we take that new idea. Beat is very important because what we play is to let people dance to it and feel the music.'[2]

While there are Seychellois communities in Melbourne and Sydney, many end up in Perth where there are two Seychelles clubs. A number of the Seychelles Polytechnic teachers were educated in Perth and pass on their love and knowledge of the city to students, who in turn, come to the city to complete their education. After finishing study, many of the students return to live permanently, creating a growing network of friends and family which encourages even more Seychellois people to move to Perth rather than other parts of Australia. Giovana Neves, manager of Seychelles Rhythms, followed a similar path when she came to live in Perth to attend university some ten years ago and then stayed.

Giovana became concerned that Seychellois youth were not attending social functions held within the Perth Seychelles community and would thereby lose their cultural heritage and identity. Combining her love of her culture, dance, and music, she formed the Seychelles Cultural Troupe in 1997 as a means of engaging and involving young Seychellois people. The original members, Giovana, Grace and Joelle Barbe, and Jacqueline Anacoura started by performing traditional dances to a tape and guitar while they saved up for a drum set and other band equipment. The group incorporated in 1999 as the Seychelles Cultural Troupe WA Inc. Remaining under this banner, the band evolved into a distinct identity, naming itself Seychelles Rhythms in 2000. Members have changed and numbers fluctuated over the intervening time. At present, the band consists of Grace, Joelle, Jacques L'Etourdie and Michael Laporte while Giovana continues as their manager.

Grace, currently studying business and e-commerce at university, plays bass and sings lead vocals. Joelle, her younger sister, has recently

FIGURE 5: Performing at Kalamunda, WA. From left: Grace Barbe and Giovana Neves dancing. *Photo courtesy of John Shave.*

finished high school. She combines playing drums and guitar with singing back-up vocals. Tall and slender, hair often braided, Joelle frequents the dance floor when the band takes a break and the DJ commences. Jacques, a professional musician for fifteen years, plays keyboard, lead and rhythm guitar. The final member, Michael, an accomplished rhythm guitarist, has only recently joined the band. The band calls on various people to perform traditional Seychellois dances at some of their performances and works closely with Luan Ladouce, who DJs during the band's breaks. Luan plays music with 'island vibes'[3]: music which is vibrant and with a strong beat that demands dancing rather than attentive sitting and listening. He includes old island songs unearthed at Cannington or Subiaco markets, the latest in club music that he brings in from the Seychelles, but also music from America or Aotearoa/New Zealand—anything that keeps the dance floor full and moving to the beat.

When the Seychelles Cultural Troupe incorporated, it instigated a five-year strategic plan that included specified goals. These aim to promote Seychelles Culture, providing an awareness and understanding of the social, cultural and economic contributions made by Seychellois to the wider Australian society, create a platform for social and cultural interactions and sharing of ideas with other cultural groups and businesses, and provide a total Seychelles experience through ways of life, arts, music, literature, cuisine and cultural exchange. Seychelles Rhythms has actively sought to achieve these aspirations. In 1999 and 2001, the band played at the Minnawarra Festival, a celebration of multiculturalism held in Armadale. They have also taken part in the multicultural Festival of Light at Murdoch University and the Perth Youth Festival.

In March 2001, as part of Harmony week, the group organised the Gosnells Multicultural Festival, attracting large numbers of people. In the weeks leading up to the festival, they undertook workshops in collaboration with other artists—Fikki Pitts from African Heartbeat, and Adriano de Souza, a South American dance instructor. This series of free workshops taught close to 150 people dances from South America, Africa, and the Seychelles. On the day of the festival, held under Perth's brilliant blue sky, many of the 500 people attending were dancing the salsa and the sega on the podium and around the stage. Not only did this create a wonderful atmosphere on the day but it also enabled those attending the workshops to gain an extended insight into diverse music and rhythms. Interest generated by the event led to a six-month series of workshops being undertaken with Adriano.

The band continues to hold four or five dances throughout the year—the most important being held on New Year's Eve. This night is a direct link to the most festive occasion in the Seychelles where, over a week, families that might be spread throughout the islands for the rest of the year come together in order to celebrate the past year and welcome in the next. It is a time of friendship, family activity and unity.

Links with other Perth cultural communities are currently being forged. Seychelles Rhythms is performing at a number of weddings in the East Timorese community, their popularity increasing through word of mouth and the band members being multi-lingual (in the official Seychellois languages of English, French and Creole), while Grace also sings in Portuguese. Connections also exist with the Samoan community, which asked the band to play at the Perth welcome for the Samoan team who played in Perth for the last Rugby World Cup.

Together with their desire to bring Seychelles culture out into the wider community and to work with other cultural groups, the members of Seychelles Rhythms also wish to establish themselves as part of Australia, not an excluded community. The desire to translate, build, and create dialogue has a powerful social and political energy and importance. In 2001, this goal led to the band taking part in the Federation celebrations. As Giovana declares, 'We wanted to be part of the moment and *be* Australian...We've a different culture, a different background but yet we are people living in Australia, who have embraced the culture. And it is very significant in that it is the same process of embracing the culture and being accepted as well.'[4] The band successfully applied for a Gosnells City Council grant to write an appropriate song and perform it at the Gosnells Centenary Fayre. They brought in Alan Webster, a seasoned professional musician, to mentor and workshop with them. The group decided on sega but, feeling the Australian community would not sufficiently identify with it, they also included elements of jazz and rock. The 'Federation Song' incorporates sega in the drumbeat, a reggae rhythm through the keyboards and a rock bass line. Overlaying this hybridity is a potent melody and, as Grace suggests, 'the most important thing: a catchy chorus for people to pick up and sing.'[5] The group's belief in the song was vindicated when they played it on the day, and those attending were singing and dancing along with them.

The performance of this song at the Gosnells Centenary of Federation celebrations contained both irony and hope. The irony stems from this group of young people of colour writing and performing a song that celebrates Australian Federation. This is the same Federation that, through the *Immigration Restriction Act 1901*, instigated the White Australia Policy which would have effectively barred their immigration to Australia. However, there is also hope because the last vestiges of this policy were finally abolished under the Whitlam Government in 1973. Even when barriers and exclusions are resurrected through government policy, a popular multiculturalism has changed Australia and Australians. This band of Seychellois people, singing a song about a unified Australia, with English lyrics accompanied by music influenced not only by rock and jazz, but also Caribbean and Indian rhythms, actualises the multicultural project. The gratitude of being able to live in Australia and the enthusiasm expressed in this song are sentiments that may well resonate for other Australian migrants who currently make up almost a quarter of our population, and an even greater proportion of Perth's citizens.[6] A city of people with diverse origins, languages and musics creates a hybrid backbeat of plurality, diversity and dialogue.

The group's efforts appear to have more than met the goals set out in their strategic plan, so it comes as a surprise when Giovana describes the last four years as a 'long and frustrating journey. It is full of disappointments and, I would say, some despair.'[7] This attitude has developed through the group finding themselves at the mercy of institutions that are neither supportive nor understanding of the group's goals. Local councils, trying to maximise income, insist on charging high fees for venues despite the group actively promoting multiculturalism and better understanding between different communities. This problem is exacerbated by the cost of both equipment and practice venues, a difficulty shared by many groups throughout Perth. When band members are either studying or on low wages, the cost of putting on an event can seem overwhelming.

Giovana is coming to see multiculturalism as something that is talked about by the Federal Government, but which is not a lived experience for everyday Australians. Cultural groups, such as the one she is involved with, are tethered to their own communities or become known through personal contacts. Indeed, local cultural groups are noticeable by their absence in *X-Press*, the bible of the live music scene in Perth. While some councils do try to promote and encourage diverse music, there has often been a lack of consultation and communication. These systematic and institutional concerns suggest a lack of value placed on creative development.

It has reached the stage where Giovana is seriously questioning whether it is worth the effort and the disappointments, despite her love for her country, her music, and the young people in her community. There is little reward or recognition for the members, despite skill and talent. While Perth is still perceived as the main base, there is a feeling that they need to look beyond its boundaries in order to reach their potential. This has meant that Seychelles Rhythms is now seeking to build cultural exchange not only within Perth but also with other cities. It was part of this inter-city cultural exchange that brought Jean-Marc Volcy, one of Seychelles' most talented and biggest selling artists, to Perth in 2003. The Seychelles Social Club of Melbourne hosted him and then negotiated with Seychelles Rhythms to bring him over to Perth to play live with them. He also played at Kulcha and held workshops on sega and moutya. Inter-city exchange with Melbourne will increase, with trips planned for the future. They hope to include up to twenty people in such self-funded tours, including not only the band but also Luan as DJ, and several dancers. The band is also turning to look overseas and is developing its links with the Seychelles and East Timor. As a long-term plan, they are looking to tour the Seychelles and the Pacific region, along with a trip to France. In the meantime, they are seeking ways to develop their music through entering international competitions.

Here in Perth, we talk the multicultural talk. The UWA Perth International Arts Festival has been bringing international theatre, music, film, art and literature to Perth since 1953. But it is centred in the city, rather than the suburbs, while the pricing takes it out of the reach of many people. It is wonderful that Kulcha, which brings world performances to Perth, is celebrating its twentieth anniversary. However, situated in Fremantle, it too is separated from the suburbs—and marginalised from the city.

This discrepancy between policy and lived multiculturalism is even more important when we consider the New Agenda for Multicultural Australia tabled in Federal Parliament on 9 December 1999.[8] This framework aimed at making multiculturalism relevant to all Australians, to ensure that the social, cultural, and economic benefits of our diversity are fully maximised. It refers to strategies, policies and programs designed to make Australia's administrative, social and economic infrastructure more responsive to the rights, obligations and needs of its culturally diverse population. It is also intended to promote social harmony among the different cultural groups in our society and to optimise the benefits of cultural diversity for all Australians. This overall strategy does not appear to be working for Giovana and Seychelles Rhythms. Perth does contain the fabric and rhythms of multiculturalism, but there needs to be structural change and political commitment if we are to recognise, encourage, and celebrate diversity. Cultural and creative development should be taken seriously so that cultural groups such as this can be resourced—and not just financially. They can make many communities—in the many meanings of that word—dance. Through this movement, Perth's citizens can learn the steps of difference, diversity and social change.

CHAPTER 18

Another Side of Life: Downsyde

Leanne McRae

> Coz our mission is to get girls working, b-boys turning, spinning and burning, MCs battling, DJs dissing, writers trashing...[1]
> *'Keep It Alive' Downsyde*

It is 10 pm on a rainy Sunday night in a middle-class pub in suburban Perth. The venue is at about half capacity, filled with young urban white men and women who have paid their fifteen dollar cover charge to see hip hop act Downsyde. Although a large part of the audience consuming hip hop, rap and R 'n' B is young white men, the absence of blackness, Asianness or Middle Easternness within the crowd of a multicultural country is startling to someone schooled in cultural studies. I find this disconcerting: the unproblematic appropriation of the gamut of gangster gestures and expressions representin' the crowd. But then again, I am a white urban woman, present to see that very same hip hop act, so my position to judge is ambivalent and unstable. I am complicit in a consumption of difference, but also watching and thinking about the differences moving before me.

Downsyde is a band comprising six young men, with diverse backgrounds and interests.[2] The range of faces on stage is startlingly contrasted to the largely homogenous audience. This plurality brings to the group a special blend of styles and sounds that shapes the unique signature of their act. Being a hip hop band in Perth is a conundrum. Alternative, indie and dance music acts have benefited from particular visibility in the Perth scene. With only one dedicated hip hop venue, (the nightclub Soul City), rap and R 'n' B acts have struggled to crack the contained and cautious music market. Yet in the past few years, with the mainstream success for R 'n' B through Craig David, Alicia Keys, and Destiny's Child and hip hop like Jurassic Five, NERD, Missy Elliott and The Black Eyed Peas, there has been more openness to the Australian hip hop acts Two-up, The Hilltop Hoods, Koolism, 1200 Techniques and The Herd. Downsyde rap with Australian accents and Perth loyalty. They speak to the conditions encountered in this city. They represent a shift in the state's music market and citizenry.

A crucible of popular music is currently bubbling away in the suburban silence of Perth. The intervention of hip hop is a singular sign that the market is opening to diversity and dynamic tunes. The interjection of a distinctly multicultural hip hop voice shadows thirty years of public policy. These new noises mark the emergence of Perth popular music. For the first time in 2003, an R 'n' B/hip hop category was included in the WAMI awards.[3] National and international trends in musical memories and melodies have filtered through the landscape, forcing the birth of vibrant voices and vocal vibes capturing a depth of talent in this state.

There is a tight knit between difference, diversity and Anglo-Celtic identity in Downsyde's lyrics and visuality. There is a startling ease with which they are able to mediate the liminality of otherness into the everyday mainstream of Australian icons and ideas. For identities on the margins, these skills are taken for granted. Yet these abilities are less common in a conservative and consensual musical culture. In hip hop (and other musical genres) these everyday negotiations are found outside the official oratory of politicians. Downsyde's ability to translate the conditions of marginalisation into the consciousness of Australianness means they reveal the gaps and absences in public policy. The significance of this intervention is demonstrated by Fiona Allon who argues that 'translation addresses the very impossibility to translate. It assembles and produces the materials of memory and history into partial, incomplete, local instances of (literally) making sense.'[4] Downsyde access the unclear and ambiguous consequences of multiculturalism for Anglo-Celts, immigrants and Indigenous peoples. Their sense of multiculturalism takes place outside of the parameters of party demographics and political posturing. They track conditions of struggle through writing, music, living and working—moments of incomplete meaning that require high levels of literacy in social relationships to survive. That this multiliteracy emerges and thrives in Perth is both predictable and marketable.

MULTICULTURAL MATTERS

Multiculturalism is a public policy aimed at generating a social consciousness of difference. It was introduced in the 1970s as a way to facilitate and frame the relationships between Australia's Anglo-Celtic and Southern European immigrant populations. As a significant deviation from the White Australia Policy, its anti-racist and pro-social justice ethic was welcomed. The core trope of multiculturalism is to generate understanding and validate 'immigration, equal opportunity, affirmative action and anti-racism.'[5] Its ultimate desire is to provide a bridge between identities from different diasporas—later also including Asian and Middle Eastern and African identities. Attached to its core ideology is a project of nation-building designed to normalise diversity and construct a coherent consciousness of collectivity. Multiculturalism 'imagines a culturally hybridised national culture'[6] and foregrounds the potential of liminality as a legitimate community construct.

Despite its most noble efforts, multiculturalism has largely failed in Australia. The reasons for this stem from a series of structural problems. The multicultural policy has opened a wound of national consciousness that has not been reconciled or redefined. Miriam Dixson argues that 'no other Western country has experienced demographic transformation as fast as Australia, and upon so small and relatively homogenous a base.'[7] The sharp turn of social and economic policy from 'White Australia' to one of ethnic diversity has exerted great strain upon the institutions supporting the nation state. The efforts to mend this modality have been seriously hampered by the tendency for public policy to remain relatively absent in the real lives of everyday people. It lacks structural programs to integrate its new consciousness into everyday lives. It remains a binarised policy that defines two coherent groups—Australians and immigrants. Consequently it allows little fluidity or communication between these two positions.[8] But in local spaces and local musics, transitory reconciliation may occur. Jennifer

DeVere Brody argues that the tendency for multicultural (or plural) nations to foreground the 'hyphenated' identity—African-American, Italian-American, Greek-Australian—can represent a desire to capture and negotiate difference through fluidity. The 'hyphen marks the ever-emergent space between two distinct terms and negotiates a space of (distantly) connected difference.'[9] It offers potential for flexibility and has been claimed by particular groups to destabilise coherent categories. Yet the hyphen retains the focus on two separate and somehow opposing ideas, objects or groups. Hyphenated categories most often emerge from empowered localities and are imposed outwards onto others, maintaining conventional power structures. Ghassan Hage has demonstrated the persistence of whiteness and Anglo-Celtic power in the Australian multicultural model.

> No matter how much multiculturalism is maintained to reflect the 'reality' of Australia, the visible and public side of power remains essentially Anglo-Celtic: politicians are mainly Anglo-Celtic, custom officers, diplomats, policemen/women and judges are largely Anglo-Celtic. At the same time, Australian myth makers and icons, old and new, are largely Anglo-Celtic, from shearers and surfers to TV and radio 'personalities,' to movie stars and rock 'n' rollers.[10]

The inability of multiculturalism to make real changes in the construction of power in the nation is a significant flaw in the policy. But its death-blow was dealt with the election of the conservative Howard Government. By 1996, the Prime Minister had dramatically reshaped the public service by abandoning the Office of Multicultural Affairs, replacing it with the Bureau of Immigration, Multicultural and Population Research. Under his government a new approach was adopted.

> Diversity and equity programs continued to operate, but structural multiculturalism was no longer actively promoted, and Government-funded bodies such as the Federation of Ethnic Communities Councils of Australia took up a lower public profile.[11]

The consequences for immigrants have been particularly serious. Their concerns are deprioritised in current national debates. Difference has been reinscribed and rewritten along pessimistic and predatory paths. The general tone of national debate has been stripped of optimism and hope. It has also contributed to a number of misconceptions about the purpose of multiculturalism in Australia, delegitimising the economic and social ramifications for immigrants. Ghassan Hage argues that our tendency to focus on the ideology of 'cultural diversity' distracts from more serious considerations of migrant workers' rights. In other words, we assume that multiculturalism involves 'neat, middle class, aestheticised multiculturalism whose boundaries often do not go beyond the urban spheres that are of interest to the managers and professionals of investing global corporation—leisure, entertainment and consumption.'[12] When we perceive a careful and contained multiculturalism, we repeat traditional racist colonial ideologies. The tendency to ignore the conditions of diversity in a conservative consciousness means that the voices of otherness remain silent. We also lose our ability to be postcolonial and pliant. In Perth, when Premier Geoff Gallop assumed the portfolio of Multicultural Interests, he increased the value granted to difference. Even by using the word 'multicultural' in the list of his specific concerns, he granted immigration and diversity a more prominent position in the state than in the country overall.

DOWNSYDE, DIFFERENCE AND DOWN-UNDER

The capacity for multicultural policies to translate the experiences of immigrant peoples into the language and grammar of nationalism is significantly lacking. The one-way nature of this public policy means that immigrants have had to find their own methods of inserting their experiences into the social landscape of Australianness. The depth in experience, knowledge and expertise derived from migrants is too often ignored. Yet the subtle changes in consciousness, with the shifts in generations, have filtered through the Downsyde sound. Hip hop is a place where this translation can occur: it is not a site for 'authentic' cultural resistance. Hip hop is not resistive recording. It is the commercial success story of the late twentieth and early twenty-first centuries.

Jay Z, J-Lo, R-Kelly and P-Diddy do not critique capitalism or consumerist culture. They are embedded in—and complicit with—the restrictive ideologies of our time. The point made by hip hop—as a discourse as much as a genre—is that there is no 'outside' to capitalism. Social alternatives are increasingly difficult to form, and even more difficult to maintain.

Downsyde is not a resistive or radical musical group. Yet they are unique. They rap with Australian accents, which is a sonic shock. There is no desire to adopt a pseudo-American lilt to hail an authenticating audience. They verbalise these values in their rhymes.

> What's the matter?
> We represent down-under,
> Not the Star Spangled Banner.[13]

Downsyde are proud of their accents and use them to clearly differentiate their concerns within an Antipodean specificity. The significance of this defiant vocalisation cannot be underestimated. The Western Australian Music Industry website cites the struggle for this local lyricism.

> It's been a hard road for most Australian hip hop players and producers over the past few years as they battled for acceptance in their own right to define and develop a regional Australian style and sound for the genre...Downsyde are at the forefront of the movement. They have avoided the clichéd and irreverent USA gangster and crass Aussie-ocker flavours to develop a defined, refined and thoroughly Australian blend...LAND OF THE GIANTS, their second album, is a defining record for Australian hip hop...an album full of pure Australian energy, optimism, soul, pride and honesty.[14]

Downsyde remain faithful to a hip hop consciousness that is embedded in community, collectivity and empowerment. They have been able to connect this culture to a regional consciousness that is more sensitive to a fragmented and fluid identity. Most significantly, they attach liminality, localism and ambiguity to the national trope of Australianness by normalising cross-literacies of whiteness, blackness and multiculturalism. Downsyde do not work in a binary—they move between the categories in a more permeable hyphenated hailing. They blend Anglo-Australian identities and knowledges with immigrant and Indigenous experiences. They do not demonise whiteness and white cultural contexts. They remain critical of its flaws and inadequacies, but there is a great affection for white Australia in their lyrics.

Downsyde validate the influence of Australian rock and particularly Perth music history by referencing AC/DC in their song 'Bittersweet.'[15] They pay particular homage to AC/DC's 'For Those About To Rock (We Salute You).'

> For those about to top hip hop—we salute you
> For those about to break and spin wax—we salute you.[16]

A history of pub rock and white-Australian music filters through Downsyde's material. They recognise the traditions and influences of contemporary music in all its forms. The band members themselves come from a variety of genres and schools of sampling. Three MCs, Optamus, Dyna-Mikes and Dazastah, are from varied backgrounds. DJ Armee is a producer. They have a 'sampologist' Cheeky, who operates the sampler and loops live while also playing bass and keyboards. On drums is Salvatore who used to be with Perth punk rock band Beaverloop. The depth of talent and influences is present in the diverse nature of their sound—from old school hip hop to funk, jazz and even Latin flavours. They hail alternative memories and histories that have often travelled alongside traditional white and conservative ideologies. They create a connective thread between the coherent and clean ideologies that shape our world, and the unclear moments of ambiguity that reveal alternative ideas about life, identity and politics.

In 'Kingswood Country,' Downsyde demonstrate a dual literacy in both disempowered immigrant histories and memories and dominant Anglo-Celtic imaginings. *Kingswood Country* was a television sitcom screened from 1980 to 1984 that featured the relationship between a conservative working-class white man, Ted Bullpit, (Ross Higgins) and his 'ethnic' or 'wog' neighbour, Bruno Bertoluci (Lex Marinos).[17] The 'Kingswood' in the title refers to a series of General Motors Holden cars that have come to signify white and masculine Australia. The humour of this situation was embedded in the clash of cultures between the Bullpit and Bertoluci families—Anglo-Celtic Australianness and ethnic immigration. Downsyde call on this history of dialogue between differences to demonstrate the struggle for alternative ideas and unpopular products to find space within a society. Yet their song is also a celebration of 'the Kingswood Country' and its capacity for reflexivity and humour when they state that they are 'Kingswood Country born and bred.'[18] The ease with which Downsyde move through and blend different ideas, identities and styles demonstrates that Australia is changing. While power structures struggle to present crisp categories to placate our fears of border transgression and terrorism, Downsyde presents a model of inclusion and cross-literacies.

Downsyde trace forgotten histories, memories and moments. They connect dispossession to a common consciousness of struggle. The ambiguous moments where diversity dialogues with convention are the naturalised spaces for them to speak. As a result, they vocalise the conditions of difference in Australia which are masked by the intensifying colonial rhetoric of dangerous deviants and rogue refugees. In an era that has been characterised by the solidifying categories of national identity, sparked by the fear of otherness and transgression of national boundaries, Downsyde has embroidered diversity and locality into the national. They have reanimated ambiguity and fluidity as a current consciousness and reclaimed marginalised memories of immigration and otherness now co-opted by conservative consumer-based forces. In the arena of public policy, these concerns are being met with dogmatism and parochial posturing. Through popular culture, diverse literacies are normalised. Downsyde's ability to translate many experiences into a common language makes them a powerful and unique representative of this music moment in Western Australian history.

CHAPTER 

Moving Off World After the Cabaret

Tara Brabazon

Let me tell you a short story, right?
A short sto-ree.[1]
Shaun Ryder

Perth is a city of immigrants. Western Australia is a state of immigration.[2] While Sydney and Melbourne market their multicultural hearts, actually—by proportion of population—Perth attracts more migrants than any other city.[3] What makes Western Australian immigration patterns so odd is the predominance of British citizens. When acid house 'hit' Manchester in 1987, Perth DJs picked up the swirling keyboards and divaesque vocals. Dancers raised their hands in the air. Family, friends and records flowed between the two cities.

Cultural movements are ambiguous to describe and difficult to research. While studies of population distribution result in dry works of demography, migrant memories are hot and passionate, managing a mesh of contradictions between old and new homes. The most effective way to track the gulf between hopes and disappointments is to follow a network of migrant relationships and their impact on Perth music. The point of multiculturalism in Australia, while a highly volatile term in its short history, was to recast citizenship within languages of difference and inclusivity, not homogeneity and insularity. In a time of border control and exclusion zones, it is important to humanise the process of immigration. There must be both strategies and intent to blast away the racist assumptions that solidify the unspoken truths of powerful institutions. This is not a 'management' of diversity but a remaking of citizenship as plural, textured and complex. Music is a 'system of articulation'[4] to commence such a project. The contingencies of multicultural cities offer significant and creative opportunities for building a new type of citizenship. The key is to not focus on immigrants or popular culture. The aim is to link the two. Following Shaun Ryder's directives, two short stories—encircling Pete Carroll and Stephen Mallinder—are told in this chapter, concluding with a coda and sting in the tale.

DOPPELGANGER URBANITY

> The city exists as a series of doubles: it has official and hidden cultures, it is a real place and a site of the imagination. Its elaborate network of streets, housing, public buildings, transport systems, parks and shops is paralleled by a complex of attitudes, habits, customs, expectancies, and hopes that reside in us as urban subjects. We discover that urban 'reality' is not singular but multiple, that inside the city there is always another city.[5]
>
> *Iain Chambers*

Pete Carroll occupies many roles in Perth and its music. He has been station manager of RTR-FM, the independent community radio station, formed and run littleBIGMAN Records with Gaz Whelan, and Off World Sounds with Stephen Mallinder. His decision to come to Australia, let alone Perth, was synergetic but also arbitrary and almost accidental.

> I spent a year travelling thru' India and Asia in 1986, we tagged Australia on to it because I'd seen an Australian kids program when I was growing up which inspired my interest in the place. I knew nothing about Australia apart from The Triffids, The Go Betweens, Birthday Party and The Saints. I'd never heard of Aussie Rules or Midnight Oil. I ended up travelling all over Australia and loved it. We decided to come out here for a year around 1990 working for Sony Music and we're still here so it can't be bad.[6]

While immigration policies for entry and visas into Australia are frequently rigid and uncompromising in their checklists, criteria and determinations, immigrant choices are far more equivocal. Oz Rock and Australian Rules Football, the supposed great markers of nationalism, were not involved in Pete Carroll's decision to move countries. He had travelled through Australia, enjoyed it, gained a job in Perth and decided to stay. He stressed the knowledge that travel had given him. I asked how frequently he returned 'home'.

> I go back to Manchester often—every year to catch a couple of games at Old Trafford and see my family. In the late nineties I spent a lot of time working in London developing multi-media with Premier League football clubs (Man Utd, Liverpool, Arsenal, Chelsea, Leeds) and music labels. Perth is always great to come back to because it is so relaxing, the first thing you notice when you get back is the space and everywhere looks so clean. You tend to come back fired up with ideas.[7]

The movement between the cities is important. His employment has not only permitted an annual return to Manchester, but a continual trading of ideas. Complacency rarely develops through such exchanges. The question is whether disadvantages emerge through this mobile strategy to manage difference.

> No, I think if you can afford to take the best of both, you emerge with an experience that can only enrich your life. I think it's all about gaining experience. That's why I always placed a lot of importance on travel. But it can be very costly, financially and emotionally.[8]

In a post-Tampa environment, the costs of immigration to the immigrant are ignored. Rarely is there mention of migrants who settle in Australia, only to return 'home' in despair or disgust. With family and friends located permanently in another place, the melancholic pull to return is strong. Pete Carroll expresses this duality of immigration: experiences are gained, but there are profound costs.

Perhaps the most difficult question to ask any immigrant—no matter what their original location—is whether they made the correct choice in moving countries.

> It's a question I ask myself almost daily. Sometimes I think it was right but there's still a strong yearning for home, particularly family and football. But Australia is a beautiful place and Perth is very laid back. The downside is the isolation.[9]

Of all the research conducted for this book, Pete Carroll's understated answer to this question has moved and troubled me most. The consequences of every day asking whether he should have stayed in Manchester—whether he made the right decision—are profound both personally and socially. The silent acknowledgement within migrants is that another life could have been lived if immigration had not taken place. They will never know whether that alternative life could have been better. The irony is that this isolation and ambivalence have made Carroll both productive and proactive. He has brought Manchester to Perth.

The centrepiece slogan for the 2001 Federal election campaign was John Howard's motto that 'we decide who comes to this country and under what terms.'[10] The membership of this 'we' is rarely specified. There is no sense in this statement that, as in the case of Pete Carroll, there may have been advantages in staying in England or any former home. Such questions are redundant, as immigrants are not part of 'the us' or 'the we'. The inability to recognise the social and economic benefits of living in a place that is not Australia emerged in an academic newspaper the week after Pete Carroll supplied me with this moving reflection on the last fifteen years of his life. Dr Deborah Gare is writing the biography of one of the longest serving premiers of Western Australia, Sir Charles Court. His parents left England in 1912. Yet she is imposing a simplistic framework over this immigration history, where a shabby old world is departed for a new, gleaming, egalitarian Australia.

> England has surprised me on closer inspection, and it is not difficult to see why so many Brits are still keen to take up a new life in such warm, exotic locations as Spain, France and Western Australia. And it is not only to do with the weather, the television or the motorways, though they are reason enough in my mind… Gone now are the idyllic countrysides of pre-war England, the parish communities and the simple lifestyles. And I can only guess at the reasons that compelled Walter and Rose Court to leave England with young Charles in 1912. But it's not hard to guess why they and so many others might leave now.[11]

Historians love sagas and mini-series of big families, particularly when punctuated by upwardly mobile political success. But the assumptions about England—let alone English class structures and regionality—after 'spending a few months in Manchester, en route from Canada to Australia'[12] are not helpful in understanding the terrors of immigration, the complex community networks in the contemporary north of England and—most importantly—the inequalities and xenophobia that have developed in Australia through the last decade. Australian television is certainly not a reason to emigrate.

Considering that Perth hosts the highest proportion of British-derived citizens in the country, I enquired of Pete Carroll what he thought these immigrants brought to the city. Particularly, I wondered whether he felt Australian-born people understood the contribution of these immigrants.

> I don't think they do even though we're all immigrants really. I think those migrants who have come from around the world to settle in Perth have helped to enrich the place culturally. The place would be in grave danger of being bland if it wasn't for the diversity. You can begin to see the influence in music—the Asian community have helped to grow R&B and hip hop. Australia has always been predominantly a rock and roll kind of place, soul music and reggae don't seem to have a strong tradition here, whereas now we are beginning to see black influences emerge. We

> only have to consider the impact of the arrival of Jamaicans in England. Australia is beginning to understand the importance of R&B, hip hop, soul and funk. I think it's finally here to stay, which can only be a good thing.[13]

Pete Carroll acted as a pivotal educator and translator for these diverse musics through his former role as station manager at RTR-FM. His continued hosting of Friday night's 'Soulsides' offers insight into his near-encyclopaedic knowledge of soul and funk. The program is also a sonic carrier of northern soul into Perth.[14] The diversity of music and ideas expressed through the station more generally make it extraordinary in the history of community radio, but also in the medium more generally.[15] During his tenure as station manager, his goals were clear and important.

> I have managed the station for nearly two years. I'd like to have some impact on the station's development while I'm here. I totally believe in the station. Without it Perth would be a significantly poorer place. It is the driving force for local music and the Arts and offers a platform for a range of important environmental, social, political and community issues. It's important that the alternative nature of the station is maintained and strengthened. I'd like to see the station become more focused and financially viable and extend its reach. I want the station to sound great and deliver all its important messages as effectively as possible. In a small way it can help to effect change.[16]

As media ownership becomes more concentrated in Australia, it is startling to hear the difference and diversity of political views on RTR. From 9 to 10 am each weekday, wide ranging political communities have an opportunity to present news, debates, discussion and opinions. From 'Proper Gander', a radical and comic reinscription of news events, through to feminist, environmental, science and Indigenous programming, a diversity of voices and views are presented. Yet RTR's role in Perth music extends beyond this conventional function for community radio. The station naturalises the process of listening to local music, interviewing Perth musicians and DJs, launching CDs and supporting events. Their commitment to dance music through the 'Full Frequency' program, which features two hours of diverse electronica each day, is matched by a spectrum of dance genres featured each night and early morning. Industrial and gothic music is presented on 'Dark Wings', electro sound art forms the basis of 'Difficult Listening', moving through to 'Ambient Zone', 'Underground Solution' and 'Gettin' Hectic'. The movement in 1998 to online streaming of the station opened their programming to a worldwide audience.[17] Aural literacies are shaped, shifted and developed by the listeners of the station.

Pete Carroll has also matched this on-air commitment with the formation of other institutional structures for the music industry. He founded two distinct record labels—one for dance and the other for guitar-oriented music. His motivations for starting each overlap, but also have distinct origins.

> I started LBM with Gaz Whelan who was the drummer with Happy Mondays, we started it soon after the Mondays' final gig, which happened to be in Perth. It's difficult to launch a label from Perth—it would be easier from Timbuktu. We're isolated from the rest of Australia and let alone the rest of the world. There's also that snob factor to overcome where the east coast and beyond tend to be dismissive. But that's slowly changing with the help of some great Perth music. But it's very hard to deliver a project or tour without strong financial backing. We do it on passion alone. So it's not impossible but it's about as close as it gets.[18]

In 2003 at a musical industry seminar, I asked Sydney and Melbourne A&R executives directly about LittleBIGMAN Records. Pete Carroll's suspicions were confirmed. They were not aware of the label's existence. This is not only an oversight, but also unwise. LBM has offered an innovative solution to the MP3 panic of the major labels, offering and publicising the downloading of their major signings, using the label's website as a portal.

Through Whelan and Carroll's experience, they recognised that The Panics—if given an opportunity—probably have the ability to become an extraordinary international musical formation. Their first album, *A House on the Street in a Town I'm From*, juts out of the banal soundscape with incisor-sharp creativity and energy. Their follow up EP, *Crack in the Wall*, released within months of the first album, confirms the stark quality of their songwriting and musicianship. It is also obvious what attracted Whelan and Carroll to the band. The Panics pluck around the last fifty years of guitar-based music, appearing enclosed in a musical bubble, gliding effortlessly from the 1960s to the 1980s, and on to the 2000s. Or, to change metaphors, they are a mobile sponge, soaking up the sounds of history as if they have heard them for the first time. Importantly, the recording for The Panics' first album used Whelan and Carroll's connections in Manchester, with the songs being recorded between the two cities. Through such a process, it is no surprise that *A House* sounds like the 'great' second album that The Stone Roses never recorded.[19] It is important to remember that the two Stone Roses albums were separated by five years. When released, *The Second Coming* was seen as 'a noticeable jump forward; it was, as some pundits promptly pointed out on its eventual release, like listening to the third album and missing out on the second one.'[20] The Rosetta Stone linking the two records has been produced—some ten years later and in an Antipodean city. The Panics' effect on an audience is similar to the Roses. As John Robb realised,

> The truth is The Stone Roses became massive without anyone's permission; they became massive because this was a great album, an album that friends played to friends and raved about in a breathless whisper.[21]

Similar responses are derived from The Panics. When I saw them live soon after the release of their album, the audience was both hushed and in awe. Watching The Panics perform was the only time in my life when I knew—implicitly and definitively—that I was watching musical greatness. They seem aware of their moment. As Jae Laffer of

The Panics realised, 'it's a great time to be a Perth band…and it's a great time to be a pop band. So take it now or else.'[22] The Panics are trans-local, trans-genre sonic historians. It would take a band from Perth, signed by the drummer from the Happy Mondays and a cousin of Shaun Ryder, to provide a fitting conclusion to The Stone Roses story, a denouement that Ian Brown never managed or imagined.

Because of Pete Carroll's diverse musical knowledge and experience, he carries forward both elements of the Manchester musical revolution. The guitar bands—many of which signed to Tony Wilson's Factory Records—are only half the story of the city. The other dance trajectory of Manchester's history, sometimes described as the clichéd 'Madchester', has been perpetuated through Off World Sounds.

> I started OWS with Stephen Mallinder in 1996. It's a label devoted to electronic music and was originally set up as a label for some of the newly emerging Perth producers. There was no focus in Perth for electronic music at the time. I believe we helped to break new ground over here and created some opportunities for a few producers and started to get a bit of recognition nationally and internationally. Having said that we have never really been recognised in our home town. WAM only recognised our existence in the past year or so. There are so many problems attached to being based in Perth—location/isolation means you need a lot more money to get your message out. We've never had the financial backing to market ourselves or tour. I guess the problem is huge really. But we've always looked good—great packaging, great artwork and I think we've tried to build a proper label that is an identifiable entity. In the tradition of the great labels.[23]

The Western Australian Music Industry Association has historically neglected and frequently ignored the electronica community.[24] Yet the lymphatic model used by OWS and dance music generally, where a secondary series of channels and networks moves through the metaphoric pop body, is a successful marketing strategy. The sheer quality of OWS recordings, from Soundlab to Gripper, the Ku-Ling Brothers to

Shaun Ryder, is breathtaking. They blow most electronica recordings in Australia off the dance floor through the chill-out room and into the car park. The production values—both aurally and visually—are high. Central Station Design, based in Manchester and most famously associated with the Happy Mondays album covers and Factory designs after Peter Saville's tenure,[25] have created stylish interventions in the increasing bland visual presentations of pop.

Pete Carroll has made a wide-ranging and unwritten contribution to Perth's music and popular culture. Therefore, I was pleased when his name—along with Shaun Ryder's—was listed at the conclusion of the report as a contributor to the Western Australian Contemporary Music Taskforce. I asked about the nature of this involvement.

> To be honest I'm not sure that I contributed anything to the report, I certainly don't recall being asked for any input and Shaun certainly wasn't involved. I think I could have offered some insights into what would be an effective approach to building a sustainable industry. I haven't seen the report so I can't comment. The Perth scene has matured in some ways over the years. There is a more focused approach from some areas of the industry and greater confidence. Perth bands occupy a high profile nationally but it's important industry figures do not become complacent and believe the hype. I have seen it happen previously in the mid-nineties. The highs come and go. The key is building something that is sustainable.[26]

Obviously the findings and recommendations of the Taskforce Report need to be more widely circulated. Other writers and contributors to this book, investigating the night-time economy and 78 Records in particular, have also expressed ambivalence about the level of 'input' by 'stakeholders'. The difficulty is the size, scope and diversity of this creative industry. Finding a representative sound, organisation or institution is impossible. Significantly though, Pete Carroll has conveyed a desire to ride through 'the hype' of Perth's momentary celebrity to create the structures and institutions that can sustain the industry and initiate growth. As this book reveals, the 'scene' and its history are far larger than currently recognised by the formal policies and institutions of the popular music industry.

There was a disturbing and unsettling part of the Taskforce's research base that will have consequences for the industry unless corrected. In the Market Equity study that formed the evidential base for the report—which also attempted cultural mapping of the industry—a statement was made by the authors Matthew Benson and Poppy Wise that needs to be addressed.

> The solution lies in the industry becoming more outwardly focused, and to do this, it must seek the input of successful professionals who have proven track records in the marketing of music nationally and globally. In the main, these individuals reside offshore or on the East Coast. Their knowledge of how to leverage our local talent, how to conduct effective marketing campaigns, and importantly, how to build profitable relationships, and with whom needs to be sought.[27]

Considering the experience and profile of Pete Carroll and Stephen Mallinder being outlined in this chapter, the rationale for ignoring already existing expertise is puzzling and damaging. As is common in Australia more generally, there is a bland and blind unawareness of the skills and experiences that immigrants have brought into Perth. Dave Haslam, in tracking the musical history of Manchester, recognised that power—like talent—is in the ears of the beholder.

> Wherever the music business moguls may be in all probability behind desks in London, answerable to more senior executives in Japan or New York, Manchester has been at the heart of English pop music creativity for at least three decades.[28]

Converging creativity and commerce reduces the power differential between institutions and instrumentation. Perth has a model for this fusion in its midst. Pete Carroll has already watched creativity against the odds in Salford. Through all the inequalities of class and space, A Guy Called Gerald pushed 'Voodoo Ray' out of Hulme. Oasis cut 'Wonderwall' out of Burnage. The Panics pumped 'This Day Last Year' out of Perth.

Pete Carroll has brought knowledge and experience to this city via management of RTR-FM and the founding of two record labels. Yet this expertise is ignored in the search for successful professionals 'off-shore or on the East Coast'. With an effective mobilisation of Western Australia's diverse population, this search can shift from off-shore to Off World.

BEYOND THE BOWL: (POST) PERTH MUSIC

> Perth is like a goldfish bowl—everything inside the bowl looks massive in relation to the external environment but at the same time we can't shut out the world outside that bowl. It's not an Australian city. Why do you think I called the label 'off world'?[29]
>
> *Stephen Mallinder*

Off World Sounds was founded in 1997 by Pete Carroll and Stephen Mallinder. The label's name was a not only a tribute to *Blade Runner* but a description of how the city relates to the rest of the planet. Soon after the label was formed in February 1997, Mallinder explained the rationale for the name: 'Perth is Off World, it's like it might as well be in outer space. In terms of how it relates to other people, it is an Off World Community.'[30] He has the expertise to make these judgments. Like all immigrants, his life has many parts that cannot be concisely compartmentalised or reconciled in the present. He is known internationally as one of the founders, with Richard Kirk and Chris Watson, of Cabaret Voltaire. Playing with sound and tape recorders in Sheffield in 1973, they built tape loops and created sonic manipulations that shifted commonsensical understandings of music. Releasing their first EP on Rough Trade in 1978, in all there were eight albums produced. The group's base in Sheffield was Western Works, rented rooms above a superfluous former northern sweat shop. In this space, sound sources were both recorded and recoded. Chris Watson left the Cabs in 1981 to become a sound engineer for Tyne Tees Television. The duo then moved to Virgin's Some Bizarre label, and set up a video and record label, Doublevision. Looking back on their body of work from the 2000s,[31] the influence of Cabaret Voltaire is obvious. The 'rules' of popular music were broken through the avoidance of song structures, storylines or acceptable images and narratives. Like the Dadaists after which the group were named,[32] the Cabs did nothing less than broaden the range of acceptable sounds (and visions) in popular music. Their positioning between genres, styles and sounds was always unstable. As Fish and Hallbery discussed in the only full-length survey of Cabaret Voltaire:

> Their happy-go-lucky attitude had set them apart from the pretensions of 'rock' musicians, or the cosy, insular cliqueiness of jazz or the avant garde, or the secular elitism of the independent scene. Cabaret Voltaire were to find themselves plunged into a grey area between the three, caught in the throes of commerciality versus creativity—an area that was to close up and become less of a comfortable place to sit as time went on.[33]

As the 1980s progressed in Britain, capitalism became the greatest of all experimental art movements, creating new and odd alliances and dissonances between neo-liberalism and neo-conservatism. Experimental and industrial music—when it was as innovative, quirky and funny as Cabaret Voltaire—would always be a bit too clever for a citizenry that believed in individuals, families and profit, not society, communities and justice. Mallinder realised this, even in the 1980s. He stated that 'we are just ordinary working class Northern people and perhaps we should have hidden it better.'[34] Being on the left or even progressive in politics since the early 1980s has been difficult to establish, and even harder to maintain. Mallinder left Sheffield for London in the late 1980s.

The jackhammer beats and clavicle-cracking bass of industrial music from Cabaret Voltaire were crucial to the rhythmic developments to later emerge from Chicago. House music reclaimed the history of the instrumental in popular music. Soul breaks became house hooks. The 1980s, although often framed as a time of bubble skirts, shoulder pads and water-stained taffeta, was a pivotal moment in the history of electronica as it punctuated the two lo-fi decades of the 1970s and 1990s. The sequencing, digitisation and automation of recording in the 2000s are based on the initiatives and recordings of the 1980s. The innovations of synthesised sounds that came from Sheffield—particularly when remembering that Human League,[35] Heaven 17 and Cabaret Voltaire were all derived from the city—have shaped subsequent sonic histories. Dance music—through sampling—has honesty, carrying its history through the mix. It offers a mode of referentiality, reflexivity and citation. Through this process, Sheffield's 1980s still breathes and moves on contemporary dance floors.

Sheffield's electronica was and is important. Andrew Blake recognised Cabaret Voltaire's influence in particular.

> Even now hard to characterise, their music lacks the careful complexity, the layered sonorities, of the Art of Noise; but like the Art's clever use of the Fairlight, Cabaret Voltaire's pioneering electronics proved important to the dance music revolution of the later 1980s, and it has been celebrated as such; one of the band's final outings featured the work of house pioneer Marshall Jefferson.[36]

Cabaret Voltaire did something significant. Slamming together punk and dada, they created a more democratic interpretation of sound, noise and music. The Cabs, like Kraftwerk,[37] were important not only for what they produced musically but for their cultural function. They held a transformational role in popular music, translating the everyday into the extraordinary, rhythmic and complex. Paul Morley included them in his list of 'definitive original British electropop pioneers.'[38]

Stephen Mallinder is in the unusual position of being part of two cities that have experienced a musical boom (of publicity if nothing else). Sheffield and Perth have both been associated with an innovative sound or scene. He offers a special insight to assess how these city musics are formed. Sheffield was a context for ABC, Heaven 17, Human League and Cabaret Voltaire to emerge, and harbours specific musical influences.

> I think the interesting statistic would be to analyse music sales, between 1973 and 76. The sales of Roxy Music albums in Sheffield were disproportionate to the rest of the UK. Add to that an environment that offered little in terms of inbuilt entertainment—like London and Manchester—meant people sought their own outlets and loads of bands began to spring up (all of whom had at least one Brian Eno in there).[39]

Similarly, it would also be an interesting study to monitor the sales of northern English-derived electronica in Perth. While researching and writing this chapter, I flicked through and played my vinyl and compact disc collection. The frequency of Sheffield-based electronica and post-acid house musics from Manchester is revealing. Before interviewing Stephen Mallinder, I never realised the scale of this influence. The sharing of this musical vocabulary, and how it moves between cities, can only be tracked through a series of oral histories as presented in this chapter. Music is mobile. We hear difference before we meet it.

Beyond the mobility of music, Mallinder also found social connections between Sheffield and Perth, based on isolation.

> Perth again was the result of people with little entertainment so you do it yourself—isolation has to be a factor which was suddenly broken by global technology and a club boom at a time when Sydney and Melbourne were caught up in their own cultural millstones—the Mardi Gras and Nick Cave respectively have a lot to answer for in those cities…These sound like glib simplifications but in a young city something had to erupt. Hedonism and sunshine are ingredients in this cocktail.[40]

With Sydney and Melbourne music communities looking inward, Perth clubbers and DJs had a flexibility to look elsewhere. Geographical isolation within Australia led to a capacity to turn from the East and towards wider cultural landscapes.

Dance music denies the authentic and the singular origin. Electronica is not pure, but creates a hybrid soundscape. Samples and remixes circulate and recirculate musical memories. Consumerism and capitalism are carriers of contradiction and resistance. Little Australianism—that is insular, white, male, bland and based in the south-east corner of the continent—rarely incorporates such volatile and fluent music. For example, a study conducted on the state of Western Australian music in December 2002 reported that:

> The boom in the electronic/dance genre is a major global trend and WA is no exception. Whilst most of the activity is non-original and non-WA music…contemporary WA musicians in the genre are starting to emerge.[41]

This report betrayed little understanding of the complex and overlapping dance histories and trajectories that have passed through Perth for the last twenty years. Many of these stories have emerged through this book. The political economy of electronica is unstable, particularly when monitoring the role of newer technologies in the production, distribution and reception of music. Instead of relying on—and perpetuating—national 'rock' modes for pop success, dance is a far more effective method for initiating success in a trans-local, digitised, post-Fordist environment.

When Stephen Mallinder moved to Australia and formed Off World Sounds, two musical projects were also initiated: Sassi & Loco[42] and the Ku-Ling Brothers. The latter was formed by Mallinder and Perth resident Shane Norton. Best known for his Soundlab project, Norton would become a crucial part of not only the Ku-Ling Brothers, but Shaun Ryder's *Amateur Night in the Big Top*. His expertise in dark electronica has cut through both Soundlab and the Ku-Ling Brothers. What commenced as a remixing moniker for Ammonia, Jebediah, Header and Yummy Fur, the Ku-Ling Brothers began producing their own material from 1997, building into *Creach*. Remixing discredits notions of the original and the authentic, cutting away and then re-weaving a track through a hook, a lyric or break. Remixing is important because it decentres a single musician or performance and transforms every soundscape into a work in progress, not a definitive presentation.

The Ku-Ling Brothers have released two profoundly important sets of remixes, *Flat Back Four* in February 2002 and *Eat the Rich* in May 2002. However *Creach* is the album that demonstrates the spread and scope of Mallinder and Norton's collaboration. Released in 2000, it was included in the *Ministry of Sounds* '101 Crucial Albums'.

> The combination of Cabaret Voltaire member (and regular MINISTRY contributor) Stephen Mallinder with young Perth musician Shane Norton proved a winner from the off. Their breaks driven, percussion-heavy sound peaks on 'To Rock the Rhythm,' 'Evolution of a Dope Fiend' and 'Octagon Head,' but this is an album best heard in its entirety.[43]

Listed alongside Massive Attack, Portishead, Primal Scream, The Prodigy and New Order, this review of dance history shows the importance of the Ku-Ling Brothers to the future of electronica. When I raised the significance of this album and the *Ministry* recognition with Stephen Mallinder, his response was customarily modest but also provides some insight into the frequently spontaneous and unplanned nature of generating music.

> Hah...I must have missed that one I only read the first 70 albums and had to get off the bus. That's great but I'm not sure how to dance to the whole album. Working with Shane has been fun, rewarding and full of mad incidents. The hardest part is trying to sustain it but we do. Sometimes I think I find it hard to carry on but then we do a gig and we have such a ball or we'll manage to get a day in the studio and turn something out and I realise why it's special. Respect to Shane.[44]

As with Pete Carroll's testimony, it is clear that there are great difficulties in finding the time and space to actually record. The quality and innovation of the releases produced through such difficulties incubates a diversity of rhythms, loops and styles.

Mallinder's experience in and through music has provided a pathway to understand the movement from Cabs to Ku-Ling. I asked him to reflect on this music journey and how he feels about the process now.

> It's difficult for me to say as I think being in a band is difficult enough in this day and age. I'm lucky enough to have done all this in a more naïve and adventurous time to give me a different perspective, I think perhaps time is more significant than place. I may not be known as much for Ku-Lings as my other stuff but that's due to more than location. I shouldn't say it but money is the hardest part. We have to do so many jobs just to survive but I think the pressures are no easier elsewhere just expectations differ in different situations. I gain as much satisfaction from my achievements with Ku-lings even though they don't seem as grand as my earlier times and let's face it we do these things cos it's what we do, not to gain laurels.[45]

The lack of recognition for the Ku-ling Brothers in Western Australia is odd. They have not been supported by policy documents or governmental directives. Yet even without this assistance, OWS is important for maintaining outward thinking and sounds while affirming local communities and commitments.

Off World Sounds recordings are a complex amalgamation of dub, trance, hip hop, soul and house genres. Shane Norton remembers the process of its formation.

> We started it off just to get our own music out, more than anything, because I had the soundlab album and he wanted to put that out. So that was the first release on there. We had a lot of

> friends who were DJs and bedroom percussionists as well, and they were doing stuff. It's just a way for all of us to make music and put it out there without having to sign contracts with record labels and get ripped off.[46]

It was crucial that a quality, thoughtful and evocative space be found for the release of these recordings. OWS provided this outlet and sonic port. As Stephen Mallinder realised, Perth is not an Australian city, and OWS does not rely on a single city's potential. It is—literally—Off World, using Perth as a base for international music to land, be remixed, recut, resewn and released back to the world. Just as Wellington is the capital of Tolkien's Middle Earth as well as New Zealand, Perth can be a remix capital for Paris or New York-based performers.[47] Gripper and Ooblo from Manchester, Little Egypt from Brooklyn, Looped for Pleasure from Sheffield and DB Chills from Sydney are examples of the diversity of sounds and spaces that are part of the Off World register. Similarly Central Station Design in Manchester has created objects of art out of the CD packaging, providing extraordinary visual accoutrements and landscapes.

Stephen Mallinder's experience in travelling and making music means that he is able to place the Ku-Ling Brothers in the context of the last twenty-five years of electronica.

> When I started making music here the last thing I wanted to do was get signed and go through the whole process again I just wanted to keep control and also give an outlet for anyone I met along the way plus I wanted to set things up for friends in England to bring out music in Australia. I was stupidly naïve to think sales here could justify this approach, but still it was fun till I nearly bankrupted Pete and myself and we had to stop bringing loads of albums out. Pete and I thought this was something we had to do and we still believe if we had been over east we would have [succeeded] fantastically. In this respect Australia is a rather stupid country. To be frank I don't think we'll ever be recognised for what we achieved and released,

> Perth is seen as a backwater and our efforts were trivialised by the majority but as I said Australia is rather unsophisticated in this way. The goldfish bowls of Sydney and Melbourne can't see beyond the murky glass which holds them.[48]

Mallinder has a right to express concern and surprise at the lack of interest in Off World recordings in Sydney and Melbourne. The only comparable model for the release of dance music in Australia is Vicious Vinyl.[49] Specialising in breaks, house and deep house, Colin Daniels, Andy Van and John Course formed the label in the late 1980s. Best known for Madison Avenue's 'Don't Call Me Baby,' a compilation of their work was *A Night Out with Vicious Grooves*. This is not a remarkable compact disc—it is not bad—but it is bland house. Almost all the producers are from Melbourne, except for Mobin, a DJ from Adelaide. The sounds are located on a smaller sonic landscape when compared with the complexity, humour and innovation of Off World Sounds releases. OWS are operating in a different league musically, aesthetically and socially.

Mallinder's influence and expertise with OWS is not the limit of his contribution to Perth's music. Soon after his arrival, he became involved in RTR as 'it was an interesting way to get me involved in the city without having to make a big deal out of my past.'[50] This transformative effect of immigration is important. The movement to Perth meant he could transcend an association with Cabaret Voltaire, while acknowledging his experience with electronica. In July 2003, Stephen Mallinder became RTR's talks producer.

> I take great pleasure in doing talks production probably cos I can marry all my interests: music, politics, culture, art etc. but perhaps as much from enjoying talking to people, everyone has a story, I just want to hear it. Plus I am passionate about broadcasting and the role RTR plays—it is to my mind quite unique. Isolation has produced this anomaly of media, a fantastic barometer of a bizarre city as it evolves during an interesting period in history.

Mallinder's expertise with sound has allowed him to present politics, the arts and sport through an innovative mix. RTR has been able to catalogue the changes to the city, aligning the sonic with the social.

Through OWS and RTR, Mallinder has given much to Perth. The question is why he came to Western Australia in the first place. It is always interesting to track why immigrants decide to take the leap of faith to a new country. Pete Carroll's decision was based on a job being available and enjoying travel. As with all immigrants, distinct push and pull factors emerge for different people. For Stephen Mallinder, it was an overt desire to move into a new period of his life.

> I'd visited Perth in 1991 and was strangely drawn, I found the isolation quite intriguing and when my second daughter was born a few years later I decided I'd like to spend some time there. I'd had enough of London after 13 years and wanted to spend some time living outside the UK. Although I'd travelled a lot before then I hadn't spent much time in residence elsewhere, I wanted to leave my past behind and be anonymous for a while.

Aligning personal and professional aims, isolation was desirable as it created a distance from expectations and notoriety. Considering such triggers for movement, I asked him if there were any regrets.

> Oh, I don't know whether there is such a thing as a right or wrong decision it was just a path we choose and then you spend your time adapting to that, I'd like to think we make the most of any situation. I strangely enough didn't intend staying in Perth, it just worked out that way and who knows if I'd have stayed in London I could have ended up as an international terrorist, driving a bus or even getting knocked down by one. Every situation offers a plethora of possibilities not all of which are self-determined.[51]

It is important to note the tenuous and fragile decision in moving countries. Intention does not always lead to outcomes. Distinct from Pete Carroll, who reflexively—and daily—asks if he was correct in moving to Perth, Stephen Mallinder is aware of the alternative lives that could have emerged if he had stayed in London. He focuses on flexible adaptation, while recognising that immigrant choices—like those of the citizenry generally—are not always self-determined.

It is extraordinary, both inside and outside music communities, that a man of Stephen Mallinder's knowledge of electronic soundscapes has not been utilised more by Western Australian marketers, music organisations or policy makers. He was not approached by the Western Australian Contemporary Music Taskforce to offer comment. It is no surprise, considering this exclusion, that the resultant document argued that the industry needed to look to Sydney and Melbourne for knowledge of 'international' markets. Cabaret Voltaire—internationally—is recognised for revolutionising music. Stephen Mallinder has continued creative and productive work through OWS and the Ku-Ling Brothers. The Western Australian Government is not going to find a better exponent or expert in electronica with a higher international profile unless they lured Ralf Hutter from Düsseldorf. I asked Mallinder why there has been a discrediting of the presence, expertise and contributions of immigrants to the music industry.

> Poms are poms. We are white trash, despite seeing themselves as sophisticated the general perception of English people is hooligan class. It's only recently that they have been seen as culturally worthwhile, I think there's a denial of who second and third generation Australians, who they actually are and assisted passage has placed a stigma that will not be removed for some time.

'White Australians' born in this nation are liminally positioned through colonisation, being both colonised by British masters and colonising an Indigenous population. One of the reasons that Australian racism is so virulent is because the word 'Australian' needed to be rewritten from a nineteenth-century application to Indigenous communities and transformed into a noun for a white national citizenry. In one century, the word 'Australian' transformed from signifying blackness to connoting whiteness. The semiotic violence required to change the racial ideologies of national vocabularies is of a breathtaking scale. The selective forgetting of White Australians creates ambiguous and damaging relationships with Indigenous peoples, but also a convoluted affiliation with immigrants. English immigrants live in an ambivalent ideological zone. With so much pressure and attention placed on the limits and 'exclusion zones' of Australia and Australians, those migrants who are a reminder of prior belongings are uncomfortably positioned.

It is important to explore what happens when Englishness travels. Music acts as a carrier for memories, disappointments and expectations. Pete Carroll and Stephen Mallinder both offer alternative trajectories and histories of immigration in Perth that are rarely told. However one more layer of musical movement—almost inevitably—provides a coda to this story of difference, change and influence.

SHAUN AND YOKO

The immigrants who gain respect or publicity in Australia either box, run or play rugby. There is little tracking of the contribution that immigrants make to the creative industries, bringing forward knowledge, ideas and experience. Pete Carroll and Stephen Mallinder set up OWS, transporting the expertise and sounds of Manchester and Sheffield with them. It is appropriate that the greatest Salford lad of them all—Shaun Ryder—recorded his first solo album in Carroll's garage in Perth. The cousins Ryder and Carroll also utilised the enormous talent of Shane Norton along with inputs from Stephen Mallinder, to create an innovative, strange and fascinating album. Through the recording of *Amateur Night in the Big Top*, Ryder claimed a second home, not only launching the album in Perth's Velvet Lounge, but wanting to share his time between Manchester and Perth. This type of musical chain migration is difficult to track and research, but OWS is the method, metaphor and model of the productive nature of musical and population movements.

Shaun Ryder was the lead singer of the Happy Mondays and therefore maintains an important place in the history of popular music. As a fulcrum for dance culture and indie-rock, they created new musical languages through translation, transposition and creative hybridity. Shaun Ryder was the street urchin with an attitude, expressive, organically intelligent[52] and with a sense of the extraordinary in the midst of banality. The Happy Mondays swirled in a series of interlocking familial and social relationships. As Dave Haslam realised, the

> Happy Mondays were Salford street-corner society on a stage, carrying their friends around them, keeping their community close knit. Shaun's brother Paul was in the band, his father Derek worked behind the scenes, and Shaun's cousins Matt and Pat ran Central Station Design.[53]

Pete Carroll, the brother of Matt and Pat, continues this network of family and social relationships which moved Ryder into new musical territory. What makes Ryder remarkable in the pantheon of celebrity was his capacity to make lightning—and fame—strike twice through his band after the Mondays, Black Grape. His influence is of such a scale that in the August 1999 edition of *Q Magazine*, which listed the 100 greatest musical stars of the twentieth century, Shaun Ryder was number 68. Thankfully, and rightly, he polled above Sting. The top five were predictable—Lennon, McCartney, Presley, Cobain and Dylan—but Ryder's placing demonstrates his influence for a generation. The difficulty is that court battles between Ryder and Black Grape's former managers, Gloria and William Nicholl, have blocked his capacity to maintain a musical career.

To gain a living through this period, he re-formed the Happy Mondays for a world tour. But as the dates and months continued, Ryder 'started drinking again and…started having a sniff again.'[54] At the tour's conclusion in Perth, Ryder decided to stay with his cousin Pete Carroll to recover. The album was a synergetic accident emerging from this time.

> The idea was just to relax and take some family time, but eventually he got curious about the noises coming from Pete's home studio and he began sitting in and telling stories. These stories, set

> to hypnotic dub-electro backing are now out on Pete's label under the title *Amateur Night at* [sic] *the Big Top*.[55]

The result is either Shaun Ryder's *Dark Side of the Moon*, or his Plastic Ono Band period.[56] *Amateur Night* is a dub album which is distinct from the beats-based styles of the Mondays and Black Grape. 'Scooter Girl' carries forward some of the Mondays' magic with spry horns and sharp groove. 'Clowns' is probably the album's masterpiece,[57] capturing the humour and rhythmic innovation of the eight tracks. His voice—which speaks more than sings—is able to summon images and ideas. The humour and word-play make it a postmodern oral history for Generation X, carried through the dub. The result is a funny, quirky, musically innovative and well-produced album.

While oral history has been used to capture immigrant stories, such as Michal Bosworth's remarkable *Emma*, there are other ways to convey these stories beyond prose. This chapter has been filled with tales of movement, change, expectations and outcomes. The capacity to live in many places and carry the lessons learnt to each subsequent location is the great gift that immigrants give their chosen new home. Shaun Ryder's *Amateur Night in the Big Top* pieces together these shifting stories, songs, rhymes and rhythms. Not surprisingly, in the era of 'fifteen minute celebrity' reality television, some music reviewers did not have the critical framework or expertise to situate the innovative nature of what they were hearing. As with Yoko Ono's music, there was belated recognition of her contribution in musicological terms through the fusing of avant garde and popular culture.

The recording process for the album was innovative in and of itself. Ryder remembered that 'the idea of doing a couple of stories came from Pete and The Story was the first track we recorded and it moved us into the record—we'd sat and talked about a lot of stories so it seemed right to drop them in.'[58] Pete Carroll recognised the importance of Ryder living in Perth during the making of *Amateur Night*.

> The album was entirely conceived in Perth and wouldn't have been made in the UK. There would have been too much resistance

> because it isn't a commercial record and we wanted to make something that was totally uncompromising, without any commercial considerations...He's [Ryder's] spent the last few years in court fighting with his old managers and has been unable to earn a living for years. It was a difficult record to make. We decided not to cut out the swearing or reduce the length of the tracks even though we realised it was commercial suicide. The music industry particularly in today's money-focused environment doesn't allow for these kinds of records. Shaun and I spent many hours talking about music and the business and the appalling situation he is in. He spent the best part of a year with me in Perth and I have no doubt this record would not have been made had the studio not been in my garage. I also think it was a very brave move for Shaun to make. Most artists would never have done it and no record company would have released it. It's today's equivalent of the first John Lennon Ono band album or Neil Young's *Tonight's the Night*. We've lost a lot of that in today's music. Everything is safely targeted and marketed with only one thing in mind—sales.

Shane Norton was instrumental in the production of the entire album, having written, produced and engineered the music, and remembered that Ryder's arrival coincided with the period of Ku-Ling Brothers creativity. He stated that 'Last year Mal and I sat down and began to start writing the follow up to *Creach* and then Shaun came over and we got sidetracked by that.'[59] Similarly, Stephen Mallinder was equally generous with his time and praise: 'It's been a buzz doing the Amateur Night project and I have so much respect for Shaun as a writer and icon.'[60] This is important music and a significant album, aligning the creative forces of this city and enabling Ryder to work through a difficult relationship with the corporate elements of the music business. Andrew Drever realised the significance of this creative collaboration.

> *Amateur Night in the Big Top* isn't a Shaun Ryder solo album; it's a curious collaboration between the Off World Sounds team and the Manchester singer, and is another fascinating twist in the life

> of one of modern rock music's most colourful and charismatic figures.[61]

The sounds, images and production of *Amateur Night* confirm the mobility of both people and music. Yet in a time when Australia's immigration policies have been restrictive, it is no surprise that even Shaun Ryder became caught in the xenophobic net. Forgetting to renew his visa while staying with Carroll's family, he was given a three-year ban from entering Australia while being deported from the country. Only when Pete Carroll made special representations to the Australian embassy in London was the issue resolved so that Ryder could return to Perth for three months to complete the album.

New Zealand has gained enormously from making itself a base of film production through the *Lord of the Rings* trilogy. It is ironic but predictable that Australian government policy cut off at the knees the formation of an album that has the potential to showcase the calibre of dance culture and production in the country. It was only family networks and substantial personal energy from Pete Carroll that allowed *Amateur Night* to be completed. Incredibly, considering Ryder was actually deported from Australia, he holds such a strong affiliation with Perth that he actually wants to return to the city more frequently.

> Perth's not isolated. I think it's a lot cooler than anywhere else in Australia. There's plenty going on. I really like the place and want to come back. Would love to spend six months in England and six in Perth. I suppose it had some effect on the record more by the people I was with and the stuff that was in my head. It was a chilled place…I want to come back to Perth and record the solo album. I want to get the legal stuff sorted and get back to working. I want to get back to making music. It's the reason I got into it in the first place. Definitely want to make another record and I want to make it in Perth. Looking forward to coming back.[62]

Not surprisingly, the man who has brought together new beats, fashions and images has also foreshadowed a new way of living and moving between cities. He is becoming a trans-city citizen, using music as a bridge.

A synergy of all the moments and movements tracked in this chapter occurred on a Friday night, 22 August 2003. Replacing the usual 'Soulsides' program, Shaun Ryder appeared on RTR-FM with Stephen Mallinder and Pete Carroll, playing the music that influenced his development. Mallinder and Carroll quietly exposed more of Ryder's remarkable musical knowledge and life in two hours of radio than in countless journalistic and biographical treatments. During this program, these three Englishmen took listeners on a journey through a jukebox history of the last twenty years. City sounds bobbed through the discussion.

Pete Carroll: New Order were important?
Shaun Ryder: New Order gave us our first break in front of big audiences. They were from Manchester. They dressed right. They acted right. You know, mixing electronics again, beats, guitars and all sorts. Going back to 1989, there was no British electro or whatever. No hip hoppy or electronic sound. It was Mancunian and it wasn't copying what was going on in New York. It was fresh, really fresh…We was really interested in mixing the electro sound that we picked up from Human League and Heaven 17 and Cabaret Voltaire—Mal eh?—you know mixing all that stuff with the Rolling Stones.[63]

Ryder was generous, acknowledging his influences, including Stephen 'Mal' Mallinder in a way not replicated by Perth's musical policy makers. Building on Ryder's narrative, Perth does not copy Manchester music. It makes music distinctive and fresh in ways that only a new context can initiate. There is a creative function for rhythm when dancing on the edge of the acceptable, the benevolent and the safe. On one night in a Perth radio station, these three northern Englishmen revealed the tissue-like web connecting new and old sounds, showcasing a world where cities mean more than nations and clubs mean more than local governments.

Pete Carroll asked Ryder about the role of Perth in his music, and his opinions of the place.

Pete Carroll: You're becoming a bit of a resident over here, eh? This is your third trip?
Shaun Ryder: Yeah, I'm sort of, you know, attached to Off World Records, doing my bit.
Pete Carroll: Do you like the place? What do you think of the place?
Shaun Ryder: Yeah right. I love Aussie, but I really dig Perth. You know it's sort of cool. You know, it's really cool. It's not stereotyped. There's no sort of hats with cork screws on, or anything like that.[64]

The man(i)c imagery and phrasing of Ryder punctuated the program, of which this exchange is an example. Perth, as a city, became something distinct from the rest of Australia, occupying a different space. In a dadaist turn—mediated through Shaun Ryder-speak—the corked hats of the Australian 'stereotype' bushman transformed into hats swinging with cork screws, certainly a more dangerous proposition. But Perth's specificity and difference were noted.

The tragedy is that this opportunity to recognise Perth's music and sell it to the world has gone unnoticed within governmental policy or music industry initiatives. While worrying about Free Trade Agreements and threats to tourism after September 11, the musical gifts that have been given free by Ryder have gone unacknowledged. When launching *Amateur Night in the Big Top*, Shaun Ryder could have chosen any city in the world. He decided to return to Perth to launch the album on his birthday. The value of this trip is probably incalculable. A BBC film crew followed him to Perth, looking at how the album was made and discussing the city. This documentary offers Perth musicians, film-makers and producers enormous opportunities.[65] The type of publicity created for Perth through *Amateur Night* would be difficult to buy, but its value is unrecorded.

Music has changed in the last twenty years. The sixties are over and Oz rock is redundant for a large proportion of Australia's population. There is a generation for whom Shaun Ryder is more influential than John Lennon, and Factory Records is more important than Mushroom. In this time and place, it is important to conceptually abolish Australia's musical exclusion zones. Even a Pacific Solution is not enough. It is time for Perth to move Off World.

CHAPTER 20

Endings: Not of London Anymore

Tara Brabazon

> Tonight I dream of home
> and not of London any more.[1]
> *The Waifs, 'London Still.'*

Ironic melancholy punctuates The Waifs' 'London Still.' Despondency is the group's best emotional suite. There is something poetic about finally performing in the centre of the world's culture and commerce—London—only to dream of home. So many of us, crouched at the western edge of this continent, dream of being elsewhere—anywhere—except in Dullsville where the sun always shines, the beer is cold and the wine is cheap. Only when leaving Perth can we dream of home once more. As The Waifs moved through 2003, touring with Bob Dylan in the United States, they returned to Australia to collect ARIAs for the best independent release[2] and best blues and roots album. Their achievement was important, showing that following their own path and principles can create extraordinary success. Operating 'under the radar'[3] proved triumphant.

When Geoff Gallop's Labor Party entered office in Western Australia, they desired change in the language of cultural policy. Borrowing from Tony Blair's creative industries matrix, film, television, design, architecture, fashion and especially music were summoned as a future for the State's economic development. *The Contemporary Music Direction Statement*, released from Minister Sheila McHale's office in 2000, called for research into the local industry to provide insight into past specificities and future developments. This document confirmed that researching the industry was an absolute priority, and this absence was blocking potential growth.

The Contemporary Music Ministerial Taskforce met eight times, and released their recommendations in September 2002. Their task was to transform creativity into a commercially viable career path and recognise the importance of infrastructural development in supporting a viable and sustainable music industry. Funding was to be distributed through Arts WA 'to the industry',[4] targeting audience and skill development strategies.[5] In other words, the Taskforce maintained a grants-oriented cultural industry approach, rather than the institutional facilitation role for the creative industries. The difficulty confronting the Taskforce was that their brief focused too narrowly on 'original bands',[6] leaving out many of the musical potentials and successful genres incorporated into this book. Further, they argued that 'music is less tied to physical infrastructure and consequently less tied to particular locations.'[7] While there are concerns with some of the findings and research apparatus,[8] the symbolic importance of this Taskforce must not be discredited. It provided an important foundation and framework for research. Certainly, the second report into another industry—Fashion—configured itself more strongly within the creative industries portfolio.[9] In the longer term, I hope there will be a greater aggregation of these creative industries sectors and a movement between fashion and music, design and dancing, tourism and sport. But the project of this book has been more limited: to bring Perth back to Perth music, to show how important location is to the formation of a creative environment.

It is a significant recognition—both rhetorically and socially—to affirm creativity as an engine of economic growth. Writers such as Richard Florida, whose *The Rise of the Creative Class* offers a new type of management and leadership in the information age,[10] recognised that creative communities are integral to economic success and technological development.

> It's often been said that in this age of high technology, 'geography is dead' and place doesn't matter any more. Nothing could be

> further from the truth: Witness how high-tech firms themselves concentrate in specific places like the San Francisco Bay Area or Austin or Seattle. Place has become the central organising unit of our time...Access to talented and creative people is to modern business what access to coal and iron ore was to steelmaking.[11]

Creativity is not an individual product of genius, but is a social process built within a community. To foster creativity—like intelligence—requires the making of connections. It is remarkable how often creative cities are also musical centres: Seattle, Austin,[12] Dublin, Toronto and Manchester. A musical environment creates lifestyle options and leisure alternatives for an outward, consumerist, urban workforce. Global centres like Auckland, Sydney, London, Paris, Tokyo and New York have much in common, creating a corporate sameness to the cities. If diversity and creativity drive population growth, then it is no surprise that 'everything interesting happens at the margins.'[13] Perth's popular music is integral to a suite of other projects, particularly city imaging and urban regeneration. The growth in the music industry creates entrepreneurial opportunities in music journalism, promotion, management, mixing and policy development. Creativity and commerce are neither disparate nor mutually exclusive in a night-time economy. Perth is both a marginal city and a city of margins.

SCRIBBLING ON THE MARGINS

> 'What is a margin?' I asked a friend recently. 'You know what a margin is,' she replied, 'it's outside the body of the text. It's what holds the page together. Also,' she added, 'it's where you write your notes.'[14]
>
> *Jody Berland*

I type these words at thirty-four years of age, older than most of the contributors to this volume. The pleasure in showcasing and compiling the writing of these diverse, interesting and passionate people has meant that the editing process has been mediated through a secret smile. It has been a pleasure researching and writing about a creative class and community while seeing it form—organically—through this book. None of the research was funded by governments, universities or community organisations. It was an independent release not owing its arguments or interpretation to a benevolent paymaster. It is appropriate and credible to write about DIY creativity, passion and diversity from such a basis.

Each day as an academic, I conduct professional scholarly work in a suited shell—attending meetings and delivering lectures, only later to wait in queues in supermarkets and clean the house—but there is something extraordinary that propels my identity beyond this everyday banality. Through all the hardships of living in a post-Fordist, change-fatigued society, there are lucid memories at my core that can never be taken away. I would not trade one day of my life if it meant losing the period from 1987 to 1994. During this time, Perth was a dance capital of the world. House music has never been an underground or marginal culture. Instead, it is a dominant cultural formation in very specific locations. During this time, the world came to Perth. The 'famous' DJs and precious white labels flooded our clubs. 'Pommy techno', as it was sometimes called, was a phrase that recognised Perth's English and Scottish immigrants who received white labels from their relatives in Manchester or Glasgow within days of issue. This was not cultural colonisation by outsiders. This was sonic appropriation that created one of the most knowledgeable dancing audiences in the world.

Experiences—like personal memories—are often flawed and frequently redundant. But it is impossible to understand the motivation for this book without going back in time to moments on a dance floor—even if that dance floor was a field of dodgily uneven turf—where Perth seemed a musical centre of the world. Dave Thomas shared this network of influences and impressions.

> I attended my first 'rave' at age 15 in 1991. In the years following this initiation, I saw the best in the world, literally. Carl Cox, Sven Vath, Derrick May, Jeff Mills, Joey Beltram, Sasha and Digweed, the Space DJs, LTJ Bukem, Grooverider, The Prodigy, Ground Level, Quench, Danny Rampling, DJ Heaven, Boy George, Jon of

> Pleased Wimmin, to name just a few. All in Perth, and on many occasions, on weeknights, to packed houses. What am I trying to say? For a period in the early 90s, Perth was simply the pinnacle of dance music in Australia. Outside of the UK, it was probably at the forefront of the rest of the world. At the height of Carl Cox's career, he chose to come to Perth on consecutive NYE parties. The Pet Shop Boys, who toured during this period, were astounded by the depth and following of the Perth rave scene. International guests spread the word throughout the UK dance communities and the names among names continued to make the trip to Perth.[15]

This time and place created dancers and DJs literate in popular music and intrinsically understanding of city cultures and the relationship between local musics. The hub on which the current boom in Perth music turns is a knowing audience who creatively move through their space and time, remembering a moment of dancing on the margins, yet feeling at the centre of the world. Perth seemed to synergise rhythms, labels, songs and DJs. Through this seizure of sounds, that were mixed and remixed for our pleasure, something new was created, something better. We were never dancing on the edge. The world came to us through incessant beats per minute.

Perhaps readers of this book may now understand my complete dismay that Perth has been termed Dullsville or a cultural backwater. Perhaps perusers of these pages may grasp my anger and disgust when music industry executives from Sydney or Melbourne come to this city and make judgments without awareness of a bigger history and context. The point of this book is to demonstrate that movements in sounds and people make this city and its music vibrant, exciting and changeable.

Popular music in Perth requires cultural mapping to assist the generation and support of creative clusters. It is an evocative and important industry to develop because it can so profoundly narrate a city's development. But the pattern of this narrative can—and should—change. Julian Tompkin, in the street-press publication *X-Press*, outlined the shape of this tale:

> With very few exceptions, the popular music history of this fine city remains unchanged—bands battle it out on the local stages and either make it through alive or perish, along with their dreams. Those that make it through get to take their crusade to a national and international level, and the rest slip into the normality of the human existence.[16]

There is now an increasing number of performers, DJs, producers and audiences who sing, dance and play against the rules of this tale. The Hampdens commenced as an electronica project, based in a studio. Playing 'live' was not their priority. The Panics record and play between Manchester and Perth. The Waifs have made their own way for ten years, and moved from touring inland Australia in a VW kombi van to supporting Bob Dylan through the United States. Shaun Ryder travelled to Perth, recorded an album and claimed a second home, even while the Department of Immigration and Multicultural and Indigenous Affairs was deporting him from the country. Following The Waifs' example, we need the courage, confidence and commitment to live the dreams of home, and not of London any more.

Notes

You've got about a year: An Introduction. ***Tara Brabazon.***

1 P. Morley, *Words and Music: A History of Pop in the Shape of the City*, Bloomsbury, London, 2003, p. 118.
2 The Simpson sisters are originally from Albany. They met the future third member of The Waifs, Josh Cunningham, in Broome, Western Australia.
3 There is much important work in Australia to be conducted around city-regions. The concept has incredible applicability, particularly in the states of Western Australia and Queensland. For a discussion of the theoretical framework encircling city-regions, please refer to Jane Jacobs, *Cities and the Wealth of Nations: Principles of Economic Life*, Vintage Books, New York, 1985, and Allen Scott's edited collection *Global City-regions: Trends, Theory and Policy*, Oxford University Press, Oxford, 2001.
4 Kazaa is a company which provides software that permits the sharing of sound files via the World Wide Web. But it is important to critique a technologically deterministic stance towards music, as if Kazaa has destroyed an industry. Music has been shared for decades through taping, but digitisation through MP3 sharing has increased its speed. There are other reasons for the decline in CD sales, including the popularity of DVDs and computer games. Also, the record industry majors are sending out mixed corporate messages. While Sony Music has attacked file sharing of music, Sony Hardware sells MP3 players.
5 A. Gregory, 'Perth to fight Dullsville tag,' the *West Australian*, 20 September 2003, p. 52.
6 P. Toohey, 'Perth: another coast, another country,' *The Weekend Australian*, 13–14 September 2003, p. 26.
7 P. Hook from C. P. Lee's *Shake, Rattle and Rain: Popular Music Making in Manchester 1955–1995*, Hardinge Simpole Publishing, Devon, 2002, p. 1.
8 S. Sassen, 'Locating cities in global circuits,' from S. Sassen, ed., *Global Networks Linked Cities*, Routledge, New York, 2002, pp. 1–36.

9 To monitor how these similarities and differences are studied, please refer to the Social Sciences and Humanities Research Council of Canada-funded project, 'Culture of Cities,' <http://www.yorku.ca/culture_of_cities>, 10 November 2003. Particularly, they are interested in researching the links and distinctions between Montreal, Toronto, Berlin and Dublin.

10 For example, the Sydney Olympics utilised sport and tourism to restructure the city and its marketing. Gordon Waitt realised that such 'place promotion is inextricably bound up with the presentation and promotion of ideology,' from 'Playing games with Sydney: marketing Sydney for the 2000 Olympics,' *Urban Studies*, Vol. 36, No. 7, 1999, p. 1073.

11 Phil Hubbard researched this process for the city of Birmingham. Please refer to his 'Urban design and city regeneration: social representations of entrepreneurial landscapes,' *Urban Studies*, Vol. 33, No. 8, 1996, pp. 1441–61.

12 A. Blake, 'The echoing corridor,' *Soundings*, No. 1, Autumn 1995, p. 175.

13 Dave Haslam realised the importance of students to Manchester's music. He described it as 'an intriguing working-class and art student mix: a very punk collision,' from *Manchester England: The Story of the Pop Cult City*, Fourth Estate, London, 1999, p. 117.

14 Sara Cohen's study of Liverpool's music scene disagrees with my argument here. She stated that 'the contribution of students in higher education to the cultural life of the city has always been small.' She made this argument in *Rock Culture in Liverpool*, Clarendon Press, Oxford, 1991, which was based on her PhD from several years earlier. Obviously, the formation of LIPA (the Liverpool Institute of Performing Arts) by Paul McCartney would alter her analysis. Further, there has been little research into the role of student populations as audiences for popular music. In the last fifteen years, theories of audiences and readerships have changed enormously since Cohen's study. Also, she was furthering an argument in her book that economic decline creates a thriving musical culture. Obviously, in promoting a creative industries agenda, a thriving economy allows the development of successful film, television, design, fashion and popular music industries.

15 *Making Music: Findings and Recommendations of the Ministerial Taskforce into Contemporary Music*, Department of Culture and the Arts, Perth, September 2002, p. 5.

16 I am offering a critique here of Stuart Cunningham's argument in *Framing Culture*, Allen & Unwin, St Leonards, 1992. In this important book, Cunningham argued that 'without a national cultural infrastructure, and a workable rhetoric to sustain it, the sources for enlivening community, local, regional or ethnic cultural activity would be impoverished,' p. 43. In the case of electronica and hip hop in particular, a 'national' policy framework cannot track, promote or grow these genres.

17 P. du Noyer, *Liverpool: Wondrous Place, Music from Cavern to Cream*, Virgin Books, London, 2002, p. 1.

18 The port has been profoundly influential for musical development, with Fremantle offering venues for music as many close in Perth. Mojo's is a pivotal venue for Western Australian music. Also, The Waifs' recent song 'The Bridal Train,' is the story of Vikki Simpson's grandmother who married a US sailor in 1945 in Fremantle, and later settled in Albany. On their 2003 tour of the United States with Bob Dylan, The Waifs returned his ashes to the United States. For discussion of The Waifs' relationship with Fremantle, please refer to Julian Tompkin's 'Rousing homecoming for western wanderers,' *The Australian*, 25 September 2003, p. 14.

19 B. Shank, *Dissonant Identities: The Rock 'n' Roll Scene in Austin, Texas*, Wesleyan University Press, Hanover, 1994.

20 ibid., p. x.

21 Shank argued that disco and its derivatives never gained a strong presence in Austin because of the city's race-based history. The limited presence of an African-American culture constrained the applicability of disco.

22 B. Dickinson, 'There is a light that never goes out: Joy Division,' from C. Hutton and R. Kurt, eds, *Don't Look Back in Anger: Growing up with Oasis*, Simon & Schuster, London, 1997, p. 10.

23 Haslam, op. cit., p. xi.

24 ibid., p. xvi.

25 ibid., p. xxvi.

26 Phil Johnson plots some of this history through *Straight outa Bristol: Massive Attack, Portishead, Tricky and the Roots of Trip-hop*, Hodder & Stoughton, London, 1996. He also questions—like the writers in this book—why particular musical formations arise in particular places. He confirms that 'trying to find reasons for the sudden growth of a new musical culture in Bristol is a difficult business,' p. 45.

27 T. Mitchell, 'Flying in the face of fashion: independent music in New Zealand,' from P. Hayward, T. Mitchell & R. Shuker, eds., *North Meets South: Popular Music in Aotearoa/New Zealand*, Perfect Beat Publications, Sydney, 1994, p. 36.

28 Xpressway then took over as a Dunedin-based label. To monitor the range and scale of Dunedin music, please refer to the three disc Yellow Eye Music compilation of 1996, *...but I can write songs okay: Forty years of Dunedin popular music.*

29 D. Hebdige, *Subculture*, Routledge, London, 1979.

30 S. Redhead, ed., *Rave Off*, Avebury, Aldershot, 1993.

31 Another fascinating theme to be explored in future work is the role of women in Perth's music industry. The distinctive voices of the Simpson

sisters and Katy Steele follow in the footsteps of Suze DeMarchi, lead singer of the Baby Animals.

32 The Stems deserve a book of their own. They should have been 'big' in 1987. About to embark on a European tour, the band broke up. There is a remarkable denouement to this tale, where The Stems re-formed in 2003 and finally went on a tour of Europe.

33 There is an argument that all writing about popular music walks in the footsteps of Greil Marcus's *Stranded: Music for a Desert Island*. Written in 1978, it was a collection of essays about the one album that writers would take to a desert island.

34 D. Haslam, op. cit., p. 187.

35 R. Palmer, from G. Marcus, *The Dustbin of History*, Harvard University Press, Cambridge, 1995, p. 6.

Chapter 1: The Wide Open Road—Filling the Potholes. *Felicity Cull.*

1 David McComb, 'Wide Open Road,' *Born Sandy Devotional*, Mushroom Records, 1986.

2 'Biography: Bon Scott' <http://members.aol.com/JDB8797/bon.html>, 23 July 2003.

3 ibid.

4 Jo Ryan & Rex Barker, 'The Mushroom Scene', *The Local Scene Newspaper*, 21 July 1967, p. 10.

5 Interview with Merv Cull, 7 November 2003.

6 'Biography: Bon Scott' <http://members.aol.com/JDB8797/bon.html>, 23 July 2003.

7 ibid.

8 Greil Marcus, *The Dustbin of History*, Harvard University Press, Cambridge, 1995, p. 24.

9 Liam Phillips, 'Covered in reflected glory', *The West Magazine*, 16 August 2003, p. 14.

10 Mike Ticher, 'The Triffids,' *Snipe Fanzine*, No 1. May 1985, <http://home.tisclai.be/the.triffids/interviewsnipe.htm>, 23 July 2003.

11 Mark Molotov, RAM, 5 January 1984, <http://home.tiscali.be/the/triffids/reviewram.htm>, 23 July 2003.

12 Niall Lucy, 'Noise works—an Interview with The Triffids', <http://home.tiscali.be/the.triffids/noise_works.htm>, 23 July 2003.

13 David McComb, 'Wide Open Road', *Born Sandy Devotional*, Mushroom Records, 1986.

14 Mike Martin, 'The Triffids', *Rough Guide to Rock*, <http://home.tiscali.be/the.triffids/biografie.htm>, 23 July 2003.

15 Tony Barass, 'Beautiful waste', The Big Weekend in *The Australian*, Saturday

17 April 1999, <http://home.tiscali.be/the.triffids/articleaustralian.htm>, 23 July 2003.

16 Stuart Cope, 'The Triffids—Just another (great) casual tragedy?', RAM, January 1984, <http://home.tiscali.be/the.triffids/articleram.htm>, 23 July 2003.

17 Mike Ticher, op. cit.

18 Stuart Cope, op. cit.

19 Tony Barass, op. cit.

20 Stuart Cope, op. cit.

21 ibid.

22 ibid.

23 Paul Kelly, *Mushroom 25 Live*, performed on 14 November 1998, Mushroom, 1999, tape two.

24 Tony Barass, op. cit.

25 Dom Mariani, 'For Always,' *At First Sight...Violets Are Blue,* Mushroom Records, 1987.

26 'The Stems: A brief history', <http://www.the.stems.com.au/bib.html>, 23 July 2003.

27 Interview with Rebecca MacGregor, 8 November 2003.

28 'The Stems and Dom Mariani,' *NFH*, No. 21, Winter 1991, <http://nkvdrecords.com/stems.htm>, 23 July 2003.

29 Sergio Del Vecchio, *The Great Stems Hoax*, CD Booklet, Off the Hip, Melbourne, 2002.

30 ibid.

Chapter 2: Selling a Music Landscape. ***Debbie Hindley.***

1 < http://www.78records.com.au/>, 30 November 2003.

2 Christopher Hudson, Sandi and Hud's son, plays in the band The Tigers.

3 The 78 Records website comprehensively covers the local music scene. It provides information on the Local Top 10, recent local releases, links other local music sites including venues, street press and local media that support the local scene. It also shows the full list of local music stocked.

Chapter 3: Party People in the House(s): The Hobos of History. ***Christina Lee.***

1 Greil Marcus, *The Dustbin of History*, Cambridge, Harvard University Press, 1995, p. 17.

2 The participants interviewed range from 21 to 34 years old. All have had extensive experience in the rave scene or the local clubbing culture.

3 http://www.glbtevents.com/travel/perth.html#scene, 11 November 2003.

4 The parties organised by Mulvaney and Hutchinson have ranged from small-

scale events with a few hundred attendees, to larger ones of several thousand—such as the highly successful *Emotions* (February 1993) and *Desert Storm* (October 1994). Hutchinson is also a freelance DJ and mixes regularly on *Beats Per Minute* on RTR-FM 92.1.

5 According to the *2001 Census Basic Community Profile and Snapshot* (Australian Bureau of Statistics), the figures for states and their respective capital cities are as follows:

   Perth, 201,517 (11.0%). Western Australia, 164,488 (12.4%).
   Sydney, 183,991 (4.7%). New South Wales, 275,130 (4.4%).
   Melbourne, 158,139 (4.7%). Victoria, 205,542 (4.5%).
   Brisbane, 92,643 (5.8%). Queensland, 183,722 (5.1%).
   Adelaide, 100,314 (9.4%). South Australia, 124,014 (8.5%).
   Hobart, 9,381 (4.9%). Tasmania, 21,306 (4.7%).
   Darwin, 5,024 (4.7%). Northern Territory, 7,929 (3.9%).

6 <http://www.inthemix.com.au/p/np/viewnews.php?id=5481&printstory=1>, 11 November 2003.

7 See <http://www.flipsideDJs.freeserve.co.uk/Rachel%20Harvey03.htm>, <http://www.inthemix.com.au/reviews/top10/darrenbriais.php>, <http://www.inthemix.com.au/p/np/viewnews.php?id=4304>, 11 November 2003.

8 At the time of writing, I was informed by James Anthony of the opening up of new mid-week gay clubbing nights that would find (transitory) residence in such places as The Ruby Room at Burswood Resort and Rise Nightclub in Northbridge. Anthony commented that in addition to themed costume nights: 'At the moment, we're trying all different forms of entertainment. At the moment we've been having magicians on, and we've had a couple of the losers from "Australian Idol" singing.'

Chapter 4: Breaking down Barriers: B-boys and Girls. ***Leanne McRae.***

1 Different b-boys and girls have different strengths. The ideal achievement is to be proficient at all spheres of b-boying. Abilities can be divided into two broad categories—style and power. Style refers to the more dance-oriented elements of b-boying—footwork, top rocking, popping and locking. Power includes the most difficult strength related moves like twists, 90s, flares, windmills, swipes and head-spins. The most respected b-boys and b-girls are able to combine power with style and freezes.

2 The year of breakdancing was 1984 which was mainstreamed when it featured as part of the Olympic Games opening ceremony in Los Angeles.

3 D. Toop, *Rap Attack 3: African Rap to Global Hip Hop*, Serpent's Tail, London, 2000, p. xxx.

4 Battle of the Year is an international non-profit event that takes place each

year in Germany. Fourteen to sixteen crews compete each with six minutes to impress the judges. The event embraces youth culture and social justice. The website at <http://www.battleoftheyear.net/> affirms 'Battle of the Year is a platform for b-boys and hip hop culture in general and an opportunity for all participants to express themselves in a peaceful and non-racist environment.' The event has grown so large—it now includes workshops and conferences—that the organisers are struggling to find venues and funding for its continuation.

5 In the track 'South Bronx' *Criminal Minded*, KRS-One rhymes: 'The Nine Lives Crew, the Cypress Boys; The real Rock Steady takin' out these toys,' Boogie Down Productions, 1987, track two.

6 Planet X is an Australian-based extreme sports competition formed in 1998. It now has franchises in the US and Europe. The breaking competition held as an accompaniment to the sporting events is unique in that crews do not prepare routines. Their material must be improvised on the day to the music being played.

7 Taka Tsuzuki interviewed by Leanne McRae, 18 November 2003.

8 ibid.

9 B-boying has always been embedded in this competitive consciousness. In the US, to be able to join the Rock Steady Crew a new b-boy had to beat a member of the crew in a battle—an extraordinarily difficult task.

Chapter 5: After Dark: Perth's Night-time Economy. *Kathryn Locke.*

1 *Young People in Northbridge Policy*, June 2003, Office of Crime Prevention, Department of the Premier and Cabinet, Government of Western Australia <http://www.crimeprevention.wa.gov.au/files/publications/> 24 August 2003.

2 *Direction Statement—Contemporary Music,* 2001, The Department of Culture and the Arts, Government of Western Australia, <http://www.ministers.wa.gov.au/policies/contemporary_music_DS.pdf> 18 September 2003.

3 ibid., p. 12.

4 *Young People in Northbridge Policy*, op. cit.

5 ibid., p. 1.

6 K. Healy, 'What's New for Culture in the New Economy,' *Journal of Arts Management, Law and Society*, Vol. 32, No. 2, 2002.

7 S. Tepper, 'Creative Assets and the Changing Economy,' *Journal of Arts Management, Law and Society*, Vol. 32, No. 2, 2002.

8 ibid.

9 P. Hall, 'Creative Cities and Economic Development,' *Urban Studies*, Vol. 37, April 2000.

10 P. Hubbard, 'Urban Design and City Regeneration: Social representations of entrepreneurial landscapes,' *Urban Studies*, Vol. 33, No. 8, 1996.
11 ibid.
12 ibid.
13 *Northbridge Action Plan, 2003–2007*, September 2003, City of Perth, Government of Western Australia, <http://www.perth.wa.gov.au/html/pub03_.php#northbridge_action> 29 October 2003.
Direction Statement—Contemporary Music, 2001, Department of Culture and the Arts, Government of Western Australia, <http://www.ministers.wa.gov.au/policies/contemporary_music_DS.pdf> 18 September 2003.
14 *Northbridge Action Plan*, op. cit.
15 *Young People in Northbridge Policy*, op. cit., p. 1.
16 D. Eggington, interview with Kathryn Locke, East Perth, Western Australia, 5 November 2003.
17 D. Eggington, quoted in 'Calls for end to Perth kids curfew,' D. Weber, ABC Local Radio, <http://www.abc.net.au/worldtodaycontent/2003/s968701.htm> 3 November 2003.
18 D. Eggington, interview with Kathryn Locke.
19 B. Simpson & C. Simpson, 'The Use of Curfews to Control Juvenile Offending in Australia: Managing crime or wasting time?', *Current Issues in Criminal Justice*, Vol. 5, No. 2, 1993.
J. Ferrell, 'Youth, Crime and Cultural Space,' *Social Justice*, Vol. 24, No. 4, 1997.
20 *Young People in Northbridge Policy*, op. cit., p. 1.
21 ibid.
22 ibid.
23 M. Turnbull, interview with Kathryn Locke, West Perth, Western Australia, 24 October 2003.
24 *Northbridge Action Plan*, op. cit.
25 B. Simpson & C. Simpson, op. cit.
R. White, 'Ten Arguments against Youth Curfews,' *Youth Studies Australia*, Vol. 15, No. 4, 1996.
J. Ferrell, op. cit.
R. White, *Public Spaces for Young People*, Australian Youth Foundation, Canberra, 1998.
M. Turnbull, interview with Kathryn Locke.
D. Eggington, interview with Kathryn Locke.
26 B. Simpson & C. Simpson, op. cit.
27 M. Turnbull, quoted in 'Gallop blasts curfew critics,' C. Manton & P. Magill, *The West Australian*, 21 October 2003, p. 5.
28 D. Eggington, interview with Kathryn Locke.

29 National Crime Prevention, *Hanging Out: Negotiating young people's use of public space*, National Crime Prevention, Attorney-General's Department, Canberra, March 1999.
R. White, op. cit.
30 D. Eggington, interview with Kathryn Locke.
M. Turnbull, interview with Kathryn Locke.
31 *Findings of the Youth Forum*, November 1997, Council Minutes, City of Perth, <http://cityofperth.wa.gov.au/html/cou_minutes/website_coumins1997/MN971125.pdf> 29 October 2003.

Chapter 6: Heritage and Hard Rock: Silencing the Grosvenor Hotel.
Rebecca Bennett.

1 S. Redhead, *Unpopular Cultures*, Manchester University Press, Manchester, 1995, p. 2.
2 'Grosvenor Hotel,' <http://www.abc.net.au/triplej/morning/archive/archive2002_November2002.htm>, 5 November 2003.
3 'Arson Link in Hotel Blaze' *Daily Mail*, Thursday 4 May 1989, p. 7.
4 J. Bell et al., 'Grosvenor Hotel' in J. Bell et al. (eds), *Statewide Survey of Hotels 1829–1939 Southern Region, Western Australia*, Cultural Environment Committee National Trust of Australia (WA) Vol. 1, Part 1, November 1997.
5 ibid.
6 'Live bands silenced by a lone local' <http://www.sundaytimes.news.com.au/printpage/0,5942,5589787,00.html>, 7 November 2003.
7 G. Marcus, *The Dustbin of History*, Harvard University Press, Cambridge, 1995, p. 18.
8 Interview with Kavian Temperley, 9 November 2003.
9 Interview with Raelene Gill, November 2003.
10 *Environmental Protection (Noise regulations 1997)* <http://www.slp.wa.gov.au/statutes/regs.nsf/Current+Legislation+Version2?SearchView>, 8 November 2003.
11 'The Grosvenor Hotel', <http://www.abc.net.au/triplej/unearthed/bands/wa.htm> 7 November 2003.
12 Active Perth, Webcast news, p. 11, <http://www.active.org.au/perth/news/front.php3?group=webcast&page=10>, 7 November 2003.
13 J. Savage, *Time Travel*, Vintage, London, 1997, p. 7.
14 Active Perth, op. cit.
15 Interview with P. Bodlovich, 12 November 2003.
16 ibid.
17 *Liquor Licensing Act 1988*, <http://www.slp.wa.gov.au/statutes/swans.nsf/Current+Legislation+Version2?Openview&Count=600&RestrictToCategory=L>, 8 November 2003.
18 Interview with P. Bodlovich, 12 November 2003.

19 ibid.
20 Z. Bauman, 'Space in the Globalizing World,' *Theoria*, June 2001, p. 6.
21 Interview with Kavian Temperley, 5 November 2003.
22 S. Brand, *The Clock of the Long Now*, Basic Books, New York, 1999, p. 26.

Chapter 7: The Ass-End of the World: Perth, Music, Venues and Fandom. *Carley Smith.*

1 Jebediah, 'Leaving Home,' *Slightly Oddway*, Sony Music Australia, 1997.
2 Erika Jellis, interviewed 6 November 2003.
3 Maryanne Cull, interviewed 6 November 2003.
4 Derek Pereira, interviewed 9 November 2003.
5 Erika Jellis, interviewed 6 November 2003.
6 Jemima Wright, interviewed 6 November 2003.
7 Maryanne Cull.
8 Erika Jellis.
9 Stacey Walker, interviewed 6 November 2003.
10 Jemima Wright.
11 Kirsty Paganini, interviewed 6 November 2003.
12 Jemima Wright.
13 Derek Pereira.
14 Erika Jellis.

Chapter 8: Home-grown: Music from the Backyard. *Rebecca Bennett.*

1 'Triple J Oz Music Month,' <http://www.abc.net.au/triplej/ozmusicmonth/s979734.htm>, 5 November 2003.
2 'The Sleepy Jackson,' <http://www.thesleepyjackson.com/>, 5 November 2003.
3 Referring to acclaimed band, Eskimo Joe. See 'Eskimo Joe Official Site,' <http://www.eskimojoe.net/>, 3 November 2003.
4 See 'The Fergusons,' <http://www.thefergusons.com.au/>, 5 November 2003.
5 See 'Gyroscope,' <http://www.gyroscope.iinet.net.au/>, 5 November 2003.
6 See 'Little Birdy,' <http://www.littlebirdy.net/body.htm>, 5 November 2003.
7 See 'The Sleepy Jackson Reviews,' <http://www.thesleepyjackson.com/>, 5 November 2003.
8 See 'WAMI,' <http://www.wam.asn.au/>, 5 November 2003.

Chapter 9: Mapping Perth. *Amanda Evans.*

1 I. Chambers, 'Maps for the Metropolis: A Possible Guide to the Present,' in *Cultural Studies*, Vol. 1, No. 1, 1987, p. 5.

2 M. Halbwachs, *The Collective Memory*, Harper & Row, New York, 1980, p. 69.
3 Like that awful moment in *Human Traffic* where 'Egg,' from the seminal 1990s British television series 'This Life', whines to the like-minded gal in Carl Cox's club.
4 The idea of 'composure' in relation to collective and individual memory was theorised by *The Popular Memory Group* at the Birmingham Centre for Contemporary Cultural Studies—see 'Popular Memory: Theory, Politics, Method,' pp. 205–52, in *Making Histories*, Hutchinson, London, 1982.
5 Halbwachs, op. cit., p. 69.
6 Many of the clubs mentioned in this article were too early to have official websites and if they did they have subsequently closed and their sites are inactive. Extensive research has shown that the dates associated with these clubs can only be approximate and therefore difficult to ascertain with precision. The only monograph that records any dates of significance is the *Western Australia Industry Directory*, *Xpress Magazine*, Perth. This directory was published from January 1996 to 1998/1999 and does not contain opening or closing dates.
7 Obviously this, like other initialised contractions—think 'I need to use an ATM machine'—is grammatically incorrect, but it was never referred to as 'DC' by clubbers or its promoters.
8 Orsini's was located in the Sheraton Hotel complex—a site that would soon be taken over by Players.

Chapter 10: Tuesday Night at the Hydey. *Angela Jones.*

1 E. Arnold, *Perth Jazz Society's 30th Anniversary Editorial*, Perth Jazz Society, Perth, 2003, p. 3.
2 ibid., p. 1.

Chapter 11: DIY D'n'B: *Felicity Cull.*

1 Email interview with Adam Kelly, 6 November 2003.
2 ibid.
3 ibid.
4 Mystique, 'Perth Produce,' *Atmoceanic Magazine*, Issue Two, 2003, p. 16.
5 MK1, 'Pendulum,' *Atmoceanic Magazine*, Issue Three, 2003, p. 31.
6 Jeremy Gilbert & Ewan Pearson, 'Metal Machine Musics—Technology, Subjectivity and Reception', *Discographies*, London, Routledge, 1999, p. 112.
7 MK1, op. cit., p. 32.
8 Email interview with Adam Kelly.
9 Twisted Individual, 'Studio Tips,' *Atmoceanic Magazine*, No. 2, 2003, p. 10.
10 Interview with Matt Hodge aka Infinite Detail, 7 November 2003.
11 Mystique, op. cit., p. 18.

12 Trafik Perth Producers Night, Heat Nightclub, 12 September 2003.
13 Interview with Matt Hodge aka Infinite Detail.

Chapter 12: He's Electric: How Perth's Electronic Musicians Gear Up *Angela Jones.*

1 <http://www.livejournal.com/community/musictech/3458.html>, 11 October 2003.

Chapter 13: 'It's Not My Fault You Hate My Band': Perth Art-Rock: *Adam Trainer.*

1 Roy Wilkinson 1998, 'Weird Science,' *Select Magazine*, EMAP Entertainment Network, London, January, p. 40.
2 Tim Gane in ibid.
3 Snowman victim #362 2003, *first past the post*, No. 2, 2003, p. 18.

Chapter 14: Writing the Perth Music Scene. ***Carrie Kilpin.***

1 Ed Needham, as cited by Blaine Greteman, 'So, How Does It Feel? Brash Young Brit Ed Needham Takes Over at that U.S. Icon Rolling Stone,' *Time International*, 8 July 2002, Vol. 159, No. 26, p. 65.
2 Julian Tompkin, interviewed by Carrie Kilpin, 10 October 2003, Perth, Western Australia.
3 *Today* is an entertainment section of *The West Australian*. As well as music, its features include articles and guides to television, cinema, film, theatre and art.
4 Simon Collins, interviewed by Carrie Kilpin, 28 October 2003, Perth, Western Australia.
5 Tompkin, 2003.
6 Craig Mathieson, 'Rock of Pages', *The Bulletin*, 21 May 2002, p. 71.
7 Collins, 2003.
8 Tompkin, 2003.
9 ibid.
10 ibid.
11 Collins, 2003.
12 ibid.
13 Tompkin, 2003.
14 Jessica Carroll & John Connell, '"You Gotta Love This City": The Whitlams and Inner Sydney', *Australian Geographer*, Sydney, July 2000, Vol. 31, No. 2, full text.
15 Tompkin, 2003.
16 ibid.
17 ibid.

Chapter 15: Breaking with Beni Benz. ***Leanne McRae.***

1 These studios are located on Murray Street in the city centre of Perth.
2 B-boying or b-girling is the preferred term to what is called breakdancing in the mainstream. B-boying/girling demonstrates a consciousness of community and hip hop culture as a whole. Breakdancing is a commercialised term applied by the media in the early 1980s when Rock Steady Crew and the New York City Breakers popularised the pastime on television broadcasts and shows culminating in the 1984 Los Angeles Olympic Games.
3 aka Third Degree Burns.
4 The winner of the Australian heat travels to Germany to compete in the Battle of the Year competition against crews from the US, Japan, France, Benelux (Belgium, Netherlands, Luxemburg), New Zealand, Spain, Germany, Scandinavia, Eastern Europe, Italy, Switzerland, the Balkans and South Africa. In 2003 Russia received a direct invitation.

Chapter 16: A Crooked Crooked Reign. ***Adam Trainer.***

1 George Lipsitz, 'We Know What Time It Is: Race, Class and Youth Culture in the Nineties,' in A. Ross & T. Rose, eds, *Microphone Fiends: Youth Music & Youth*, Routledge, New York, 1994, p. 20.
2 ibid.
3 Johan Fornas, Ulf Lindberg & Ove Sernhede, *In Garageland: Rock, Youth & Modernity*, Routledge, London, 1995, p. 253.
4 *Dead Set*, 1998, dir. Rob Payne, Siren Entertainment.
5 *Hype!*, 1996, dir. Doug Pray, Helvey-Pray Productions.

Chapter 17: A Seychelles Rhythm. ***Rachel Shave.***

1 Giovana Neves, Manager of Seychelles Rhythms, videotaped interview, 15 October 2001.
2 Grace Barbe, lead vocalist, Seychelles Rhythms, videotaped interview, 15 October 2001.
3 Luan Ladouce, DJ, telephone interview, 30 October 2003.
4 Giovana Neves, videotaped interview, 15 October 2001.
5 Grace Barbe, videotaped interview, 15 October 2001.
6 Australian Bureau of Statistics, <http://www.abs.gov.au/>, 17 December 2003.
7 Giovana Neves, audiotaped interview, 20 October 2003.
8 'Abolition of the "White Australia" Policy', Australian Government's official website for the Department of Immigration and Multicultural and Indigenous Affairs, <http://www.immi.gov.au/facts/08abolition.htm>, 17 December 2003.

Chapter 18: Another Side of Life: Downsyde. ***Leanne McRae.***

1 Downsyde, 'Keep It Alive,' *Land of the Giants*, Hydrofunk, EMI, 2003, track nine.
2 There are a number of interviews and articles that cite varying versions of the ethnic make-up of Downsyde. Australian, Middle Eastern, Indigenous, South American, Asian and European identities comprise the band. For more information on Downsyde, please see their website at <http://www.downsyde.com.au/>.
3 Downsyde won most popular local original album, most popular local original music video for 'El Questro' and most popular local original urban music act.
4 F. Allon, 'Translated Spaces/Translated Identities: The Production of Place, Culture and Memory in an Australian Suburb,' in Gabriella Espak, Scott Fatnowna & Denise Woods, eds, *Jumping the Queue*, University of Queensland Press, Brisbane, 2002, p. 107.
5 T. O'Regan, *Australian Television Culture*, Allen & Unwin, St Leonards, 1993, p. 105.
6 ibid., p. 106.
7 M. Dixson, *The Imaginary Australian*, UNSW Press, Sydney, 1999, p. 6.
8 It also ignores Indigenous concerns.
9 J. DeVere Brody, 'Hyphen-Nations,' in Sue-Ellen Case, Philip Brett & Susan Leigh Foster, eds, *Cruising the Performative*, Indiana University Press, Bloomington, 1995, p. 149.
10 G. Hage, 'Anglo-Celtics Today: Cosmo-Multiculturalism and the Phase of the Fading Phallus,' *Communal/Plural*, Vol. 4, 1994, p. 44.
11 K. Betts, 'Immigration Policy under the Howard Government,' *Australian Journal of Social Issues*, Vol. 38, No. 2, 2003, p. 187.
12 G. Hage, *Against Paranoid Nationalism: Searching for Hope in a Shrinking Society*, Pluto Press, Annandale, 2003, p. 111.
13 Downsyde, 'Gifted Life,' *Land of the Giants*, Hydrofunk, EMI, 2003, track three.
14 Western Australian Music Industry Website, 'Band Profiles' <http://www.wam.asn.au/scene/profiles/downsyde.htm>, 25 November 2003.
15 Bon Scott, original lead singer for AC/DC lived, and is buried, in Fremantle, Western Australia.
16 Downsyde, 'Bittersweet,' *Land of the Giants*, Hydrofunk, EMI, 2003, track two.
17 The show was created by Tony Sattler and Gary Reilly and screened for five seasons. It contrasted an excessive 'ocker' Australianness with equally extreme 'ethnicity' or Italianness. The Bullpits lived at 14 Wombat Crescent in Goanna Heights—imagery of traditional Aussie lore. The intervention of the

Bertolucis functioned to demonstrate the absurdity of an amplified Australian national identity, but ultimately never destabilised any power structures in national imagining, gender or generational politics.

18 Downsyde, 'Kingswood Country,' *Land of the Giants*, Hydrofunk: EMI, 2003, track ten.

Chapter 19: Moving Off World after the Cabaret. ***Tara Brabazon.***

1 S. Ryder, 'The Story,' *Amateur Night in the Big Top*, OWS, 2003, track one.
2 In the 2001 Census, Western Australia had the highest percentage of people who were born overseas, at 27%. These statistics are derived from '2001 Census Basic Community Profile and snapshot,' Australian Bureau of Statistics, <http://www.abs.gov.au>, 19 November 2002.
3 Perth's population has 190 different regions of origin within its citizenry. To observe the musical consequences of this diversity, refer to Natalie Schmeiss's 'Worldly Delights', *X-Press*, No. 874, 13 November 2003, p. 28.
4 W. Straw, 'Systems of Articulation, Logics of Change', *Cultural Studies*, Vol. 5, No. 3, 1991, p. 369.
5 I. Chambers, *Popular Culture: The Metropolitan Experience*, Methuen, London, 1986, p. 183.
6 Pete Carroll, email interview with Tara Brabazon, 28 November 2003.
7 ibid.
8 ibid.
9 ibid.
10 J. Howard, 'We decide who comes to this country,' Liberal Party advertisement, *The West Australian*, 9 November 2001.
11 D. Gare, 'Farewell to Old England,' *Campus Review*, 26 November–2 December 2003, p. 30.
12 ibid.
13 Pete Carroll, email interview with Tara Brabazon.
14 An outstanding history of the role of black American music in Manchester is Keith Rylatt & Phil Scott, *CENtral 1179: The Story of Manchester's Twisted Wheel Club*, Bee Cool Publishing, London, 2001.
15 The recent history of RTR warrants a research project of its own. As a non-profit organisation, based on subscriptions and run by volunteers, its previous incarnation was 6UVSFM. What made it distinct from other community stations was that much of the programming was based on electronic music. This focus radically lifted the listener base. While Australian radio has moved to more nationally networked formats, RTR becomes even more important. A diversity of listening populations is served, cutting through the homogeneity of radio formats. The station has a pivotal function in transmitting to local communities.

16 Pete Carroll, email interview with Tara Brabazon.
17 <http://www.rtr.com.au>, 10 December 2003.
18 Pete Carroll, email interview with Tara Brabazon.
19 To hear this tissue of connectiveness, compare The Stone Roses 'Waterfall' from 1989 with the Panics' 'Don't Be Kind' from 2003.
20 J. Robb, 'Louder than Bombs: Happy Mondays', in C. Hutton & R. Kurt, eds, *Don't Look Back in Anger: Growing up with Oasis*, Simon & Schuster, London, 1997, p. 215.
21 J. Robb, *The Stone Roses and the Resurrection of British Pop*, Ebury Press, London, 1997, p. 137.
22 J. Laffer in J. Tompkin, 'The Panics the Last Laffer,' *X-Press*, No. 860, 7 August 2003, p. 34.
23 Pete Carroll, email interview with Tara Brabazon.
24 Such a stance was continued through 2003. Dan Stinton was made the Presidential Chair and Executive Director of WAM. His background includes the editing of *Scoop* Magazine, DJ-ing and hosting several programs on RTR. He made a public statement that during his time at WAM that there would be greater acknowledgement of electronica and remixing by the organisation, in a desire to increasingly involve DJs in WAM's operation. Swiftly though, the WAM website intervened in this shift, reporting that, 'If you've seen that article and been a bit alarmed, then rest assured that WAM's focus is and will continue to be the development of the original music industry in WA.' <http://www.wam.asn.au/news.htm>, 9 November 2003. Dan Stinton went on to become the Station Manager for RTR-FM, replacing Pete Carroll, in May 2004.
25 The political goal of Pat and Matt Carroll was also clear. When interviewed for the 1992 Sublime: Manchester Music and Design 1976–1993 exhibition, their aim was 'opening doors…into art galleries, into a career in art and design for working-class youngsters, and not least for the ambitious ways they see their own work developing,' *Sublime Catalogue*, Cornerhouse, Manchester, September 1992, p. 45.
26 Pete Carroll, email interview with Tara Brabazon.
27 M. Benson & P. Wise, *A Study into the Current State of the Western Australian Contemporary Music Industry and Its Potential for Economic Growth*, Department of Culture and the Arts, Government of Western Australia, December 2002, p. 9.
28 D. Haslam, *Manchester England: The Story of the Pop Cult City*, Fourth Estate, London, 1999, p. xxvii.
29 Stephen Mallinder, email interview with Tara Brabazon, 2 December 2003.
30 Stephen Mallinder, interviewed by Steven Quinn in February 1997, *Thinking on Your Feet*, PhD Thesis, Murdoch University, 2000, p. 294.

31 Recently, some outstanding reissues of Cabaret Voltaire's work have emerged. The three CD set, *Conform to Deform '82/'90. Archive;*, Virgin, 2001, is an excellent starting point to explore the range of Cabaret Voltaire's influence on sound, dance and electronica. For a sample of their more commercial singles and mixes, please refer to *The Original Sound of Sheffield 78/82*, released on Mute Records in October 2002. Cherry Red Recordings, based in London, also released a DVD of *Cabaret Voltaire, Live at the Hacienda* in 2002.

32 The Cabaret Voltaire was formed by a group of artists—the Dadaists—in Zurich in 1916.

33 M. Fish & D. Hallbery, *Cabaret Voltaire: The Art of the Sixth Sense*, SAF, Harrow, 1989, p. 13.

34 Stephen Mallinder, in ibid., p. 74.

35 Phil Oakey formed the Human League in 1977 with Martin Ware and Ian Craig Marsh. The latter two men went on in 1980 to form Heaven 17.

36 A. Blake, 'Making Noise: Notes from the 1980s', *Popular Music and Society*, Vol. 21, No. 3, Fall 1997, p. 29.

37 Remarkable writing has been produced which tracks the influence of Kraftwerk on contemporary electronica. Best known is Lester Bangs' 'Kraftwerk feature', in G. Marcus, ed., *Lester Bangs: Psychotic Reactions and Carburettor Dung*, Minerva, London, 1988. Also, refer to the evocative research by Tim Barr, *Kraftwerk: from Düsseldorf to the Future (with Love)*, Ebury Press, London, 1988. He asks if we have ever 'wondered why nobody ever talks about the UK/US domination of pop music any more…then, somehow, somewhere, Kraftwerk have become the ghost in your machine.' p. 3.

38 P. Morley, *Words and Music: A History of Pop in the Shape of the City*, Bloomsbury, London, 2003, p. 236.

39 Stephen Mallinder, email interview with Tara Brabazon.

40 ibid.

41 Market Equity, *A study into the Current State of the Western Australian Contemporary Music Industry and its Potential for Economic Growth*, p. 6.

42 Sassi and Loco are made up of Stephen Mallinder and Travis Calley. Their *Bibleopoly* was the first release of Off World Sounds, OFF 1, 1997.

43 C. Barker, S. Connolly, T. Boskus, D. Corvini, Mike G, M. Hebblewhite, S. Hitchings, D. Jones, G. King, T. Levy, G. Mitchell, T. Hardaker, L. SickBitch, '101 Crucial Albums', *Ministry Magazine Australia*, No. 10, October 2003, p. 36.

44 Stephen Mallinder, email interview with Tara Brabazon.

45 ibid.

46 S. Norton, *Ku-Ling Brothers*, <http://www.ozbang.com/Kuling%20Brothers.htm>, 1 November 2003.

47 The *Ministry* magazine website described Off World Sounds as 'a truly international concern, with an artist roster spanning Australia, the US and Britain,' 'West Koast Ku-Ling', *Ministry* 09, <http://www.ministryofsound... cfm?page_id=37773801112961003&SE_id=112>, 1 November 2003.
48 Stephen Mallinder, email interview with Tara Brabazon.
49 Vicious vinyl now has four imprints: Vicious vinyl, Vicious grooves, Vicious urban and Vicious. They also have partnership labels with Vapour, Bamboo and Cosmetic.
50 Stephen Mallinder, email interview with Tara Brabazon.
51 ibid.
52 Shaun Ryder's imagination and verbal loquaciousness were not well recognised within his formal schooling. He admitted in an interview with Sheryl Garratt that he suffered from dyslexia: 'When I was at school they didn't really look for it, so when I started off at 11 years old, I was in the top set. By the time I was 13, 14 I was in the remedials, and that's when I left school. I could write a great story but I'd get bad marks for it because the spelling was ridiculous,' from Sheryl Garratt, 'What's the Story behind Shaun Ryder Killing All Those Pigeons?' *Word*, No. 6, August 2003, p. 8.
53 D. Haslam, op. cit., p. 178.
54 S. Ryder, in Garratt, p. 8.
55 Sheryl Garratt, ibid., p. 8.
56 Shaun Ryder recognised the importance—and the difference—of this album from his other musical contributions. He stated that 'at first I called this my "Dark Side of the Moon," but now I think it's Yoko Ono,' quoted in A. Street, 'Shaun Ryder', *dB Magazine Online*, <http://www.dbmagazine.com.au/309/iv-ShaunRyder.html>, 7 September 2003.
57 Of particular note is the Gripper mix of 'Clowns' included in the 'Scooter Girl' CD single, OWS, 2003, track two.
58 Ryder in Street.
59 S. Norton, in D. O'Keeffe, 'Ku-Ling Brothers interview, 26 May 2002, *residentadvisor*, <http://www.residentadvisor.com.au/features.asp?ID=128>, 1 November 2003.
60 Stephen Mallinder, email interview with Tara Brabazon.
61 A. Drever, 'Amateur Night in the Big Top,' *The Age*, 11 July 2003, <http://www.theage.com.au/articles/2003/07/11/1057783329672.html>, 7 September 2003.
62 S. Ryder, interviewed by G. Savage, 'Shaun Ryder', *X-Press*, No. 857, 17 July 2003, p. 13.
63 P. Carroll & S. Ryder, 'Soulsides', RTR-FM, 22 August 2003.
64 ibid.
65 For a discussion of this documentary, please refer to 'Reality TV Show to Star

Shaun Ryder', RTE Entertainment, 10 December 2003, <http://www/rte.ie/arts/2003/1210/riders.html>, 17 December 2003, 'BBC3 to Air Documentary on Shaun Ryder', <http://www.ananova.com/entertainment/story/sm_805153.html?menu=entertainment>, 17 December 2003.

Chapter 20: Endings: Not of London Any More. ***Tara Brabazon.***

1 The Waifs, 'London Still,' from *Up All Night*, Jarrah Records, 2002, track three.
2 The Waifs' fourth album, *Up All Night*, went platinum without the support of a major label. Donna Simpson stated, in reviewing their success, that 'it's nice to know that our music is getting out there on its own through merit rather than wild crazy promotion and media and stuff, 'cause it has got some really bad reviews and it's not everyone's cup of tea,' from P. Coufos, 'The Waifs', *X-Press*, No. 866, 18 September 2003. Importantly, The Waifs booked their own gigs, and funded and recorded compact discs themselves.
3 This was Josh Cunningham's description of The Waifs' strategy for success, 'Channel 10 News', 25 September 2003.
4 *Making Music: Findings and Recommendations of the Ministerial Taskforce into Contemporary Music*, Perth, September 2002, p. vii.
5 For example, the Department of Culture and the Arts, the Department of Education and Training and ArtsEdge, funded a project administered by the Western Australian Music Industry Association which produced the *Music W.A. Education Pack*, including CD, CD ROM and curriculum materials.
6 *Making Music*, p. 2.
7 ibid., p. 5.
8 Theories of audience and reception practices are a very important part of cultural studies methods and its history for the last thirty years. It is interesting to note that the audience analysis conducted by Market Equity, the research firm hired to gather data for the Taskforce, was limited. In their report, they stated that 'due to the budget and time constraints, an on-line survey was conducted using Market Equity's on-line database. This database contains over 3,500 individuals and while not perfectly representative of the general population provided a robust sample of 661 completed responses.' Clearly, the number of responses was not the problem, but greater information was required about the identity profile of this audience. No sample size can ever be 'representative,' but only provides a starting point for evaluation and interpretation. Refer to Market Equity's report, *A Study into the Current State of the Western Australian Contemporary Music Industry and Its Potential for Economic Growth*, Department of Culture and the Arts, Government of Western Australia, December 2002, p. 22.

9 For example, the Ted Snell-led committee reported that 'Creative Industries have a vital role in the future global success of Western Australia because they harness the creativity and talent of Western Australians and generate wealth through intellectual property. They have the potential to take the economy of our State into a future where we no longer limit ourselves to success in our traditional industries of strength,' *The Premier's Fashion Industry Taskforce Report*, August 2003, Government of Western Australia, p. 4. It should be noted that the Popular Music Taskforce was under the leadership of the Minister for Culture and the Arts, while the investigation into fashion fell into the Premier's jurisdiction.

10 While Florida's book has become a best-selling guide to a new economy, it is also important to recognise how many of his ideas have their origin in Daniel Bell's work, *The Coming of Post-Industrial Society: A Venture in Social Forecasting*, Basic Books, New York, 1976.

11 R. Florida, *The Rise of the Creative Class*, Basic Books, New York, 2002, p. 6.

12 South by Southwest (SXSW) transforms Austin Texas into the base for global music for a week each March. It is a musical and media conference, with over a thousand performers from around the world performing over five nights. Similarly, Manchester's 'In the City' festival features 'unsigned' acts, including The Panics and Spencer Tracy.

13 Florida, op. cit., p. 184.

14 J. Berland, 'Space at the Margins: Colonial Spatiality and Critical Theory After Innis', *Topia*, No. 1, Spring 1997, p. 65.

15 D. Thomas, personal email to Tara Brabazon, 15 October 2003.

16 J. Tompkin, 'The Hampdens House of the Setting Sun', *X-Press*, No. 862, 21 August 2003, p. 17.

Select Bibliography

Cohen, S. *Rock Culture in Liverpool*, Clarendon Press, Oxford, 1991.

Dixson, M. *The Imaginary Australian*, UNSW Press, Sydney, 1999.

du Noyer, P. *Liverpool: Wondrous Place, Music from Cavern to Cream*, Virgin Books, London, 2002.

Florida, R. *The Rise of the Creative Class*, Basic Books, New York, 2002.

Haslam, D. *Manchester England: The Story of the Pop Cult City*, Fourth Estate, London, 1999.

Hayward, P., ed., *From Pop to Punk to Postmodernism*, Allen & Unwin, Sydney, 1992.

Hayward, P., Mitchell, T., & Shuker, R., eds, *North Meets South: Popular Music in Aotearoa/New Zealand*, Perfect Beat Publications, Sydney, 1994.

Hebdige, D. *Hiding in the Light*, Routledge, London, 1988.

Hebdige, D. *Subculture*, Routledge, London, 1979.

Hutchinson, T. *Your Name's on the Door*, Australian Broadcasting Corporation, Sydney, 1992.

Johnson, P. *Straight outa Bristol: Massive Attack, Portishead, Tricky and the Roots of Trip-Hop*, Hodder & Stoughton, London, 1996.

Lee, C. P. *Shake, Rattle and Rain: Popular Music Making in Manchester 1955–1995*, Hardinge Simpole Publishing, Devon, 2002.

Marcus, G. *The Dustbin of History*, Harvard University Press, Cambridge, 1995.

Morley, P. *Words and Music: A History of Pop in the Shape of the City*, Bloomsbury, London, 2003.

Redhead, S. ed., *Rave Off*, Avebury, Aldershot, 1993.

Ross, A. & Rose, T. eds, *Microphone Fiends: Youth Music & Youth*, Routledge, New York, 1994.

Scott, A. *Global City-regions: Trends, Theory and Policy*, Oxford University Press, Oxford, 2001.

Shank, B. *Dissonant Identities: The Rock'n'roll Scene in Austin, Texas*, Wesleyan University Press, Hanover, 1994.

White, R. *Public Spaces for Young People*, Australian Youth Foundation, Canberra, 1998.

Index